Future of Business and Finance

The Future of Business and Finance book series features professional works aimed at defining, describing and charting the future trends in these fields. The focus is mainly on strategic directions, technological advances, challenges and solutions which may affect the way we do business tomorrow, including the future of sustainability and governance practices. Mainly written by practitioners, consultants and academic thinkers, the books are intended to spark and inform further discussions and developments.

More information about this series at http://www.springer.com/series/16360

Uwe Seebacher

Predictive Intelligence for Data-Driven Managers

Process Model, Assessment-Tool,
IT-Blueprint, Competence Model
and Case Studies

 Springer

Uwe Seebacher
Graz, Austria

ISSN 2662-2467 ISSN 2662-2475 (electronic)
Future of Business and Finance
ISBN 978-3-030-69402-9 ISBN 978-3-030-69403-6 (eBook)
https://doi.org/10.1007/978-3-030-69403-6

Preface

Most books end with acknowledgments. I would like to begin this book with one of them, namely that to Rolf-Günther Hobbeling of Springer Verlag, because without his initiative I probably would not have summarized my experiences on this topic in a book. In the course of his research, he had found several posts in various social networks about my lectures, among others at the Annual Strategy Conference in Königstein of the German Engineering Federation (VDMA) in autumn 2019, at Europe's largest B2B event "IGNITE 2020" in London[1] or the Industrial Communication Day 2020[2] of the German Association of Industrial Communication.

I would also like to thank my colleagues and comrades-in-arms, especially Lukas Strohmeier, Philipp Danninger, and Thomas Geiger. Together with Lukas, I started the groundwork in the summer of 2017, which subsequently led to the emergence of Predictive Intelligence. We gave our self-developed Excel-based application the melodious name "Market Intelligence Cube (MIC)." Lukas and I had never thought about the scope of our work. In the fall of 2017, Philipp joined the team and gave the entire activities an enormous boost. He is the prototype of a future data science professional. In the meantime, he has given up his former job, as he decided to pursue postgraduate studies in Data Science. Congratulations, dear Philipp, it was exactly the right decision!

At the beginning of 2018, Thomas joined us as a student assistant. Once again, my philosophy has been confirmed that students are a good choice when it comes to new, innovative, and interesting topics. Very soon Thomas had become deeply involved in the field of Business Intelligence and developed more and more sophisticated algorithms, dashboards, and models. In the first business unit, we had the first interactive dashboards online after about 6 months. Our internal customers no longer had to wait days and weeks for numbers, data, and facts, as it was previously the case, but were able to view and use the relevant information interactively via the intranet after a short training session. After another 12 months, we had also connected the data from the CRM to our Business Intelligence solution and were able to implement specific focus campaigns quickly and effectively on this basis.

---

[1]https://b2bmarketing.b2b-ignite.net/speakers/uwe-seebacher/. Accessed: August 18, 2020
[2]https://bvik.org/tik-2020/programm/. Accessed: August 18, 2020

In the summer of 2018, I was then assigned to optimize and reposition the global marketing of another business unit with regard to predictive profit marketing (Seebacher 2020). Based on the already realized work regarding Business Intelligence, Thomas was able to put the MIC for the next division online in only 3 months. This way we realized a de facto cost saving of about 75% compared to the first MIC. We established a MIC *Key User Network* and were thus able to focus our scarce resources within marketing on the further development of MIC but also on business-oriented activities such as short-term cash flow optimization, medium-term business planning and market entry strategies as well as ongoing strategic corporate management.[3]

Over time, we were able to connect more and more validated data sources to the MIC, which thus no longer only contained market data, but also information on customers, competitors, and projects. Thus, we had developed a 360° perspective to interactively and dynamically oversee our internal and external business environment. Based on the rapidly growing data pool, we were able to dynamically update the data using regression, correlation, and extrapolation, thus providing the entire organization with an increasingly accurate basis for decision-making. More and more studies, such as the recent study by Fujitsu in cooperation with Freeform Dynamics, prove that data-driven companies perform significantly better than those companies that operate "data-less." This makes it even more important to mention that in the DACH region, just 5% of companies have sufficient capabilities to continuously draw information from their data in real time and use it in the appropriate context throughout the entire organization.[4] This means that 95% of companies in Germany, Austria, and Switzerland obviously lack the necessary database to develop, monitor, and plan their own business.

In this context, I like to use the following comparison: companies today act like a pilot who knows that he has to fly to Singapore, but who lacks any data on the loading of the aircraft, special features of the route, or current and dynamic weather data. Would you like to sit in this aircraft? Data-driven corporate management based on the predictive intelligence model is therefore an absolute must today when it comes to the responsibility toward the employees and stakeholders of a company because unconstrained and uncompromising corporate management is irresponsible and highly risky. Particularly against the background of the applications and technical possibilities available today, it no longer seems comprehensible why the majority of companies are still flying "blind" in data technology.

I have decided to write this book in order to describe the complex and unsolvable topic of predictive intelligence in a simple and comprehensible way. In this way, I want to give you, the reader, an instrument to effectively and efficiently initiate this important topic yourself and to implement it in a sustainable and cost-minimizing

---

[3]See also the various case studies in the remainder of this book.

[4]https://blog.wiwo.de/look-at-it/2020/08/17/digitalisierung-nur-fuenf-prozent-der-firmen-in-deutschland-mit-ausreichender-datenreife/

way in order to maintain and expand your own entrepreneurial competitiveness. There is no shortcut to success because success is the result of many small steps.

With this in mind, I wish you an exciting and enriching read. Stay healthy and grateful.

Graz, Austria   Uwe Seebacher
March 2021

Reference

Seebacher, U. G. (2020). *B2B marketing essential – How to turn your marketing from a cost into a sales engine*. Graz: AQPS Inc..

Contents

Predictive Intelligence and the Basic Economic Principles

1

1.1 Where Do We Come from?

Anglo-American management historians agree that the exercise of management functions in the sense of corporate management in the modern sense of the word was first demonstrated in the course of industrialization from 1750 onwards (Pollard 1965; George 1972; Wren 1979). However, they are the ones who make it clear that there were already functions in antiquity that can be called management from today's perspective. At that time, however, there was still a lack of economic orientation. The background for this was the general disregard for economic and performance-oriented thinking, caused primarily by religion and philosophy as well as feudal social conditions.

Problems in the area of organization and leadership at this time arose primarily in the pursuit of religious, political, and military goals. Thus, management historians point out that management principles and techniques were already being applied with the emergence of the first conglomerates with formal structures, from the Egyptians in the area of large irrigation and pyramid projects, the Hebrews in the area of the laws of Moses, but also the Chinese in terms of advice from the staffs, the Babylonians and Indians in terms of recording for the purpose of tax collection, the Greeks in terms of the division of labor in crafts and also the Romans in the development of the infrastructure of the Roman Empire.

In the course of the Crusades, economic interests came to the fore for the first time, in addition to religious and power-political ones. During this period, trade and banking developed from Northern Italy, and especially from Venice, but even in the extensive production of weapons, ships, and clay products, people still relied on artisan production methods. It was thus only the social, political, technological, and economic changes of the eighteenth century that led to industrialization, thus creating the necessity and the prerequisite for the development of management in economic organizations (Michel 1953; Bendix 1960).

© The Author(s), under exclusive license to Springer Nature Switzerland AG 2021
U. Seebacher, *Predictive Intelligence for Data-Driven Managers*, Future of Business and Finance, https://doi.org/10.1007/978-3-030-69403-6_1

1.2   How Industrial Management Came About

The industrial revolution can thus be considered the birth of industrial management and thus of modern business management. Starting with industrialization in England in the middle of the eighteenth century, industrialization in Germany also took place towards the end of the eighteenth century. At that time, 85% of the population still lived in rural areas (Kocka 1983). Industrialization in Germany led to the unification of the currency and economic policy as well as to the creation of a large economic area, because at the beginning of the nineteenth century Germany was still fragmented into a large number of individual states. The improvement of hygienic conditions, health care, and nutrition led to a significant reduction in the mortality rate. Population growth led to declining wage costs due to a high demand for labor. Flanking government measures, such as the abolition of official concessions for factory operation, the facilitation of capital procurement through the legal form of the joint-stock company, and measures of state social policy, continued to promote industrialization in a targeted manner. The expansion of transport routes also enlarged sales markets and facilitated supra-regional trade.

At the beginning of the nineteenth century, industrialization also began in North America, which is sometimes wrongly regarded as the country of origin of management. At that time, no comparable preoccupation with management issues to that in England can be identified, because until about 1840, small production facilities with a high proportion of child labor predominated in North America due to the latent shortage of labor. Around 1900, immigrants accounted for 40% of population growth and over 70% of industrial workers. From 1850 onward, significant industrial growth is observed, triggered by large immigration flows and high capital inflows. The most important growth sectors were mining, steel, textiles, leather, meat preserving, and above all oil. These sectors brought the USA the big business and the first "Robber Barons" like Vanderbild or Rockefeller. Supported by a laissez-faire capitalism and a lack of social legislation, they were able to dominate the country for a long time.

In the further course of global industrialization, the forms of production changed from artisanal, small-scale production facilities to large-scale production facilities in the form of factories. With industrial growth and in the course of the changes in production activities described above, management tasks also changed. Originally, the management's area of responsibility was the execution of the planned work preparation, allocation, and monitoring. Due to the changed production forms, the tasks also became relevant for all other functional areas of the companies, such as purchasing, personnel administration, research and development, financing, accounting, and sales.

1.3 The Separation of Ownership and Management

This expansion of the tasks of the company management is also accompanied by the separation of ownership and management, especially as a result of the continuously increasing size of the company. The constant local, but also the functional expansion of the company's activities and the associated higher complexity of management tasks force entrepreneurs as owners or capital providers to call upon particularly qualified executives. A process of gradual detachment of management from capital ownership and its inherent decision-making power therefore began at that time (Berle and Means 1932). This gradual detachment, which can be found today in almost all medium-sized and large companies, made it possible for the manager to become the representative of a new professional group, a new social class. Although the *"managerial revolution"* prophesied by Burnham (1941) never occurred, the manager type is now an indispensable part of everyday professional life.

It is important to note that in German companies at the top management level, a division into a commercial and a technical directorate could already be observed in the middle of the nineteenth century, although initially no separate position was planned for a general directorate or *general manager*. It was not until the beginning of the twentieth century that there were isolated departments for general administration or a general management and thus a three-tier system. A further significant impulse with regard to the development of modern management theory came at the end of the nineteenth century (from 1870), when publications on production management and cost accounting appeared in British engineering journals. In the USA, the year 1886 is regarded as the beginning of the new discipline of management. On May 26, 1886, the president of the *American Society for Mechanical Engineering*, Henry Towne, gave a speech to the Society, which was founded in 1880 and of which F. W. Taylor was a member, on the subject of "The Engineer as an Economist." This is celebrated by management historians as the beginning of the management sciences (Bluedorns 1986), which, following Staehle (1994), can be divided into three groups of models or approaches

- Traditional approaches:
  - Engineering-economic approaches
  - Administrative approaches
  - Bureaucratic approaches
  - Physiological-psychological approaches
  - Social psychological and sociological approaches
- Modern approaches:
  - Disciplinary specialization (behavioral and formal science approaches)
  - Systems theory approaches (natural and social science approaches)
  - Situational approaches (classical situational and behavioral situational approaches)
  - Consistency Approaches
- Organizational etymological approaches:

- Cybernetics
- Positivistic approaches
- Antipositivist approaches
- Constructivism

Research results in the field of corporate governance and management are available in many different disciplines, such as psychology, sociology, political science, but also in engineering and law. Irrespective of their own research contribution, the disciplines of business administration in the Anglo-Saxon world and business administration for the German-speaking world are considered predestined to impart knowledge in the fields of corporate management, corporate governance, and management respectively. In any case, when searching for management knowledge, *managers* cannot limit themselves to one of these disciplines alone but should always take into account the relevant research results of neighboring disciplines. Without the appropriate management training and competence, an engineer will not be able to sustainably manage a modern company with the corresponding complexity, dynamics, and networking. As mentioned above, this fact was already known in Germany in the middle of the nineteenth century, when commercial and technical management positions were first created.

1.4   What Are the Current Challenges?

The modern era in management is characterized by an ever-increasing number of fashion waves, as Byrne (1986) already pointed out in an editorial in the magazine *Business Week*, in which he criticized American management. While in the fifties approaches such as *Computerization, Theory Y, Operations Research* or *Management by Objectives*, in the sixties one spoke of *Matrix Organizations, Conglomerates* and also of *Centralization* and *Decentralization*. In the course of the seventies the management keywords were then *Zero-Base-Budgeting, Experience Curve* and *Portfolio Management*, which were replaced in the eighties by *Theory Z, Intrapreneurship, Lean Management, Restructuring, Organizational Culture, Management-by-Walking* Around or also *One-Minute Managing*.

Especially the last approach, which was first published in the book of the same name by Blanchard and Johnson (1983), is symptomatic of the criticized form of management fashions and books as a recipe for successful leadership. Byrne called on science and practice, for the protection of employees and capital providers, not to be increasingly led or tempted by management fashions, which in most cases were pushed into the market by sales-oriented consulting firms. The emergence of innumerable and ever new models of corporate management went hand in hand with the boom of the entire consulting industry.

In stark contradiction to this are statement systems that deny any reference to organizational etymology and thus lay claim to spatio-temporally unlimited validity and universal applicability as far as the object area is concerned. In principle, representatives of this line of thought, such as Fayol (1916), among others, assume that the same applicable management models must always be available for all forms of organizations such as private and public enterprises, churches, schools, prisons, theaters, political associations, and others.

With regard to today's challenges regarding corporate management, it is crucial to take a closer look at the two schools of thought of the analytical-functional and the empirical-action-oriented. The first school of thought goes back to the work of Fayol (1916) and refers to the functional organization of the enterprise. The empirical-action-oriented approach has its origins in an empirical study by Carlson from 1951. In any case, both approaches have in common that they assume that the function of management in the sense of corporate governance and corporate control is subject to essential target criteria. These are the long-term protection of the workforce and capital providers while at the same time adhering to basic economic principles such as profit and return.

1.5   The Basic Economic Principles Are also Disrupted

However, these basic economic principles were fundamentally disrupted at the turn of the millennium when the rapid spread of the Internet and the associated possibilities and technologies gave rise to the so-called *New Economy*.[1] Suddenly, capital providers, now called investors and venturers, were willing to invest their money even in loss-making companies as long as an "e" or "Internet" could be found in the *pitch deck*. The managers of these companies were suddenly between 20 and 30 years old and some of them did not even have a completed education. Not that I would like to deny these young companies the appropriate competence at this point, but for the entire ecosystem of economic activity, it was in any case a disruption to suddenly see 25 year olds with supposedly billion-dollar companies listed on their own trading floors, such as the *"Neuer Markt"* Index on the Frankfurt Stock Exchange. As many history books of the financial industry show, it did not take long for the *New Economy Bubble to* burst, leaving behind many loss-making investors.

Only a few years later, we were hit by the banking crisis in 2008, caused by a completely new type of financial products, which in turn were only made possible by new technologies and the Internet, and increasingly risky speculation even by the most prestigious financial institutions of the time. The result was a devastated Deutsche Bank and a Commerzbank, which had to slip under the rescue umbrella of partial nationalization. I have described in detail the developments of the last

---

[1]https://en.wikipedia.org/wiki/New_Economy. Accessed: November 17, 2020.

decades in my book "Template-based Management" (2020) and interpreted the effects.

The phenomena that we have to deal with today in the context of modern business management are multi-layered and complex. New technologies make it possible to act and react more and more quickly. Global networking enables a global shift of capital. Being able to do everything from your own smartphone often makes existing inhibitions disappear too quickly. Only recently, the Wirecard case has shown that we are in a time of *technology-based de-ethnization*. Enron and Worldcom prove this as well. The question arises as to why fundamentally honest and ethical managers and executives are drifting into supposedly legal illegality. The question arises how in today's world 1.9 billion euros can be faked over a period of years, as was the case with Wirecard.

It seems that the interplay of forces in economic systems with the capital providers, hedge funds, and shareholders on the one hand and the boards and managers on the other, with the vanity and uncompromising striving for prosperity of more and more managers, is turning into a dangerous cocktail. The supposed transparency of global networking in combination with increasingly complex and sophisticated control mechanisms seems to fall victim to the *complexity paradox* of ever-increasing loopholes. The current example of Wirecard is proof of this, since Wirecard as an IT company was not subject to banking supervision and therefore these transactions could not be uncovered earlier. One could assume that with a less complex control structure, Wirecard as a listed company would automatically have been subject to banking supervision and thus the scandal could have been avoided or the extent and damage could have been minimized by disclosing the transactions earlier.

Against this background, I see two major challenges for corporate management in the twenty-first century:

1. The first big challenge is the uncompromising return to the original economic principles of classical management research, as I mentioned before:
   (a) Long-term protection of the workforce and capital providers
   (b) Compliance with basic economic principles such as profit and yield
   Today more than ever, it must be possible to stringently pursue these two basic economic principles with the technical achievements. And this is where the topic of this book comes into play, namely Predictive Intelligence. In order to be able to fulfill these two basic economic principles permanently and lastingly stringently, it is also necessary to be aware of the fact that healthy growth can only be realized continuously and persistently to a manageable degree. Everything that rises too fast and grows too fast is unstable and runs the risk of tending downwards again very quickly. *Perseverance, patience*, and *reflection* are three further qualities that make it easier to adhere to the two basic economic principles.

Fig. 1.1 Triangle of trust
[based on Frei and Morriss
(2020)]

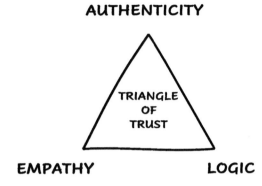

2. The second great challenge of our time is to return to the basic principles of
   ethical action of the individual. Managers have to recall the *triangle of trust*
   (Fig. 1.1) consisting of *authenticity*, *ethics*, and *logic*—but also and above all the
   fact that a manager can only assume his multi-layered responsibility if he also has
   a fundamental command of the aforementioned knowledge in the neighboring
   disciplines of his own core discipline. In this respect, management boards and
   their supervisory boards must proactively strive to establish dual management
   structures not only at the highest corporate level, but also again at the second
   level, at the divisional and business unit level. On the basis of my almost 25 years
   of professional experience, I could give you numerous examples where professionally "one-dimensional" managers have brilliantly failed to successfully manage the business units left to them. Too often the saying "arrogance and ignorance
   dance a dance" unfortunately has to be strained in these cases.

1.6   What Role Does the Corona Pandemic Play?

Against this background, the current corona pandemic may, in addition to all the
terrible effects on humanity, possibly also have a positive effect, namely in terms of
deceleration and recollection, as described above. Jeremy Rifkin even goes a
decisive step further and proclaims the *New Green Deal* and predicts a paradigm
shift in terms of business models, but also management models.[2] Rifkin (2019)
announces a hydrogen revolution as well as a zero marginal cost society and his main
criticism is the stoicism and persistence of managers, which in turn results in a lack
of willingness to change. The new normality will lead us into the age of a *re-mocal
economy*. In such an economy companies will have to actively use and integrate
global aspects, identities, and products *remotely* due to limited global supply chains
for being independent in case of future possible lockdowns while ensuring to foster

---

[2]https://en.wikipedia.org/wiki/Jeremy_Rifkin. Accessed: August 19, 2020.

acting *locally*, for being accepted in their respective local markets. The current COVID19 pandemic is leading to a re-emergence of local identities in order to protect against the virus from outside. This also implies the increasing need to rethink global supply chains in terms of the necessary independence from foreign suppliers. Governments will no longer be able to afford not to provide protective masks for their own people because suppliers from the other end of the world cannot deliver. All this leads to a sensible and necessary process of rethinking and change.

This makes it all the more important to be able to anticipate and reflect possible developments with ever greater precision. In the 1980s and 1990s, the topic of controlling became fashionable. The main point of criticism was that only data from the past was used and processed, which according to the latest Fujitsu study is still practiced by almost all companies today. No organization can afford to operate at full throttle just by looking in the rear-view mirror, because responsible management of the new normality of the twenty-first century requires forward-looking action based on valid future scenarios for all possible dimensions, such as applications, disruptions, industries, innovations, customers, markets, regions, to name just a few.

1.7   What Do We Know?

In this chapter, the historical development was used to show where we have reached today and why we have reached this point. It is shown that we can learn a lot from history and that in earlier times some things were apparently already done better than today. The chance in our new normality in the context of a corona pandemic is now to unite the best of all worlds in order to re-orientate economic action towards the introduced basic economic principles with corresponding sustainability.

Further Reading

Bendix, R. (1960). *Work and authority in industry*. New York. 1956. Deutsch: *Herrschaft und Industriearbeit*. Frankfurt/Main.

Berle, A. A., & Means, G. C. (1932). *The modern corporation and private property* (2nd ed. 1968). New York: Routledge.

Blanchard, K. H., & Johnson, S. (1983). *The one-minute manager*. New York: Berkley.

Bluedorns, A. C. (1986). Introduction to special book review section on the classics of management. *AMR, 2/1986*, S. 442–464.

Burnham, J. (1941). *The managerial revolution*. New York: John Day.

Byrne, J. A. (1986, January 20). Business facts: What's in – and out. *Business Week*, S. 52–S. 61

Carlson, S. (1951). *Executive behavior: A study of the work load and the working methods of managing directors*. Stockholm: Strömberg.

Fayol, H. (1916). *Administration industrielle et générale*. Paris: Dunod.

Frei, F., & Morriss, A. (2020, Juni). Entfesselt. Der Leitfaden des unentschuldigten Führens zur Befähigung aller um Sie herum. *Harvard Business Review*.

George, C. S. (1972). *The history of management thought* (2nd ed.). Englewood Cliffs, NJ: Prentice-Hall.

Kocka, J. (1983). *Lohnarbeit und Klassenbildung*. Berlin/Bonn: Dietz.

Michel, E. (1953). *Sozialgeschichte der industriellen Arbeitswelt* (3rd ed.). Frankfurt/Main: Knecht.

Pollard, S. (1965). *The genesis of modern management. A study of the industrial revolution in Great Britain*. London: Edward Arnold.

Rifkin, J. (2019). *Der globale Green New Deal: Warum die fossil befeuerte Zivilisation um 2028 kollabiert—und ein kühner ökonomischer Plan das Leben auf der Erde retten kann*. Frankfurt: Campus Verlag.

Seebacher, U. (2020). *Template-based management—A guide for an efficient and impactful professional practice*. Cham: Springer.

Staehle, W. (1994). *Management* (7th ed.). Munich: Vahlen.

Wren, D. A. (1979). *The evolution of management thought* (2nd ed.). New York 1972.

Predictive Intelligence at a Glance

2

2.1 What Is Predictive Intelligence?

The term was mentioned for the first time in 2016 in the context of marketing.[1] At that time the term is defined as follows:

> Predictive intelligence is the process of first collecting data on the behavior and actions of consumers and potential consumers from a variety of sources, possibly combined with profile data on their characteristics.

Predictive Intelligence (PI) has therefore been defined as a three-step process of analysis, interpretation, and implementation rules for automated communication. One of the leading consulting firms already considered PI as an approach to predict the probabilities of an event as precisely as possible. In 2015, the Aberdeen Group conducted a comprehensive study entitled "*Predictive Analytics in Financial Services*" in which 123 financial services companies were surveyed. Even then, it was confirmed that companies using predictive analytics realized an average of 11% higher customer acquisition compared to the previous year. In addition, these companies achieved a 10% increase in new opportunities and leads compared to their competitors who had not used predictive analytics.

Forbes Insights interviewed approximately 300 executives from companies with annual sales of $20 million or more. An impressive 86% of these managers achieved significantly higher ROI when they had been running predictive marketing initiatives for at least 2 years. In summary, predictive intelligence leads to significant improvements in all marketing channels. In order to be able to derive a generally valid definition for PI on this basis, the term must be removed from the field of marketing and defined in a generally valid way:

---

[1] https://www.smartinsights.com/digital-marketing-strategy/predictive-intelligence-set-change-marketing-2016/. Accessed: August 20, 2020.

> Predictive Intelligence is the process in which first data from the past on all internal and external relevant contingency factors of an organization are collected from a multitude of validated internal and external sources, validated, linked and processed by means of defined and validated algorithms, dynamically extrapolated and modelled by means of variable parameters in terms of assumptions and occurrence probabilities for short, medium and long-term events, prepared and made available to the organization 24/7 for the purpose of sustainably securing the existence of the organization in question.

On this basis, predictive intelligence can now be narrowed down for the management area or adapted to the area of corporate management. On this basis, we define Predictive Intelligence for the management of organizations as follows:

> Predictive Intelligence is the process in which first of all data from the past on all internal and external relevant contingency factors of an organization from a multitude of validated internal and external sources are collected, validated, linked and processed by means of defined and validated algorithms, dynamically extrapolated and modelled by means of variable parameters in the sense of assumptions and occurrence probabilities for short, medium and long-term corporate management, prepared and made available to the organization 24/7 for the optimization of basic economic principles.

The decisive difference in relation to *Predictive Analytics* (PA) is that PA can be classified as a sub-discipline and one of the foundations of Business Analytics in the field of *data mining*.[2] Although PA also deals with the prediction of future developments, the results are purely descriptive and analytical, whereas predictive intelligence uses the methods and technologies of artificial intelligence, *deep learning*,[3] *machine learning*[4] and also *auto machine learning* (AutoML)[5] or *meta machine learning* (MetaML) to develop concrete options and recommendations for action in an interpretative and constructivist manner. Predictive analytics is also used to identify trends by using predictors[6] as one or more variables in an equation, which are used to predict future events. On this basis, predictive models are developed to calculate probabilities of occurrence.[7] The entire conceptual environment as well as the PI ecosystem will be discussed and debated in more detail and more comprehensively in the remainder of the book.

---

[2]https://en.wikipedia.org/wiki/Data-Mining. Accessed: August 20, 2020.

[3]https://en.wikipedia.org/wiki/Deep_Learning. Accessed: August 20, 2020.

[4]https://en.wikipedia.org/wiki/Maschinelles_Lernen. Accessed: August 20, 2020.

[5]https://de.qwe.wiki/wiki/Automated_machine_learning. Accessed: August 20, 2020.

[6]https://www.computerweekly.com/de/definition/Predictive-Analytics.   Accessed: August 20, 2020.

[7]https://www.vorteile-nachteile.info/leben/predictive-analytics/. Accessed: August 20, 2020.

2.2   The Maturity Model for Predictive Intelligence

The maturity model for Predictive Intelligence (Fig. 2.1) was developed on the basis of various implementation projects in companies. The model comprises four stages and was first presented to the public in July 2020. The model was developed within the framework of expert interviews and on the basis of the evaluations of various scientific papers.

The model shows the developments of the various relevant dimensions over time to be considered:

- Costs for data
- Validity and reliability of the data
- Time for evaluations and analyses

The model divides the development into four stages or characteristics of how data is handled in organizations. The starting point, on which around 90% of all companies are still based today, is known as reactive-static business analytics. This stage is characterized by high costs for data, long waiting times, and low validity and reliability with regard to data. In most cases, necessary analyses and studies are commissioned externally, which are used once and then do not flow into any further processing in the companies.

Development level 2 is called *Proactive-situational Business Analytics* (BA). At this level, BA is no longer only used reactively, but for the first time, it is also used proactively in relation to specific situations and questions. This means that companies already have data available, validated and prepared, but also maintained, in their own companies. No specific instruments or IT applications are required for

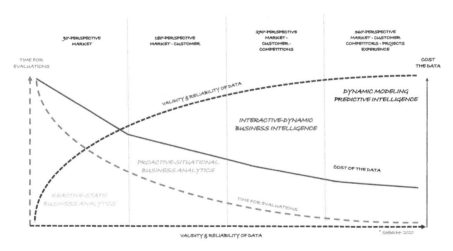

Fig. 2.1 Maturity model for Predictive Intelligence (Seebacher 2020a, b, c)

this, because in most cases conventional applications such as Microsoft Excel or Access are completely sufficient, as are data preparation applications such as MS PowerBI. It is important to note that, as PI matures, the spectrum of data considered must also evolve from an initial 90° to ultimately a 360° perspective in order to implement PI in a sustainable and meaningful way.

The third stage of development then goes hand in hand with an already 270° comprehensive data perspective and enables *Interactive-dynamic Business Intelligence.* In operational terms, this means that the PI department is constantly involved in all operational and strategic measures of the company management. In the meantime, an intensive exchange and dialog with the various internal customer groups have developed, which can provide corresponding evaluations and overviews in real time on the basis of past data, for sound and profit-optimized corporate management.

The development step towards the last and highest level of the PI maturity model is a gradual and iterative process. The *Dynamically-modeling Predictive Intelligence* combines all relevant internal and external data dimensions into a 360° perspective. This 360° view can also be dynamically computed and calculated over flexibly adaptable time periods. The decisive difference to the first three stages of the maturity model is the competence of the interpretative and concluding intelligence. This not only provides analyses and evaluations, but also enables concrete future simulations by integrating self-learning applications, instruments, and technologies, in the sense of a statement not only about the probability of occurrence of future events, but also about their applied operative design.

A comparison should clarify this difference: Predictive Analytics (PA) is comparable to predictive models in the field of meteorology. These models enable weather warnings. However, these models do not calculate any resulting causal events such as avalanches or floods, nor do they calculate mudflows or other natural disasters. Predictive intelligence in the field of meteorology would be able to evolve such causal events quantitatively predictively. In economics, this means that PI would numerically model expected causal events and thus show exactly how this would affect the company in terms of basic economic principles. The attribute "modeling" also makes it clear that PI can also calculate and design different scenarios by applying artificial intelligence. This is crucial in order to enable management to quantify and qualify even more precisely the different options in terms of their effects.

An example could be in the area of medium-term PI, for example, if the company management plans to enter a new market. The investments for the market entry with regard to sales and marketing could be simulated on the basis of three scenarios with low, medium, and high investments and then be quantitatively predictive with regard to the resulting return on investment (RoI).[8] Based on this PI maturity model, the schematic process model for predictive intelligence was developed for this

---

[8]See also the corresponding case study "Medium-term Predictive Intelligence" in the back of the book.

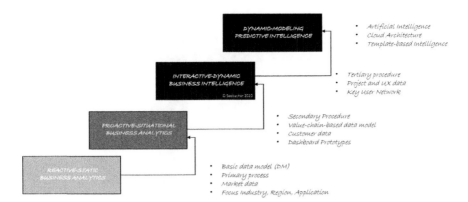

Fig. 2.2 Process model for Predictive Intelligence

publication (Fig. 2.2). The model can be used to derive the most important areas of activity for each stage of the PI development model that need to be performed in order to move on to the next maturity level. In the relevant section of this publication, the PI procedure model is described and explained in detail.

2.3 The Predictive Intelligence Self-Assessment (PI-SA)

The Predictive Intelligence Self-Assessment Instrument comprises 50 questions and is divided into three different areas. In the first section of the instrument, the potential of an organization with regard to Predictive Intelligence is assessed. This value is expressed in the form of the Predictive Intelligence Potential Index (PI-PI). In the second section, which is made up of seven segments, the current status of the company in question with regard to Predictive Intelligence is queried. The third section aggregates the seven segments previously queried and maps them cumulatively in a so-called *Predictive Intelligence Readiness Index* (PI-RI). This value links the results of the first segment to the second and therefore, in combination, relationally represents the corresponding maturity of the examined organization in terms of potential.

The PI-SA is structured in such a way that it also makes it clear to organizations if the potential to be realized through PI is correspondingly small. This might be the case due to the size of the company, the small number of markets or regions in which the organization is active or responsible for, but also the product portfolio of a company. If this is the case, this organization might be well advised to consider not to develop PI internally on its own. Especially in such cases, where the potential for Predictive Intelligence is small, the "buy" rather than the "make" would make more sense.

The PI-SA is available to all companies free of charge and can be completed online within 15 min. The QR code in Fig. 2.3 takes you directly to the analysis questionnaire. Figure 2.4 shows an example of an evaluation of an international organization with a correspondingly high potential value for PI and above-average

Fig. 2.3 QR code for Predictive Intelligence Self-Assessment (PI-SA)

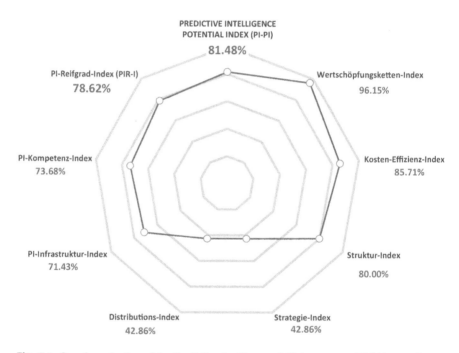

Fig. 2.4 Sample evaluation of the Predictive Intelligence Self-Assessment (PI-SA) according to Seebacher

maturity in terms of predictive intelligence. The graph shows that the organization has succeeded in very well implementing the necessary groundwork in terms of value chains (see Value Chain Maturity Index), but also the cost-efficiency parameters up to the organizational structure. The challenges or potential for this organization obviously exist in the areas of strategic positioning (Strategicness Index), market development (Go-to-Market Index), the necessary infrastructure for

Predictive Intelligence (Infrastructure Maturity Index), but also the lack of around 25% of the necessary competencies for implementing Predictive Intelligence (Competence Availability Index).

The maturity model for Predictive Intelligence will be discussed in more detail later in this book. In addition, the individual indicators of the instrument are explained in detail and also critically discussed with regard to organizational implications.

2.4   The Advantages of Predictive Intelligence

The topic Predictive Intelligence is new. In order to be able to establish it in an organization in the long term, the necessary data must be available and prepared accordingly. In the context of the recent study of Fujitsu quoted at the beginning of this book, according to which only 5% of the enterprises in the DACH region indicate to realize data-driven management today, it becomes clear, how big first of all the need for action is. Secondly, this fact also makes clear that today only few scientifically validated and provable numbers and facts regarding the advantages of Predictive Intelligence can be available due to the lack of a required number of sample companies. From a strategic conceptual point of view, three major areas can be identified with regard to the advantages of PI (Fig. 2.5). The point is to be the decisive step ahead of the other market participants through Predictive Intelligence. Predictive intelligence can also be used to produce better forecasts for business, capacity, and resource planning. In this context, reference should also be made to the work in the field of strategic workforce management (Seebacher and Güpner 2010), which also uses similar methods and techniques to attempt to predict as precisely as possible the skills and personnel requirements expected in the future. Ultimately, and this is the all-decisive and irrefutable argument for Predictive Intelligence, it has been proven that by better and more precise addressing of potential and existing

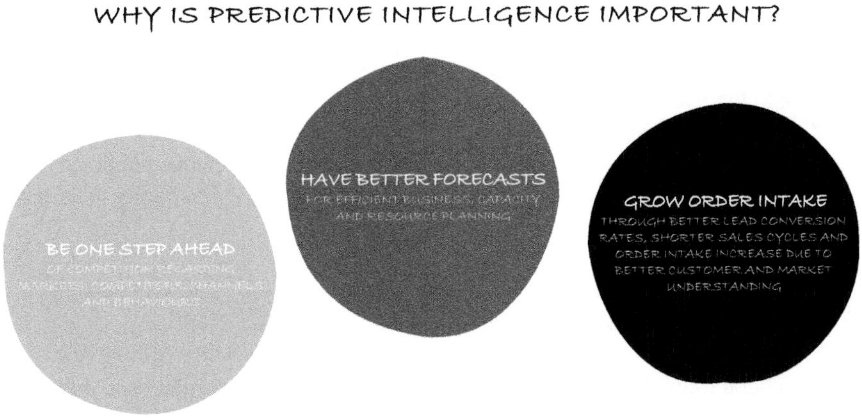

WHY IS PREDICTIVE INTELLIGENCE IMPORTANT?

HAVE BETTER FORECASTS
FOR EFFICIENT BUSINESS, CAPACITY
AND RESOURCE PLANNING

BE ONE STEP AHEAD
OF COMPETITION REGARDING
MARKETS, COMPETITORS, TRENDS
AND BEHAVIOURS

GROW ORDER INTAKE
THROUGH BETTER LEAD CONVERSION
RATES, SHORTER SALES CYCLES AND
ORDER INTAKE INCREASE DUE TO
BETTER CUSTOMER AND MARKET
UNDERSTANDING

Fig. 2.5 Reasons for Predictive Intelligence

BENCHMARK SURVEYS SHOW THAT **PREDICTIVE INTELLIGENCE...**

- Lifts website revenue by 10 percent,
- Increases email click through rates by 35 percent,
- Optimizes email conversion rates by 25 percent,
- Reduces sales cycle times by 12 %,
- Increases sales hit rates by 24 % and more, and
- Leverages A defined salesforce by 32 %

Fig. 2.6 Advantages of PI-based marketing

customers, the order intake can not only be significantly increased, but also optimized in terms of Return on Sales (RoS).

However, the area of industrial goods marketing is apparently a pioneer in this field, because in this area most companies have been storing, managing, and more or less evaluating numbers, data and facts about customers in CRM systems for some time.

Based on the maturity model for Predictive Intelligence, it becomes clear that customer data is the starting point for the sustainable development of Predictive Intelligence in companies. Due to the developments in the field of automation of marketing and sales, the automated generation, evaluation, and also use of more data became easier and faster to implement. Against this background, innovative B2B marketing managers from marketing departments have already established predictive intelligence environments in recent years. On this basis, from today's point of view, findings on the demonstrable advantages of data-driven marketing using the predictive intelligence approach can already be presented (Fig. 2.6). The following advantages, which were collected in a study with more than 1000 companies, can be derived for the area of marketing and sales support in the sense of *sales enablement* alone:

If one looks at generally valid organizational structures and thus sets marketing in relation to them as only a small part of it, the lever of the extension of PI to the entire field of corporate management very quickly becomes comprehensible in its entire extent. Any decision in the context of corporate management can be predicted more and more precisely by Predictive Intelligence and can be used as a highly valid basis for management decisions to be made.

2.5   The Conclusion

In this chapter, an attempt has been made to present these essential core messages and aspects of Predictive Intelligence for Managers for their data-driven corporation in a compact way. The aim was to present the initial situation, the basics, the development stages, and thus also the instrument for a contingency-based individual analysis in regard to the status of data-driven management using predictive intelligence. With the help of this section, I hopefully could make clear how negligent it would be on the part of top management not to deal with the topic of Predictive Intelligence for corporate management. No sensible and responsible pilot today would set his aircraft in motion without the necessary data and information about the flight and its routing. Likewise, department heads, managing directors, and board members should therefore not continue to control their organizations without the corresponding data.

Never before has it been so easy and cost-effective to implement sustainable, valid, data-based, and forward-looking planning and controlling of organizations. It is understandable that many top managers are not aware of the technical possibilities and their rapid developments today due to their complex and multilayered tasks. Data-driven management and even more Predictive Intelligence are still a black box for most business leaders today. This book is intended to reveal this black box, explain it in a comprehensible way and also show how easily sustainable Predictive Intelligence can be implemented in all forms of organizations in a cost-optimized way.

Further Reading

Seebacher, U. (2020a). *B2B marketing: A guidebook for the classroom to the boardroom*. Cham: Springer.

Seebacher, U. (2020b). *B2B marketing essential: How to turn your marketing from a cost into a sales engine* (2nd ed.). Graz: AQPS.

Seebacher, U. (2020c). *Template-based management—A guide for an efficient and impactful professional practice*. Cham: Springer.

Seebacher, U., & Güpner, A. (2010). *Strategic workforce management*. München: USP Publishing.

The Predictive Intelligence Ecosystem

3

3.1   Introduction

Predictive Intelligence has developed from the term *Business Intelligence* to meet the need not only to evaluate data with foresight, but also to relate it directly to concrete management decisions—in the sense of valid decision and action recommendations. The term "Business Intelligence" was invented by the consulting firm Gartner in 1989 and has since then become firmly established in the modern management vocabulary. Business Intelligence (BI) refers to technologies, processes, and skills that are necessary to collect and analyze data and transform data into actionable insights and information.

In recent years, the terms "Business Analytics" or "Analytics" have also come up, whereby these and similar terms are used interchangeably and confusingly. The increasing popularity of these and similar terms "Analytics" and "Business Analytics" can be attributed to the rapid developments in the field of data analysis with respect to, e.g., *in-memory*, *advanced algorithms*, *artificial intelligence* (AI) or *machine learning*, etc. which have massively increased the performance of Business Intelligence software. An ever more increasing number of new terms in the subject area of modern business management does not necessarily contribute to the necessary transparency and make it more difficult for top management to make the appropriate, necessary decisions for their own company and to initiate the right measures. Against this background, the following section describes and presents the current state of the PI ecosystem with the most important, established terms.

Note: English and German terms are sometimes used in this chapter. This selection was made in consideration of the frequency of use of the respective terms in order to show the reader the more common term in this list. Nevertheless, the various synonyms and other language mutations and versions were listed for better referencing.

© The Author(s), under exclusive license to Springer Nature Switzerland AG 2021
U. Seebacher, *Predictive Intelligence for Data-Driven Managers*, Future of Business
and Finance, https://doi.org/10.1007/978-3-030-69403-6_3

3.1.1 A/B Tests

This method describes the comparison and testing of different measures or options for action by exchanging and changing individual components, features, criteria, or parameters. The procedure plays an essential role in the allocation of resources.

3.1.2 Artificial Intelligence (AI)

Artificial Intelligence (AI) originated in the field of computer science and is therefore also a subfield of computer science. AI is concerned with the automation of intelligent behavior and learning of machines, machine learning, as this will be defined later as part of the conceptual ecosystem of PI in this chapter. An exact delimitation or definition of the term would require as a basis a precise definition of "intelligence," which does not exist.

The word "intelligence" comes from the Latin word *intellegere*, which can be translated with various terms such as "to recognize," "to see," "to understand." If you translate the word literally, it is composed of the Latin *inter*, which means "to choose between…" and *legere* for "read" or "choose." In psychology, the term is a collective term for cognitive or mental performance. Cognitive abilities are differently developed in living beings. Against this background, there is disagreement about how intelligence is to be determined, which is also the reason why there is no generally valid definition for intelligence in research on artificial intelligence (AI).

AI basically describes the reproduction of natural, i.e., human intelligence. Today's fields of application are, e.g.,

- Dynamic optimization for traffic jam detectors or route planners
- Speech recognition and machine translation
- Search engines on the Internet
- Social Bots and Chat Bots
- Signal recognition in the context of image understanding, image recognition, face recognition, pattern recognition
- Humanoid robots as, for example, at Atlas, ASIMO, Pepper
- Autonomous weapon systems
- Computer games increasingly use AI for computer-controlled opponents

Neural networks can be considered the forerunner of today's AI, as they replicate the human brain and reproduce it in the computer to simulate how the human brain works. The ever more rapid development in the performance of computers makes it possible for such artificial networks to become more and more powerful and achieve a learning ability similar to that of the brain. This is known as machine learning, which will be discussed in more detail later in this chapter. When artificial intelligence surpasses human intelligence, the state of *technological singularity* is reached.[1]

If the state of the technological singularity is reached can be determined by the Turing test.[2] In the course of the test, a human being goes through an interactive but virtual situation—without visual or auditory contact with the counterpart. If, after an intensive questioning, the questioner cannot determine which of the two interlocutors was a machine or a human, then the machine has passed the Turing test. This machine is then certified to have a thinking ability equal to that of a human being. An AI that you can test online is, e.g., the cleverbot , which is specialized in small talk.

What artificial intelligence has lacked so far is (self-)awareness and emotion. Moreover, a machine, even if it is obviously equipped with intelligent behavior, remains only an instrument until a self-consciousness and motivation to act on "own" initiative and to pursue "own" interests is recognizable and verifiable. Such a technology, which could be interpreted as emotional, would in turn raise various questions of ethics regarding the right and responsibility of such a machine. The discussion to be conducted would revolve around whether a "biological" machine should be evaluated differently from a "technological" intelligence.

With regard to predictive intelligence, the field of AI will play an increasingly important role in the applied extrapolation of data, the causal relationships based on it, and above all complex decision trees and subsequent causal events in the form of multidimensional scenarios. Only through the integration of AI can PI calculate the effects of an alternative course of action more and more precisely, extrapolate them relationally and, based on this, identify parameters that change or develop to the disadvantage of the alternative. For example, a faster realized market entry with higher investments can lead to market participants initiating countermeasures, which in turn would shift the one dimensionally and not relationally determined return on sales (RoS) or return on investment (RoI). If a company would then have a thin capital cover and be dependent on achieving the defined RoI, this could have a dramatic effect on the entire company.

Due to the ever-increasing involvement of AI in the field of PI, such multivariate models and considerations are becoming more and more precise and can thus have a significant positive influence on the quality of corporate management in a way that has never been seen before and has not been possible before.

---

[1] https://en.wikipedia.org/wiki/Technological_singularity. Accessed: November 18, 2020.

[2] https://en.wikipedia.org/wiki/Turing_test. Accessed: November 18, 2020.

3.1.3   Artificial Neural Network (ANN)

Artificial neural networks (ANN)[3] are networks of artificial neurons. They are the subject of research in neuroinformatics and represent a branch of artificial intelligence. ANN are gaining more and more importance in the field of predictive intelligence, since they significantly increase the performance and precision, but above all the resilience of applied, predictive intelligence. ANN are mostly based on the interconnection of many McCulloch-Pitts neurons[4] or slight modifications of them, such as the high-order neuron. The topology of a network in the sense of the assignment of links and nodes must be optimally structured depending on the defined project objective in order to generate information with added value from the Big Data. After the initial design of a mesh, this design must "learn" in a training phase in order to optimize itself with regard to the task at hand. Theoretically, a network can learn by using the following methods:

- Development of new compounds
- Delete existing connections
- Change the weighting within the construction
- Adjust the threshold values of the neurons, if they have threshold values
- Add or delete neurons
- Modification of activation, propagation, or output function

Especially in the field of predictive intelligence, we are operating in an environment where there is only a small amount of explicit (systematic) knowledge about the problem to be solved in most cases. This is caused by the complex and multidimensional contingency situation of corporate management and the many different internal and external influencing factors. Especially in such an environment ANN prove to be important tools to develop models even more valid and precise. Today, ANN are mainly used for text recognition, speech recognition, image recognition, but also for face recognition, where many millions of pixels have to be transformed into a comparatively small number of allowed results. But ANN are also used for the early detection of emerging tornadoes.

3.1.4   Association Analysis

To be able to recognize how objects are related to each other and thus associated, the method of association analysis[5] is applied. Within the framework of these methods, three common measures are used to determine associations.

---

[3]https://en.wikipedia.org/wiki/Artificial_neural_network. Accessed: November 18, 2020.

[4]https://de.wikipedia.org/wiki/McCulloch-Pitts-Zelle. Accessed: August 24, 2020.

[5]https://en.wikipedia.org/wiki/Association_rule_learning. Accessed: November 18, 2020.

- *Support*: This criterion indicates how often a set of objects occurs in relation to the total in which this set is involved.
- *Confidence*: This measure indicates how often a characteristic *a* occurs when characteristic *b* is present. The confidence is calculated as a relation of the total quantity with characteristic *a*, where characteristic *b* also occurs, and the total of all transactions with characteristic *a*.
- *Lift*: This value indicates how often *a* and *b* occur together but taking both individual frequencies into account.
  An important principle in the context of association analysis is the a-priori principle, which accelerates the search for frequently occurring combinations of features by excluding large data ranges of rarely occurring combinations ex antes.

3.1.5 Evaluation Metrics

Once a model is defined and implemented, it must be evaluated in terms of its precision in relation to model predictions, i.e., *Predictive Intelligence Precision* (PIP). This means that underlying PI procedures are compared with each other to identify which of several different approaches can be used to generate the best predictions for a situation or defined problem. The most commonly used evaluation metrics are the following three methods:

- *Classification Metrics*: This category includes the percentage of correct predictions as the simplest way of evaluation and the so-called truth matrix or confusion matrix.
- *Regression Metrics*: The root mean square[6] determines prediction errors as differences between predicted and actual values.
  However, since over-adapted models for a given metric produce different results for different data, (PI) models should always be evaluated using an appropriate validation procedure (see the corresponding section in this chapter).

3.1.6 Big Data

This term, which originates from the English-speaking world in the broadest sense, refers to data sets that are too large, too complex, too fast-moving, or too weakly structured to be evaluated using manual and conventional methods of data processing (Christl 2014). Big Data as a term in the narrower sense describes the processing of large, complex, and rapidly changing data sets. In the narrowest sense,[7] the term refers to firmly defined types of data, whereby "big" refers to the four dimensions

---

[6]RMS, root mean square.
[7]https://en.wikipedia.org/wiki/Big_Data. Accessed: November 18, 2020.

- *Volume* (scope, data volume)
- *Velocity* (speed with which the data sets are generated and transferred)
- *Variety* (bandwidth of data types and sources) and
- Veracity (authenticity of data)

This definition is extended by the two Vs "value" and "validity," which stand for added business value and ensuring data quality.[8] The data can come from various data sources, depending on the organization and environment.

"Big Data" is also often used as an umbrella term for digital technologies, which are being held responsible for a paradigm shift in technical terms for a new age of digital communication and processing of data and information, but also in social terms (Reichert 2014).

3.1.7 Business Analytics (BA)

The complexity of the ecosystem for Predictive Intelligence can be seen in the term Business Analytics. The similarity of terms such as business analysis and business analytics makes it clear how crucial and important a precise delimitation and coordinated definition of relevant and used technical terms is.

The goal of *Business Analysis* is to understand the structures and processes of a company   (IIBA®   International   Institute   of   Business   Analysis   2017). Recommendations for action are to be derived and recommended, which enable the organization to eliminate identified deficits with regard to structural and process organization. Examples are optimized workflows, changes in the organizational structure, and especially the use of IT tools.

Business Analytics,[9] on the other hand, focuses on the process of so-called data refinement. It is a strategic tool of modern business management and control. As an essential aspect of Predictive Intelligence, the aim is to provide answers not only to the question: "What was," but also: "What will be." In the Encyclopedia of Business Informatics[10] Felden provides the following definition of Business Analytics based on comprehensive research:

> Business Analytics is the combination of people, tasks and technology, and thus of skills, technologies, algorithms, applications, visualizations and processes that can be used internally or externally to gain insight into business activities based on internal and external data. The project-oriented use is carried out in a process to evaluate company-wide activities, so that insights are collected across departmental and company boundaries as a basis for decision-making, in order to derive current measures and future-oriented actions from

---

[8]http://www.gartner.com/it-glossary/big-data. Accessed: August 24, 2020.

[9]https://en.wikipedia.org/wiki/Business_analytics. Accessed: November 18, 2020.

[10]https://www.enzyklopaedie-der-wirtschaftsinformatik.de/lexikon/daten-wissen/Business-Intelli gence/Analytische-Informationssysteme%2D%2DMethoden-der-/Business-Analytics/index.html. Accessed: August 25, 2020.

them, which have a positive influence on the company's performance and secure the long-term development of the company.[11]

Already since the end of the 1990s, the process of knowledge discovery in databases (KDD)[12] has been the theoretical basis for an ever-increasing number of available software products on the market. These include aspects such as data selection, preprocessing, transformation, data mining and, increasingly, the interpretation of results. Business Analytics builds on these procedural steps but extends this KDD process by an initial processing of the incoming data to optimize the input and, based on this, the output quality and topic-specific measures regarding the decision to be made and its implementation. Furthermore, the underlying process model is supplemented by the evaluation step, which in turn enables the comparison of the generated model variants on the basis of a so-called quality measure.

Business Analytics thus focuses on a long-term perspective and a strategic component and provides a basis for decision-making for corporate management through the generated results. Specialist analysis requirements and technical components for the target group and task-specific support must be considered jointly in this process in order to create meaningful full automation in the context of information logistics—making data available to the right recipient at the right time and in the right quality (Dinter and Winter 2008).

Business Analytics expands the understanding of Business Intelligence to include further analysis of, for example, business activities and focuses on supporting interactive and exploratory evaluations by potential internal customers. The goal is to gain new insights and thus an organizational, context-related learning from past activities, in order to be able to recognize previously unknown patterns or structures in the data sets. Business Analytics is based on detailed data to be able to view and analyze individual activities accordingly.

3.1.8 Business Intelligence (BI)

Business Intelligence (BI) defines itself as the process of collecting, preparing, and making available data for decision-making (Chamoni and Gluchowski 2006). In the context of operational management, it is more likely to focus on a standard orientation with consistent key figures in terms of metrics and analyses. In the context of Business Intelligence, pre-defined questions are to be answered dashboard-based with congruent, pre-defined report structures. This is made possible by indirect access or either manual or partially or fully automated aggregation of multidimensional data sources, banks, and systems. Advanced BI infrastructures are available to internal customer groups 24/7 dynamically and always updated via intranets or

---

[11]Ibid.

[12]Originally, the corresponding term of the KDD process (KDD = Knowledge Discovery in Databases) was used.

similar structures. The provided information can be adapted interactively by the respective user by means of filters or *slicers*, derived from the function of extracting certain, relevant data records from an entire data set, simply and quickly to the relevant question. Modern BI infrastructures also allow for so-called *exception reporting*, which is discussed in the corresponding section in the further course of this chapter.

3.1.9 Cloud Analytics

The term refers to a service model in which parts of the data analysis are performed in a public or private cloud and the results are made available. Cloud analytics applications are usually offered with a usage-based pricing model. Cloud analytics is being transformed in terms of labor market economics by the connection between companies and users made possible by the Internet. Gartner defines six key aspects of analytics. These are:

- Data source
- Data model
- Data processing application
- Computing power
- Analysis model
- Share and save results

Cloud analytics therefore refers to all analysis processes in which one or more of these elements is or are implemented in the cloud. Examples of cloud analytics products and services include data warehouse hosting, software-as-a-service business intelligence (SaaS-BI), and cloud-based social media analytics. The most common systems in this area are currently *Mechanical Turk* from Amazon or *oDesk*.

3.1.10 Cloud-Based Social Media Analytics (CSMA)

Cloud-based social media analytics involves the use of tools to identify not only the best platforms and sites for a defined task or objective, but also individual applications for data collection, *harvesting*, storage services, and data analysis software.

3.1.11 Cloud Sourcing

Cloud sourcing is made up of *cloud computing*[13] and *outsourcing*[14] and defines an external procurement of IT services, data, and solutions from cloud environments. In practice, cloud sourcing is an important component of today's hybrid IT sourcing strategies. Cloud sourcing is comparable to outsourcing, but the costs for cloud sourcing services are today based in most cases on usage models (pay-per-use) rather than on an annual or monthly contract. In the context of predictive intelligence, this term refers to the question of which applications, data, instruments, or capacities are to be purchased externally. Aspects to be considered are security, performance, but also costs and IT strategic aspects of the respective organization, so that PI can be optimally established and rolled out in the long term, both methodically and systemically, with the right mix of internal and external hardware and software elements.

3.1.12 Clustering

Clustering as cluster analysis[15] is a method for identifying groups by means of so-called clustering algorithms. The term *cluster analysis* is derived from the graphical representation, where the result can be one or more clusters of data points. These are methods for the discovery of similarity structures in large data sets. The groups of "similar" objects found in this way are referred to as clusters, the group assignment as clustering. The found similarity groups can be graph-theoretical, hierarchical, partitioning, or optimizing.

Clustering is an important discipline of data mining with the goal of identifying new groups in the data. Important is the distinction to classification, where data to be examined are assigned to already defined and existing groups, the so-called classes. One speaks of an *uninformed procedure*, since it does not depend on previous knowledge about groupings. The newly identified groups can then be used, for example, for further measures of classification, for the recognition of patterns in image processing or for market segmentation, or in any other procedures that rely on such prior knowledge.

3.1.13 Data Analysis

Data analysis uses statistical methods to generate value-added information from data, regardless of its quality and source. There are three different models of data analysis:

---

[13]https://en.wikipedia.org/wiki/Cloud_computing. Accessed: November 18, 2020.

[14]https://en.wikipedia.org/wiki/Outsourcing. Accessed: November 18, 2020.

[15]https://en.wikipedia.org/wiki/Cluster_analysis. Accessed: November 18, 2020.

- *Descriptive data analysis*: Display data from a sample or population using key figures or graphics.
- *Inferential data analysis*: Concluding from the sample on the characteristics of the non-surveyed population.
- *Exploratory data analysis*: Identify relationships between different variables.
- *Context-based data analysis*: Identify constellations in contextually related data.

Data analysis is an old field of knowledge and is an integral part of business management. Especially in the field of marketing, data analysis on buyer behavior and customer satisfaction has been used since the 1990s, especially in the business-to-consumer (B2C) sector. With the development of modern marketing technologies, these methods have also found their way into the area of industrial goods marketing or business-to-business (B2B) marketing (Seebacher 2020a, b, c). Statistical data analysis is used in a wide range of applications, from survey research to the analysis of latent relationships in very large data sets, which in turn closes the content gap to *data cleansing* and *data mining*.

3.1.14 Data Cleansing

Data cleansing is also sometimes referred to as *Data Editing*. As the term suggests, data cleansing involves procedures for removing and correcting data errors in databases or other information systems. Data cleansing, for example, turns incorrect, incomplete, possibly originally wrong or outdated, redundant, inconsistent, or incorrectly formatted data into corresponding valid, complete, and consistent data sets. An important process in this context is the identification of so-called duplicates, which refers to the recognition and merging of identical data records—duplicates[16]—and data fusion as the merging and completion of incomplete data.

Data cleansing aims at optimizing the quality of information. Ideally, this is done at the beginning of an activity in terms of comprehensive and sustainable PI measures to ensure and guarantee that the generated results and insights will be correspondingly valid and resilient. Information quality in this context concerns many aspects of data and its sources, such as credibility, cost, relevance, or availability, which cannot be optimized even by the data cleansing process. It is therefore all the more important that organizations, with regard to data-driven corporate management on the way to Predictive Intelligence, proceed along the maturity model for Predictive Intelligence, as described and illustrated in detail in the chapter "The Process Model for Predictive Intelligence," in order to be able to ensure the required information quality from the outset for all new data sources and their data sets.

---

[16]https://en.wikipedia.org/wiki/Wikipedia:Duplication_detector. Accessed: November 18, 2020.

3.1.15 Date Lake

The term refers to a large pool of raw data for which no use has yet been defined. The difference to the classic *data warehouse*[17] is that in a data *warehouse*, the data is structured and filtered for a previously defined purpose or task.

3.1.16 Data Mining

Data mining describes the systematic application of the methods of classical statistics to large data sets. The terms *big data* or mass data are closely related to data mining. The aim of data mining is to derive new findings from the data stocks with regard to correlations, cross-connections, or trends. Due to their volume, such data stocks must be processed with the help of computer-aided methods. In the course of the developments of the past years, data mining has increasingly become a sub-area of or a sub-concept of the more comprehensive process of *Knowledge Discovery in Databases (KDD)*, as already described in the section on *Business Analytics*. While KDD also includes steps such as data cleansing and preprocessing as well as evaluation, data mining is limited to the actual processing step of the process itself (Fayyad et al. 1996).

The term data mining, which in the figurative sense means de facto "mining of data," is actually wrong, because it is not about winning new data or knowledge, but about generating new knowledge from already existing data. Also, in the field of data mining, the term is not used completely correctly, because sometimes the pure acquisition, storage, and processing of large amounts of data is also wrongly called data mining. In the scientific environment, data mining primarily defines the extraction of knowledge that is "valid, previously unknown and potentially useful" (Ester and Sander 2000) on the basis of the criteria of general statistics, but it can also be considered "to determine certain regularities, laws and hidden connections."[18] Fayyad et al. (1996) put the term directly in relation to KDD as a step of KDD, "which consists in applying data analysis and discovery algorithms that provide a specific listing of patterns (or models) of the data under acceptable efficiency constraints." The following can be defined as typical data mining activities:

- Observation
  - Identification of unusual data records
  - Clustering
- Forecast
  - Classification
  - Regression Analysis

---

[17]https://en.wikipedia.org/wiki/Data_warehouse. Accessed: November 18, 2020.

[18]https://www.duden.de/rechtschreibung/Data_Mining. Accessed: August 25, 2020.

- Association analysis[19]
- Reduction of data to a more compact description without loss of information

It is also important to distinguish it from the field of machine learning. If the focus of data mining is on finding *new* patterns, machine learning is primarily based on *known* patterns that should be automatically recognized by the computer in new data. Regarding the methodology, it can be stated that procedures from machine learning are very often used in data mining and vice versa. However, a simple separation of machine learning and data mining is not always possible, because if association rules are extracted from existing data, this in itself represents a data mining process in the classical sense. However, these extracted rules also fulfill the criteria of machine learning.

Research into database systems, especially so-called index structures, also has a significant influence on the field of data mining. Especially research aimed at reducing the complexity of data structures can significantly improve the runtimes of data mining algorithms. Typical data mining tasks such as "nearest neighbor search" are considerably accelerated by appropriate database indices.

3.1.17 Data Science

Data Science defines the extraction of knowledge from data (Dhar 2013) as an interdisciplinary science. The term has existed since the 1960s as a replacement for the term "computer science" and was first used freely by Peter Naur in 1974 in the *Concise Survey of Computer Methods*. Another important milestone was set in 1996, when the term Data Science was first used in the title of the conference of the *International Federation of Classification Societies (IFCS)* in Kobe (Forbes 2013). In 1992, the current definition was subsequently drafted at the second Japanese French Statistical Symposium at the University of Montpellier II in France (Escoufier et al. 1995). This definition is based on and relies on the use of established concepts, methods, and principles of statistics and data analysis with a focus on data of various origins, dimensions, types, and structures with an increasing use of computers.

Modern courses of study in the field of data science combine and interlink concepts, methods, techniques, and theories from the fields of information technology, mathematics, and statistics, including signal processing. Models from the fields of data storage, data engineering, machine learning, statistical learning, pattern recognition, forecasting, programming of uncertainty, and probability modeling are used.[20]

---

[19]Identification of relationships and dependencies in the data in the form of rules such as "A and B normally follow C."

[20]https://en.wikipedia.org/wiki/Data_science. Accessed: November 18, 2020.

Every data science study always contains the following four steps: first the data must be processed and prepared. Then the appropriate algorithms are selected, followed by the parameter optimization of the algorithms. On this basis, models are then derived, and from their comparison—evaluation and validation—the best situation is then identified (Ng and Soo 2018).

3.1.18 Data Scientist

The job description of a data scientist is still a very young one and only very few training courses are offered. Frequently, the training as a data scientist is linked to an already existing education in economics, computer science, or statistics, which has a positive effect on *employability* (Güpner 2015).

In most cases, Data Scientists are used in Marketing and Corporate or Central Business Intelligence departments (Strohmeier 2020). However, the demand for Data Scientists will increase strongly in the coming years, especially against the background of the developments in the area of the MarTech Stack (Seebacher 2020a, b, c) but also the SalesTech Stack[21] and the many new possibilities that come along with it.

3.1.19 Deep Learning

Deep or more in-depth learning is referred to in the current literature as *Deep Learning*. Deep Learning is assigned to the field of information processing. It is a method of machine learning using artificial neural networks (ANN) (Borgelt et al. 2003). These ANNs are equipped with several layers, so-called *hidden layers*, between the input layer and the output layer to define an extensive inner structure.

Deep Learning has only gained importance in the recent development of artificial intelligence. The background was that in the beginning, the focus in the field of artificial intelligence was on problems that were difficult to solve for natural, biological intelligence. These problems could be described by formal mathematical rules and algorithms and could thus be easily solved by computers with the appropriate computing capacity. More and more the real challenge for artificial intelligence crystallized out, namely the imitation of problem-solving processes of simple tasks of natural intelligence. It was therefore a matter of solving tasks that were easy for humans to perform but difficult to map by mathematical rules and algorithms. The seemingly simple became a challenge, such as understanding language or recognizing objects or faces (Bruderer 2018).

To meet this challenge, it was necessary to imitate experiential learning, as occurs in natural intelligence. This form of learning plays a decisive role in the development

---

[21] http://unified.vu/2018/06/11/the-ever-growing-sales-technology-landscape-sales-tech-stack-2018/. Accessed: August 25, 2020.

of methodological and structural competence within the framework of the Template-based management approach (Seebacher 2020a, b, c). It is crucial to understand the world in the context of a hierarchy of concepts. Here, each concept is defined on the basis of its relationships to simpler concepts. Such a concept cannot and must not be understood in isolation from the ecosystem of neighborhood concepts associated with it. The approach of *organizational etymology is* also based on this scientific theory and has thus enabled significant new insights in the field of organizational development (Seebacher 2020a, b, c). This experiential learning enables the machine to develop and structure the knowledge required to process a given task itself. Likewise, the formal specification is done autonomously by the machine. On the basis of *hidden layers*, the computer is able to learn even complicated contexts and concepts by aggregating them in a logically simpler way. The computer develops a method to recognize and learn structures. Deep Learning is therefore comparable in its functionality with the mechanisms and basics of the Template-based Management approach according to Seebacher (2020a, b, c).

Deep Learning can be illustrated very well by the example of handwriting recognition: It is difficult for a machine to recognize or understand non-prepared, sensory input data, as is the case with a text, for example, which initially represents only an unstructured collection of pixels. The transformation or translation of a set of such pixels into an information chain of numbers and letters is extremely compli-cated and impossible to program manually.[22] To accomplish this task, Deep Learning is used as a subset of machine learning, which in turn is one of the most commonly used techniques of artificial intelligence. In the Deep Learning method, machine learning is made possible by the previously mentioned layers in the sense of hierarchies.

The artificial neural networks used are based on the structure of the human brain. The input layer is the first layer of the neural network. It processes the input raw data, as in the example of character recognition the individual pixels of a character or a word. The data input on the first layer contains corresponding variables that are accessible to observation, which is why the first hierarchical level is also called the *visible layer.* The input layer forwards its outputs to the next layer, which in turn processes the received information and passes the generated result on to the next layer. This process is repeated over and over again. The non-visible layers of the system represent the already mentioned *hidden layers.* The features contained in these hidden layers become increasingly abstract. Instead, the system has to deter-mine which approaches are useful and valid for explaining the relationships in the data under investigation. At the end of this iterative process, the result is output in the last, then again visible layer. De facto, Deep Learning divides a complex process into many small logical observation or analysis steps in order to solve the resulting smaller, less complex tasks step by step and thus arrive at a valid result.

---

[22]Ian Goodfellow, Yoshua Bengio, Aaron Courville: *Deep Learning.* MIT Press, accessed February 19, 2017 (English). Accessed: August 27, 2020.

3.1.19.1 Excursus

At this point, I would like to give an example from my experience as a management consultant in the context of the deregulation of the energy market in Germany in the late 1990s. At that time, I was working as a consultant at Deloitte Consulting. We were involved in the spin-off of an energy company to spin off the billing management and meter management departments of the four municipal utilities in Bremerhaven, Bremen, Hannover, and Osnabrück into a new company. This had become necessary due to new legislation regarding the separation of energy supplier and network operator.

Within the scope of the project, it was of course also a question of preparing a profitability analysis in order to be able to ex antes check the plausibility of such a project. In this context, we had to deal with a lot of qualitative aspects and topics, which all had to be included in a valid profitability analysis. To make this possible, we used so-called Qualitative-Quantitative-Matrices (QQM), which we created in Microsoft Excel. The qualitative factor that had to be quantified was written in the far-left column of the sheet. After the definition, a more detailed description of the factor was written in the second column. The third column described how the spin-off and merger with the other municipal utilities would affect this factor. In the fourth column, this anticipated effect was justified and explained. On this basis, a percentage change was then defined on the basis of the three scenarios that are generally applied—negative, neutral, and positive—which in turn enabled an exact quantification for all three scenarios on the basis of the current values now transparent, objective, and comprehensible.

If Deep Learning layers are used, in my example the individual columns were in the matrix in order to be able to perform an analytic-prognostic task, which is complex in itself, in a valid and comprehensible way by dividing it into several smaller steps. I hope that this excursus in putting something highly complicated very simple helps to better understand how Deep Learning works.

3.1.20 Descriptive Analytics

In order to define the term Descriptive Analysis, the difference between *analytics* and *analysis* will first be briefly discussed here for the sake of completeness. The word *analysis is derived* from the Greek "ἀνάλυσις—analysis" and means *resolution*. Such a resolution describes a systematic investigation in which an object of interest is broken down into its elements. Analytical definitions explain a term by logical decomposition into its characteristics. The difference between analysis and analytics is that the science concerned with carrying out the analysis of a fact or an object is called analytics.

For this reason, reference is made at this point to the following term, Descriptive Analysis, in relation to the conceptual delimitation relevant to the ecosystem of predictive intelligence.

3.1.21 Descriptive Analysis

Descriptive analysis falls within the subject area of descriptive statistics. A well-performed descriptive analysis is the basis for any valid work with data. A thoroughly thought-out descriptive analysis provides a basic understanding of a relevant data pool. If there is a total data collection in the sense of a general pool of data, the task of descriptive analysis of this *raw* data is to condense the information contained in the data and to find a way to work out and present the essential and relevant to possible tasks. Descriptive data analysis has an exclusively *descriptive* character, which is derived from the Latin word "describere" in the sense of "to describe."[23]

3.1.22 Descriptive Models

Descriptive models establish quantitative connections and relationships in defined data pools. This enables groupings and classifications to be established. In contrast to descriptive models, which focus on the prediction of future events, descriptive models are concerned with the recognition and identification of resilient dependencies, relationships, and connections. It is about extracting causalities and cause-effect relationships in order to be able to prove and represent possible questions of corporate management not only one dimensionally, but multidimensionally.

3.1.23 Exception Reporting

Modern Business Intelligence infrastructures not only generate defined reports and aggregated data, but also enable *exception reporting*, i.e., the triggering of automated information provision when defined thresholds are reached or exceeded (Felden and Buder 2012, p. 17ff).

3.1.24 Extrapolation

Extrapolation is a very important method in the field of predictive intelligence. The word is composed of the Latin *"extra"* meaning "outside" and a variation of the term *"interpolate"* with the mathematical meaning to determine a value *between* two values. In general, the word has the meaning of inferring from a known state or a known development to states in other areas or to future developments. Extrapolation is an extrapolation or determination of a mostly mathematical behavior, such as a

---

[23]Further information on data analysis can also be found under the corresponding term in this chapter on the PI ecosystem.

series of numbers over a defined period of time, beyond the secured or existing (data) area.

With the help of extrapolation, existing data and resulting data series are analyzed within the framework of predictive intelligence with regard to their mathematical second derivation in the sense of the rate of increase or decrease and extrapolated into the future on the basis of these values. A distinction is made between different variants of extrapolation, which result from the combination of the extrapolated number of data series, but also from the consideration or integration of one or more contingency factors:

- *Static Extrapolation*: In the context of this procedure, a volume of data is extrapolated once and without consideration into the future to a firmly defined point in time in the future. The simplest type of this extrapolation procedure is to add a trend line in an Excel table or an Excel chart.
- *Dynamic Extrapolation*: In contrast to static extrapolation, dynamic extrapolation does not extrapolate a data series to a single point in time, but rather to a variably definable period or time frame. This allows users to dynamically interrogate possible developments depending on the situation and to query the anticipated values.
- *Monodimensional Extrapolation*: This type of extrapolation works with only one dimension of influencing contingency factors, such as the inclusion of the *Ease-of-Doing-Business Index* or the import or export rates of a country.[24]
- *Multidimensional Extrapolation*: As defined by the name of this type, this variant of extrapolation integrates two or more influencing contingency factors with—if necessary—different weightings into the algorithm. In this way, logical relations can be considered in the extrapolations with respect to possible scenarios.

3.1.25 Functional Models or Modeling

The functional model focuses on the transformation or modification of the data. To illustrate data transformation, data flow diagrams are created, which are graphs of processes, data flows, data stores, and objects of action. Functional models can also be integrated into operational applications and data products to provide real-time analysis functions. An example of this in the marketing area is so-called recommendation engines on websites of online retailers, which evaluate customer behavior based on their surfing behavior but also on their buying behavior, and on this basis suggest further purchase recommendations and point to other products.

---

[24]https://en.wikipedia.org/wiki/Ease_of_doing_business_index. Accessed: November 18, 2020.

3.1.26 Hadoop Cluster

A *Hadoop cluster* can simply be described as a coordinated hardware link to provide greater capacity for processing large, unstructured data sets. Hadoop clusters operate according to a *master-slave model*, a model for a communication protocol in which a device or process, called a *master*, controls one or more devices or processes, defined as *slaves*. The Hadoop cluster is thus a group of hardware that facilitates the use of open source Hadoop technology for data processing. It consists of a group of nodes. One node called the *Name-Node* is the Hadoop Master. This node communicates with various data node nodes in the cluster to support operations. Hadoop clusters also typically use other Apache open source technologies such as Apache MapReduce and Apache Yarn , which helps to route collaborative activities on virtual machines or containers through different nodes in the system. Hadoop clusters work in concert to handle large unstructured data sets and deliver data results.

3.1.27 Harvesting

Harvesting in the context of Predictive Intelligence means the "harvesting" of data or information. The term *Information Harvesting* (IH) was established by Ralphe Wiggins (1992) as an attempt to derive rules from data sets. In the beginning, different input variables were classified, which gave the variables in the input a certain structure. On this basis, rules were generated, and generalization was exchanged for storage. By this procedure, many more new rules could be established. This included rules and strategies to detect over-matching and to correct it if necessary. Against this background, IH can also be regarded as a form of machine learning and falls within the scope of today's *data mining*. The advantage, however, compared to other data mining products of that time and even many generations later, was that Wiggins' approach for the first time provided processes for finding *multiple* rules that not only classified the data, but could also determine the best rules to use based on pre-defined criteria.

3.1.28 Principal Component Analysis (PCA)

This term refers to the method of identifying those variables by which data points can best be broken down. It is a method for dimensional reduction, since existing data can be described with a smaller set of variables, the main components. Such principal components can also be understood as dimensions along which data points are most widely distributed (Fig. 3.1), where a principal component can be expressed by one or more variables. Each principal component represents a weighted sum of the original variables. However, in order to measure and use different variables with different units together, they must first be standardized.

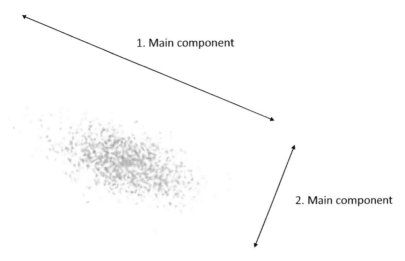

Fig. 3.1 Visualization of two main components (Source: Own illustration)

Standardization in this context refers to the process of converting or specifying each variable in the form of percentiles, allowing them to be plotted on a uniform, dimensionless standard scale. The advantage of principal component analysis (PCA) over *k-Means Clustering* is that the variables are not thrown together with trial and error, but the PCA calculates exact weights that allow the variables to be combined in such a way as to provide an optimal breakdown. PCA as a method is best suited when the most meaningful dimensions have the greatest dispersion in the data and are also perpendicular to all others.

3.1.29 In-Sample

This term refers to sample units or data sets that are directly related to a sample of data to be processed. The opposite is defined by the term *Out-of-Sample*.

3.1.30 *k*-Means-Clustering

This term defines a technique of supervised learning. The technique groups similar data points into groups, the clusters. *k* indicates how many groups should be mapped. The weak point of the procedure is that each data point can only belong to one group. Sometimes, however, data points lie exactly in the middle between two clusters and are nevertheless assigned with equal probability to one of them. Another aspect that cannot be overlooked is the fact that clusters are assumed to be circular or spherical in *n* dimensions. The stepwise and repeated assignment of data points to the next center of a cluster represents a reduction of the cluster radius, resulting in a compact sphere with 2, 3, or even *n* dimensions. But if the actual shape of a group of data points is not a circle, but for example an ellipse, then such areas might be cut off and the corresponding data points might be wrongly assigned to one of the neighboring clusters.

3.1.31 *k*-Nearest Neighbors

This method is also often called kNN or outlier detection. It is important not to confuse it with the abbreviation ANN , which stands for Artificial Neural Networks (see the section on *Artificial Neural Networks* in this chapter). *k-nearest* neighbors (kNN) is an algorithm for classifying a data point based on the properties of its neighbors. In practice, this means that a data point with an unknown value surrounded by five data points "oil presses" and one data point "pump" is automatically assigned to the "oil presses" by the kNN algorithm.

The "k" itself is again a parameter representing the set of nearest neighbors, which is used by the algorithm. Therefore, an optimal *k-value* is the one that connects the data points with a reasonable average number of neighbors. In addition, this method can also be used to predict continuous data values by aggregating the values of the nearest neighbors. In this context, the use of a weighted mean is useful, where values of closer neighbors have a higher weight compared to those of more distant ones.

kNN can also be used to detect outliers. Especially in the context of predictive intelligence, this is of crucial importance in order not to jeopardize the validity of the basis for decision-relevant recommendations for action by considering false data outliers. This outlier recognition can even sometimes lead to additional insights or even the recognition of a previously unknown predictor. Since kNN uses patterns contained in data for prediction, prediction errors reveal data points that do not fit the general trends. This means for predictive intelligence that in principle any algorithm that generates a model for the prediction can also be used for outlier detection. In the context of regression, data points that deviate significantly from the regression line would thus be immediately identifiable as outliers.

In relation to the example of the oil presses and pumps mentioned above, the introduction of another predictor would be helpful to ensure a correct allocation. For example, the addition of a further predictor as an additional sale of a certain spare part, which is essential in the case of oil presses, could provide the decisive indication for a correct allocation. In general, however, kNN works best with few predictors and classes of equal size.

3.1.32 Classification

For the term classification, technical terms like *typification* or *systematics* are also used. Classifications are used in the context of documentation and in document management in connection with indexing with metadata, whereas in merchandise management rather *commodity groups* and in science rather *systematics* are used conceptually. The goal is to establish an overview of objects ordered in a data set and to enable thematic searches to develop an order.

It is about a planned generation of abstract classes, to enable a delimitation or to develop an order. Such classes are often defined as *categories, concepts,* or *types.* This classification is usually based on the classification of objects based on certain matching characteristics. In this context, the terms *classification* or *class assignment* refer to the application of a classification to an object by selecting a matching class of a defined, given classification. In the field of Predictive Intelligence, the *typology,* often referred to as *artificial classification, is* often used, which is divided into:

- Conceptual classification based on synthetic class formation
- Deductive classification, from general to specific, and
- Qualitative classification based on situation-specific, specially selected features

3.1.33 Louvain Method

This method is a procedure to detect clusters in a network. It goes back to a group of researchers around Blondel et al. (2008) from the University of Louvain. The method tests different configurations of groupings to maximize the number and strength of edges between nodes in the *same* cluster and to minimize the number and strength of edges between nodes *in different* clusters. The degree to which this criterion is met is called modularity, where the optimal assignment to a cluster is the one with the highest modularity.

3.1.34 Machine Learning

The term refers to a technology that teaches computers and machines to learn from tasks by learning from data, rather than being programmed to do so. Machine learning is a generic term for the generation of knowledge from experience through "artificial" methods. For this purpose, special algorithms are used to learn from large amounts of data, Big Data. Corresponding statistical models are built, which are based on training data. Examples and processes are not stored and replicated by the machine, but patterns and regularities in the learning data are recognized. Through the so-called *learning transfer,* these learning experiences can be applied to unknown data and thus be evaluated. If a machine fails because of an unknown data set, the term *overfitting*is used.

In the context of machine learning, an increasing size of data sets is advantageous because the more data the machines can generate from it, the more learning experience they can provide. Machine learning offers many advantages for management in a business environment and especially in the area of predictive intelligence:

- Optimized findings
- Optimized validity of the generated results
- High adaptability

- Higher speed of decision-making
- Increased efficiency and effectiveness of all business activities
- Optimal use of resources

In terms of the predictive intelligence ecosystem, the concept of machine learning is closely related to the topics of Knowledge Discovery in Databases (KDD), Deep Learning and Data Mining, where the primary focus is on recognizing *new* patterns and laws, and machine learning uses existing patterns to train the machine to autonomously recognize known patterns in new data sets.

Machine learning is divided into *symbolic* and *non-symbolic* approaches and into algorithmic approaches, which in turn are divided into *supervised* and *unsupervised* learning. Both forms of learning are defined in the further course of this chapter. For symbolic approaches, the examples as well as the underlying rules are known and *explicitly represented*. In contrast, non-symbolic approaches refer to forms such as neural networks, which are taught computable behavior but do not provide insight into the learned solutions, and therefore the knowledge is unknown or, in technical jargon, *implicitly represented* (Langley 2011).

More and more software vendors offer corresponding software for machine learning on the market, such as Caffe[25] as a program library for deep learning, the product of the same name DeepLearning[26] as an open source software programmed in Java with a focus on unsupervised learning, which helps to accelerate algorithms by using indices, or ML.NET[27] from Microsoft as a free machine learning library. With regard to Predictive Intelligence it is crucial to have machine learning in mind, because in the further course of development, due to the maturity model on which Predictive Intelligence is based, this technology will in any case become increasingly important.

3.1.35 Feature Extraction

If suitable variables must first be drawn for a calculation, this is called feature extraction or *feature engineering*. Not only the values of a single variable can be regrouped, but also several variables can be combined, which is called dimension reduction. This process makes it possible to extract the most interesting and useful information from a large number of variables and then analyze it using a smaller set of variables.

---

[25]http://caffe.berkeleyvision.org/. Accessed: November 18, 2020.

[26]https://deeplearning4j.org/. Accessed: November 18, 2020.

[27]https://dotnet.microsoft.com/apps/machinelearning-ai/ml-dotnet. Accessed: August 28, 2020.

3.1.36 Modeling

Modeling is generally defined as the development, shaping, or production of a model. The result of the modeling is the *model delivery* followed by the *model monitoring*. Modeling is used in many different disciplines. In the field of Predictive Intelligence, two of these areas are of particular relevance: computer science and algorithms.

In the field of computer science, the term describes the discipline of model-based development of software and hardware systems. In this context, a model is used as a representation of reality limited to the essential elements. In this context, this reduction refers to the essential functionalities and occurs in representational models in the form of prototypes[28] and frameworks. Theoretical models are applied in the form of abstract models. In terms of algorithms, modeling serves to develop and optimize procedures for the logical and mathematical preparation and processing of data. Modeling is used here for all steps of the value chain of data processing, i.e., from data import, data cleansing to complex processes of extrapolation and regression. Through modeling, it is possible to continuously work on the quality of results with respect to the requirements of classical mathematics and statistics.

Especially modeling was a key factor in the first projects in the field of predictive intelligence to approach this new topic. With regard to the sustainable development of PI competence in organizations, modeling is essential, since modeling can be used to realize crucial steps of the intrinsic, organizational learning process. The *how* and the *what* with the data in the context of PI along the entire data-technical value chain represents the competence-technical backbone of such an application. Only the gradual and incremental development of this system, together with the automatically occurring knowledge development process, will enable valid and successful predictive intelligence for corporate management in the long term.

3.1.37 Model Monitoring

Model monitoring defines the machine learning phase after model provision. Model monitoring monitors models for errors, crashes, and inconsistencies, and latencies. Model monitoring must ensure that the results of the PI reach an ever-higher level of objectivity, reliability, and validity, in order to contribute in the best possible way to profit-optimized and risk-minimized corporate management. Even though machine learning will only be used in the further course of the PI maturity model, it is essential to be aware of the important function of machine learning and thus of modeling and model monitoring. The last mile of PI will only be mastered with AI and machine learning due to the big data and the complex calculations and functions. If then the involved team is not master of the underlying algorithms and models, it

---

[28]https://en.wikipedia.org/wiki/Prototype. Accessed: November 18, 2020.

will not be possible to raise this knowledge to the level of AI and machine learning. It is therefore crucial to always know exactly where the PI journey must and will go.

The importance of model monitoring results from the phenomenon of *model drift*, also known as model decay, which is based on the deterioration of the accuracy and predictive power of a model.[29] In the following, the most common metrics of model monitoring are listed, but they will not be discussed in detail at this point, since PI will require corresponding data and IT experts in the respective organization for management in the long term anyway, who will have this detailed knowledge in any case:

- Type 1 Error—false positive
- Type 2 error—false negative
- Accuracy—Accuracy
- Precision
- Remember
- F1 score—accuracy measure for tests as a harmonic mean for precision and recall
- R-square—scattering around the line of best fit
- R-square adjusted
- Mean Absolute Error (MAE)—Average Absolute Error
- Mean square error (MSE)

3.1.38 Sample Units

Sample units are units in data sets that are used to develop, evaluate, optimize, and validate models in the context of predictive intelligence. A distinction is made between sample units within the sample (see *In-Sample*) and outside the sample (see *Out-Of-Sample*).

3.1.39 Neural Networks

Neural networks are the basis of modern automatic image recognition. Three factors are essential for their relevance in terms of predictive intelligence:

- Optimized data storage and availability
- Increased and rapidly evolving computing power
- New algorithms

Neural networks use or work in layers, where the result of one layer represents the input for the next layer. The following types of layers are distinguished:

---

[29]https://ichi.pro/de/post/60196108842518. Accessed: August 31, 2020.

- Input layers
- Intermediate layers or hidden layers
- Output layers
- Loss Layers

The last type is essential for the training of neural networks. If a correct prediction has been made, the result reinforces the further inputs and layers. If a prediction was not correct, the errors are traced back and the corresponding criteria for error reduction are changed. *Backpropagation* is used as technical term in this context. This iterative training process serves to teach the neural networks to connect the input signals with the correct output applications. These connections that are then learned are called activation rules and improve predictive intelligence precision (PIP) by optimizing the components that define these activation rules.

3.1.40 Out-of-Sample

In contrast to the term *In-Sample*, samples or training units in samples with known attributes but unknown causal characteristics are referred to as *from the sample*. These *out-of-sample units* are not necessarily related to the training sample units in terms of content and logic.

3.1.41 Parameters

Parameters are ways to change the settings of an algorithm, as in a kitchen stove, where the temperature of a single hotplate is set. This fact means that the same algorithm can give different results depending on how its parameters are set. An overview of parameters of frequently occurring procedures is shown in Fig. 3.2. Since in the field of Predictive Intelligence models are very often very powerful and complex, the complexity can be kept under control by means of the regularization procedure (see corresponding section in this chapter).

3.1.42 Predictive Analysis

Predictive Analytics (PA) is a subset and also one of the pillars of business analytics, more commonly known as *Business Analytics* (BA). PA falls into the area of data mining. In the context of and with Big Data, PA has gained enormously in importance in order to be able to analyze, evaluate, and also validate large data sets in order to draw appropriate conclusions on this basis. With the help of PA, probabilities for the future should be calculated and corresponding trends should be determined. By using so-called predictors, these predictions about the future can be made very

Procedure	Parameters
Regression Analysis	• Regularization parameters (for lasso and ridge regression)
k-nearest neighbors	• Number of nearest neighbors
Support Vector Machine	• Buffer contacts • Kernel parameters • Insensitivity parameters
Decision tree	• Minimum size of the last nodes (leaves) • Maximum size of the last nodes (leaves) • Maximum depth of the tree
Random Forest	• All decision tree parameters • Number of trees • Number of variables to be selected for each division
Neural network	• Number of interlayers • Number of neurons per layer • Number of training iterations • Learning rate • Initial weights

Fig. 3.2 Overview of adjustable parameters of common methods (Source: Ng and Soo 2018)

precisely. By using several, different predictors a prediction model is created to calculate probable events.[30]

PA is an advanced analysis method that uses both new and historical data to predict future events. The most common and well-known areas are the financial sector and meteorology. In the last 10 years, PA has also established itself in the field of modern marketing (Seebacher 2020a, b, c). In general, historical data is used to create mathematical models to extrapolate trends. This predictive model is then applied to current data to predict what possible events may occur in the future or to derive actions that can be taken to achieve optimal results. Predictive analytics has gained enormously in importance in recent years, as major advances have been made in supporting technologies, including big data and machine learning.

PA involves the application of statistical analysis techniques, analytical queries, and automated machine learning algorithms to data sets. In the area of PA, the following methods are used, which are also described in more detail elsewhere in this section on the ecosystem of PI:

- *Define Project*: In order to be effective and efficient, it is necessary to define *in* advance exactly what is *in scope* and what is *out of scope in terms of* data and object of investigation.
- *Data Acquisition*: Based on the previous phase, the relevant data is acquired or collected. The discipline of data mining is often applied in this phase. This provides a complete overview of the contingency factors.

---

[30]https://en.wikipedia.org/wiki/Predictive_analytics. Accessed: November 18, 2020.

- *Data Analysis*: Data analysis describes the process of analyzing, cleansing, evaluating, validating, and modeling data with the aim of discovering useful information and reaching a conclusion.
- *Statistics*: Assumptions are made, and hypotheses are validated and tested using methods from the field of classical statistics and standard statistical models.
- *Modeling*: Forward-looking modeling enables accurate predictive models to be created for the future. In a scenario-based, multimodal assessment, different solutions can be compared, and the optimal solution identified.
- *Provision*: The foresighted provision of models and also possible scenarios make it possible to incorporate the results in the form of recommendations for action as a basis for management decisions in the daily decision-making process.
- *Model Monitoring*: Ideally, models are not only used selectively, but are evaluated and monitored continuously and dynamically to check the model performance with regard to the three scientific criteria objectivity, reliability, and validity, and to ensure that the expected results are achieved.

In the context of PA, a general distinction is made between three models, which are discussed in more detail in the various sections of the PI ecosystem:

1. Predictive models (see Predictive Models)
2. Descriptive models (see Descriptive Models)
3. Decision models

A few examples will illustrate the effects of PA:

- Innovations with Autonomous Vehicles: Automotive companies developing driver assistance technologies and new autonomous vehicles use PA to analyze sensor data from networked vehicles and to create driver assistance algorithms.
- Condition Monitoring for Aircraft Engines: To optimize aircraft uptime and minimize service costs, the aerospace industry uses PA-based real-time analysis applications that predict the performance of oil, fuel, aircraft startup, mechanical condition, and control subsystems.
- Forecasting of Electricity Price and Demand: Advanced forecasting apps in the energy industry use models of PA, to predict and monitor the availability of power plants, energy prices, seasonality, and much more.
- Development of Credit Risk Models: Banks and insurance companies use machine learning techniques and quantitative tools to predict both credit risks and the probability of loss occurrence.
- Prediction of Machine Failures: Machine and plant manufacturers are saving ever larger amounts of money every month with the help of PA-based systems for condition monitoring and predictive maintenance that reduce downtime and minimize plant inefficiencies. *Smart Maintenance* , *Predictive Maintenance* , *Smart Service* or *Predictive Service* are just a few of the many different new terms that are becoming increasingly important in the context of the "*As-a-*

Service" industry and the "*Equipment-as-a-Service*" trend (Seebacher 2020a, b, c)

• Using Pattern Recognition Algorithms to Detect Asthma and COPD: An asthma management device documents and analyzes patients' breath sounds and provides immediate feedback via a smartphone app to help patients manage their asthma and COPD

3.1.43 Predictive Models or Modeling

For prediction models, methods of mathematics and computer science are used to predict future events or results. Based on changes in the parameters of the respective model, these models predict results in a future state or at a future, defined point in time in the future. These models are developed, tested, and evaluated in an iterative process using a training data set and training patterns to determine the accuracy of the generated predictions. In recent years, predictive models have increasingly used technologies from the fields of artificial intelligence and *machine learning in* order to identify the most optimal and valid model from several models.

3.1.44 Predictors

Predictors are variables in an equation that are used to predict future events.

3.1.45 Prescriptive Analytics

Prescriptive analytics can be defined as a subset of data analysis in which predictive models are used to propose concrete actions. These recommendations for action are in turn contextually oriented towards the optimal result, which was described or specified in the initial project definition. Prescriptive analyses are based on optimization and rule-based decision-making techniques. Forecasts in the sense of load profiles for electricity networks in the next 24 h are an example of predictive analytics. In contrast, decisions or recommendations for action based on these predictions, such as how power plants should be optimally operated in a given situation, represent the results and findings of *prescriptive analytics*. Prescriptive analytics adds a real-time element to the results of predictive analytics by applying actions to events.

Artun and Levin (2015) define three methods of prescriptive analysis:

• Unsupervised learning (clustering models)
• Supervised learning (prediction models)
• Reinforcement learning (recommendation models)

3.1.46 Predictive Marketing

This term has not been used congruently in the literature so far and is not finally defined accordingly. Artun and Levin (2015) write about it:

> "Predictive analytics" refers to a set of tools and algorithms used to enable predictive marketing. It is an umbrella term that encompasses a variety of mathematical and statistical techniques used to recognize patterns in data or make predictions about the future. When applied to marketing, predictive analytics can predict future customer behavior, classify.... customers into clusters and other use cases. Predictive marketing is the perfect combination of machine learning and human intelligence.

Molly Galetto of NG Data defines predictive marketing as follows[31]:

> Predictive marketing is a marketing technique that uses data analysis to determine which marketing strategies and actions have the highest probability of success. It has its place in the marketing technology landscape (MarTech) as companies use general business data, marketing and sales activity data, and mathematical algorithms to match patterns and determine the most appropriate criteria for their next marketing actions. Companies that adopt this strategy strive to make data-driven decisions to achieve better results.

Galetto thus provides a generally applicable definition, which also provides the transfer to the wider field of corporate management and the associated strategy. It focuses on data-driven decisions in order to achieve better results—from a marketing perspective, but of course in relation to the entire company. Seebacher (2020a, b, c) introduces *Predictive Profit Marketing* (PPM) as the overall objective, that marketers have to target at in the long run as PPM is the key lever for turning any marketing department from a cost-driver into a turnover engine. This is especially essential for the area of industrial marketing considering the fact that technical sales as such will soon be dead as sales is only a click away and institutional buyers are characterized by a fast-growing willingness to even make multi-million Dollar purchases virtually and online.

3.1.47 Procurement Intelligence

Procurement Intelligence (ProcI) is closely linked to data-based corporate management but a rather undeveloped field. It is no secret that "in purchasing lies the profit!" Especially companies in the purchasing-intensive, conservative mechanical and plant engineering industry, still operate in the area of purchasing with little structured but organizationally established purchasing departments, which are by no means equipped with modern Procurement Intelligence, and thus burn millions of Euros against this background. Procurement Intelligence is a multidimensional data cube, which is set up according to applications, industries, and regions and evaluates

---

[31]https://www.ngdata.com/what-is-predictive-marketing/. Accessed: August 31, 2020.

potential suppliers 24/7 according to three target categories. In most cases, these three categories are based on what a purchasing process is geared towards:

- Price
- Speed
- Special requirements regarding size, processing, material, etc.

The ProcI is fed with data from suppliers and continuously updated. Initially, the data is entered and evaluated manually. Step by step the data is optimized and completed by modeling. Subsequently, the data input can be done automatically by WebCrawler. It is crucial that employees in sales, back office, sales support and also in purchasing have access to the data in order to obtain a ranking of the relevant suppliers based on defined requirements. The ProcI automatically weights the relevant information and thus always provides a selection of relevant possible suppliers—faster, more valid, and always up-to-date.

I define Procurement Intelligence as follows:

> Procurement Intelligence is the IT-based collection, processing and validation of 24/7 interactive data and information on relevant suppliers in order to achieve an optimal return on procurement (RoP) based on the various criteria of price, delivery time and special requirements.

Especially in the context of my Remocal Economy theorem and the New Green Deal thoughts by Jeremy Rifkin (2019), the much better, interactive, timely, and responsible management of supply chains needs to be taken care of. On this basis, and in line with Galetto's definition of Predictive Marketing as well as my Predictive Profit Marketing model described above, I define the term *Predictive Procurement Intelligence* (PProcI) as a further key element of Predictive Intelligence as such:

> Predictive Procurement Intelligence is the process in which data from an organization's Predictive Intelligence is collected, validated, linked with all internal and external data of an organization's procurement, processed by means of defined and validated algorithms, dynamically extrapolated and modelled by means of variable parameters in terms of price, delivery times and costing specifications for short, medium and long-term procurement needs, prepared and made available to the organization 24/7 to optimize the return on procurement in terms of economic efficiency and effectiveness but also the ecological footprint of the applied supply chains.

PProcI is an important part of Predictive Intelligence for corporate management in certain purchasing-intensive industries. It can be set up in parallel to the PI activities for management. It is crucial that the same methods and structures are used so that PProcI can be easily integrated into or linked to the company's PI. This is because a powerful PProcI requires a connection to the ERP system, but also to the CRM system and the data areas of the PI in terms of macro and microeconomic economic data in order to be able to apply predictions regarding price developments and availability to future procurement processes.

3.1.48 Random Forest

The term is based on the hypothesis that the combination of models improves predictive intelligence precision (PIP) as prediction accuracy. Such a combination is called *ensembling* or ensemble learning. A random forest refers to an ensemble of decision trees, where the ensemble in this context represents an aggregated, synergistic predictive model. Such a model results from the combination of many different individual models either by majority decision or by averaging.

Such a random forest can be assigned to the tertiary methods, because the input data represent the primary level and the individual models the secondary level, and thus the random forest as an ensemble of these individual models is located on the tertiary level. Therefore, a random forest usually has a better PIP than the individual models or decision trees on which it is based. However, the results generated on the basis of this procedure cannot be interpreted, but the predictors can be classified according to their respective valences to the PIP. It is also important to note in the context of random forest that two methods are used:

- Bootstrap Aggregating generates a large number of uncorrelated decision trees by randomly dropping some variables.
- Ensembling combines several decision trees or their predictions by mathematical methods, either majority decision or averaging.

3.1.49 Regression Analysis

This method identifies the so-called optimal trendline,[32] which touches as many data points as possible or comes as close as possible. This trendline is calculated using weighted combinations of predictors (see the corresponding section in this chapter), with the regression coefficients denoting the corresponding weightings in this context. The regression coefficients are a value for the significance of a single predictor in interaction with other predictors.

Regression analysis works best when there are few correlations between the various predictors, few data-related outliers and the expected trend is a straight line.

3.1.50 Regularization

This term describes a possibility to control the complexity of a model by introducing a so-called penalty parameter. Such a parameter "punishes" any complication of a model by artificially increasing the prediction error. This is crucial, since many studies and projects run the risk of using over-adapted models over time. This is

---

[32]Best fit trend line or also regression line.

done in the context of the understandable effort to minimize the prediction error, but this leads to an increasing complexity of the prediction model.

3.1.51 Reinforcement Learning

In contrast to unsupervised and supervised learning, in which the models once implemented continue to be used unchanged, a model in reinforcement learning continuously optimizes itself by directly feeding the generated results back into the model as feedback.

3.1.52 Supervised Learning

This form of learning also falls into the field of machine learning. In contrast to unsupervised learning, in supervised learning an ex ante defined learning algorithm tries to find a hypothesis that makes the most unerring predictions possible. This method therefore depends on a pre-defined task to be learned, the results of which are known. The results of the learning process are compared with the known, correct results, i.e., "monitored" (Müller and Guido 2017). The following procedures, which will not be discussed in detail here, since it would in any case go beyond the scope of the PI ecosystem, are used in supervised learning, among others:

- Linear regression
- Logistic regression
- Bayes classifier
- Naïve Bayes classifier
- Nearest Neighbor classification
- Discriminant analysis
- Artificial neural network

In this context, learning refers to the ability of an artificial intelligence to reproduce laws, which in turn must be known through laws of nature or expert knowledge in order to be able to teach the machine. If the results of the output are available in a continuous, quantitative distribution, one usually speaks of a regression problem (Gareth et al. 2017). However, if the results are available in discrete or qualitative form, one speaks of a classification problem (Smola 2008).

3.1.53 Training Patterns

Training patterns are used in the context of predictive analytics for processing and optimizing descriptive models. The available sample units with known attributes and known performances are called "training patterns." In this context, a distinction is made between *in-sample* and *out-of-sample* units, which are also defined in this section.

3.1.54 Unsupervised Learning

This form of learning is used in the field of machine learning, such as deep learning, where learning on the hierarchies or layers hidden in the system cannot be reproduced from the outside. Unsupervised learning therefore defines machine learning without ex ante known target values. The computer tries to recognize patterns in the input data that deviate from the structureless rest of the data population (Hinton and Sejnowksi 1999). An artificial neural network (ANN) orients itself by congruence to the input values and adapts the weights accordingly. In the area of unsupervised learning different things can be learned, but most of all automatic segmentation (clustering) and compression of data for dimensional reduction are applied.

3.1.55 Validation

This term describes the testing of the precision with which a (PI) model generates predictions for new data. In this context, new data sets are divided into training data and test data. Using the test data, a prediction model is created and optimized. The test data is used to estimate the predictive precision of the model in question. This procedure allows the best (PI) model to be determined, which provides the most accurate predictions for the test data set.

3.1.56 Variables

The term in logic is a formal language placeholder for different expressions. In the context of Predictive Intelligence, it defines a placeholder for the unknown, indeterminate, or variable in formulations, formulas, and even algorithms. There are four basic types of variables:

- *Binary*: The simplest type with only two characteristics, such as whether someone has purchased a pump or a separator.
- *Qualitative*: If there are more than two choices that cannot necessarily be specified with numerical values, the information can or must be defined by a categorical variable. In addition to the above example, when it comes to defining what type of pump has been purchased in relation to different models.
- *Integer* or *Discrete*: Such variables can be either natural in the sense of integers or a certain set of other "allowed" values such as ½ or ¼.
- *Continuous*: Such variables can take all real numbers, i.e., decimal places, with in principle as many decimal places as desired.

If too many variables are fed into an algorithm, this leads to long computing times or even to false statements regarding predictive intelligence. It is therefore necessary to select the relevant and meaningful variables with trial and error. A good starting point for this is simple plots to uncover correlations between variables.

3.2   The Dynamics of the PI Ecosystem

When you hold this book in your hands, many more terms will have been created. The half-life in today's practice but also in science is characterized by an increasing dynamism. In this section of the book, I have attempted to disregard "noise" and map the nucleus of terms for the PI ecosystem. My aim was to provide you with the knowledge to be able to always know so much in further discussions in order to be able to be "dangerous" in case the going gets tough.

Predictive Intelligence is a young discipline in which more and more experts from a wide range of disciplines will come together to provide companies that are flying blind in terms of data technology and their managers with the necessary basis for sustainable and responsible corporate management and control by means of the predictive intelligence approach. You as a manager must be familiar with the PI ecosystem and its most important terms, because many experts, as the research for this chapter has shown, use many of the terms mentioned inconsistently and not congruently.

I do not claim to be complete or infallible, but rather I consider this chapter to be a status quo of an ever more rapidly developing field, which is completely amoebic in itself and therefore subject to constant change. Much must first manifest itself on the basis of the developments and further results. The chapter should be regarded as a basis for discussion and as an orientation aid to provide a framework for the discussion of the subject matter and the linguistic and disciplinary perspective. I hope to contribute to an effective and efficient dialog and process in research, practice, and academia, which can be focused and results-oriented through a congruent use of terms on the basis of a coordinated understanding of content.

Further Reading

Artun, Ö., & Levin, D. (2015). *Predictive marketing—Easy ways every marketer can use*. Hoboken: Wiley.

Blondel, V. D., Guillaume, J.-L., Lambiotte, R., & Lefebvre, E. (2008). Fast unfolding of communities in large networks. *Journal of Statistical Mechanics: Theory and Experiment, 2008*(10), P10008.

Borgelt, C., Klawonn, F., Kruse, R., & Nauck, D. (2003). *Neuro-Fuzzy-Systeme—Von den Grundlagen künstlicher Neuronaler Netze zur Kopplung mit Fuzzy-Systemen*. Cham: Springer.

Bruderer, H. (2018). Erfindung des Computers, Elektronenrechner, Entwicklungen in Deutschland, England und der Schweiz. In *Meilensteine der Rechentechnik* (2., völlig neu bearbeitete und stark erweiterte Auflage. Band 2). München: De Gruyter.

Chamoni, P., & Gluchowski, P. (2006). *Analytische Informationssysteme: Business Intelligence-Technologien und -Anwendungen* (3. Auflage). Berlin: Springer.

Christl, W. (2014, November). Kommerzielle digitale Überwachung im Alltag. PDF. *auf: crackedlabs.org*, S. 12.

Dhar, V. (2013). Data science and prediction. *Communications of the ACM, 56*(12), 64.

Dinter, B., & Winter, R. (Hrsg.). (2008). *Integrierte Informationslogistik (Business Engineering).* Heidelberg: Springer.

Escoufier, Y., et al. (1995). Preface. In *Data science and its application* (englisch). London: Academic Press.

Ester, M., & Sander, J. (2000). *Knowledge discovery in databases.* Techniken und Anwendungen. Berlin: Springer.

Fayyad, U. M., Piatetsky-Shapiro, G., & Smyth, P. (1996). From data mining to knowledge discovery in databases. *AI Magazine, 17*(3), S. 37–54.

Felden, C., & Buder, J. (2012). Entscheidungsunterstützung in Netzgesellschaften. *Wirtschaftsinformatik, 1,* S. 17–32.

Forbes. (2013). *A very short history of data science.* New Jersey: Gil Press.

Gareth, J., Witten, D., Hastie, T., & Tibshirani, R. (2017). *An introduction to statistical learning with applications in R.* New York: Springer.

Güpner, A. (2015). *Ich bin ein Star—Lasst mich hier rein! Das Karrierebuch für den perfekten Berufseinstieg.* München: USP International.

Hinton, G., & Sejnowski, T. J. (Hrsg.). (1999). *Unsupervised learning: Foundations of neural computation.* Cambridge: MIT Press.

IIBA® International Institute of Business Analysis. (2017). *BABOK® v3—Leitfaden zur Business-Analyse BABOK® Guide 3.0* (3., erweiterte Auflage). Gießen: Verlag Dr. Götz Schmidt.

Langley, P. (2011). The changing science of machine learning. *Machine Learning, 82*(3), S. 275–279.

Müller, A. C., & Guido, S. (2017). *Einführung in Machine Learning mit Python: Praxiswissen Data Science.* Heidelberg: O'Reilly.

Ng, A., & Soo, K. (2018). *Data Science—Was ist das eigentlich?! Algorithmen des maschinellen Lernens verständlich erklärt.* Berlin: Springer.

Reichert, R. (2014). *Big Data: Analysen zum digitalen Wandel von Wissen, Macht und Ökonomie.* Bielefeld: Transcript Verlag.

Rifkin, J. (2019). *Der globale Green New Deal: Warum die fossil befeuerte Zivilisation um 2028 kollabiert—und ein kühner ökonomischer Plan das Leben auf der Erde retten kann.* Frankfurt: Campus Verlag.

Seebacher, U. (2020a). *B2B marketing: A guidebook for the classroom to the boardroom.* Cham: Springer.

Seebacher, U. (2020b). *B2B marketing essential: How to turn your marketing from a cost into a sales engine* (2nd ed.). Graz: AQPS.

Seebacher, U. (2020c). *Template-based management—A guide for an efficient and impactful professional practice.* Cham: Springer.

Smola, A. (2008). *Introduction to machine learning.* Cambridge: Cambridge University Press.

Strohmeier, L. (2020). Central business intelligence. In U. Seebacher (Hrsg.), *B2B marketing—A guidebook for the classroom to the boardroom.* Cham: Springer.

Wiggins, R. (1992). Docking a truck: A genetic fuzzy approach. *AI Expert, 7*(5), 28–35.

The Predictive Intelligence Maturity Model

4

4.1 Why Do We Need a PI Maturity Model?

The world is changing, and it is changing at an increasingly rapid pace. The degradation of knowledge or the decreasing half-life of business models is just some of the many signs of this. However, it seems that certain principles can withstand all these changes, as they are the basis of all further developments and changes. Just as water, despite all the incredible and increasingly disruptive innovations and technologies, will always flow downward, or an apple will always fall to the ground in the future, organizations will always develop and change according to the same criteria and processes.

Even if we speak of *agile*, *disruptive*, and *teams-on-the-fly* today, there are firmly defined rules in the area of organizational development and organizational etymology, which will continue to exist despite all new approaches and concepts. These basic principles are comparable to the two basic economic principles described at the beginning of this book. Even the most disruptive business models will only be successful in the long run if they meet the two basic economic principles.

And it is exactly the same in the area of development and maturation of companies as organizational constructs. Organizations can and will always develop or evolve according to rules that have been established since the beginning of management and organizational science and that have been continuously refined and optimized, adapted, and developed. This is due to the fact that such organizational constructs are a network of formal and informal structures. Just as chemical elements combine and dissolve in ever similar ways and thus combine to form chemical networks and systems, organizations function according to the same patterns. The chemical elements in the context of organizations are the individuals with their different characteristics and competences, which in turn connect, dissolve, reconnect, and thus change on the basis of the defined organizational and operational structures.

If such constructs were to develop completely independently, autonomously, and amoebically, the free play of forces would lead to chaos. Without a common idea or vision, the organizations would not be able to realize goal-oriented, value-added development or change through the constant inner dynamics. The only purpose of change would be intrinsic self-realization, like a small child putting its own causal needs and their satisfaction above everything else. It is only through socialization and the process of maturation that one's own behavior can be adapted to the situation in the respective context.

The maturity model for predictive intelligence provides a frame of reference in the sense of an orientation aid. The PI maturity model is the backbone and the big picture of the PI process model and should therefore be the signpost in the sense of the *common idea* and *vision*. Only through a clear, defined, and fixed picture of the goal, an organization will be able to efficiently and effectively follow and master the path toward a data-driven organization. The PI maturity model is, therefore, to be regarded as a reference model, which can be used by managers and executives to determine at any given time where their own department, division, or company is on the way to a data-driven organization with Predictive Intelligence.

The PI maturity model also shows which are the different activity fields that need to be developed and processed. In addition, the model places these different fields in relation to each other and thus helps to identify themes that build on each other and the dependencies and interdependencies that derive from them.

4.2   How the PI Maturity Model Was Created?

Many things in life just happen. When I conducted many different consulting projects with some of the most renowned companies in the years 2000–2003, I was not aware of what had come into being on the side—namely the Template-based Management (TBM) approach (Seebacher 2020). I made a virtue out of necessity and developed a way to optimize my work as a consultant and supporter of companies. *Templates* were the means to an end, with the help of which I was able to support and guide project teams of 40–50 people in a meaningful and serious way instead of the usual 10–15 team members.

Furthermore, the templates unconsciously initiated an enormous transfer of knowledge in the area of methodological and structural competence of the customer project team members. With the help of the templates, they learned how to pre-structure concrete problem-solving processes in order to be able to implement them without external consultants and supporters. It was only through various feedbacks from customers that I became aware of the fact that I had unconsciously developed a very valuable sustainable instrument or approach for effective and cost-optimal problem solving for organizations.

In a joint research project with colleagues from the fields of organizational development, organizational etymology, but also and especially from the fields of human resources management and leadership development, we defined and validated the TBM approach ex post, which led to the first edition of the corresponding management book in 2003. To this day, the book is being used in more and more companies. Why am I making this digression? Also, the findings in the area of predictive intelligence did not originate in an institute at one of the leading universities of business schools, but in business practice. They are therefore a result of applied scientific research and work.

It all started in June 2017 when I joined a leading technology group. I was responsible for the global marketing of a division with sales in the mid-triple-digit million Euro range. The initial situation was that of a classic plant and mechanical engineering company. Marketing had a low priority and was simply considered a cost factor, an approved evil. Activities were limited to organizing trade fairs and customer events and producing brochures. However, the Division Manager quickly realized that, in the context of my educational background, my entrepreneurial track record and experience, I could provide him with decisive support in terms of business development and strategy.

4.2.1 The Game Begins

After only a short time, I was therefore also given additional responsibility for strategic agendas and the field of business development. After a short time, I found myself in a meeting to which the global sales director, Sam Steiner, had invited me. When I entered the meeting room, Sam and two other gentlemen were already there. It turned out that they were the new Regional Sales Directors for North and South America. David joined the company from a competitor and was responsible for the USA. The company was previously represented there only by agents and distributors and Richard, the Regional Sales Director, wanted to develop the market there more actively. The fourth in the round was an Argentinean and his name was Jose. He also came from a competitor and could already point to many years in the relevant market segment. I got along with Jose right away, since I had lived in Uruguay and Argentina for some time, whereas I had little to do with David's "bullish" style.

The goal of the meeting was to develop the business plan for the two regions, on the basis of which the annual goals for David and Jose would be agreed upon. The targets were then also used to calculate the bonus payments for both Regional Sales Directors. Sam started with the USA and in a two-person conversation with David started writing market figures on the whiteboard like crazy. With the proverbial "hot thumb," millions of dollars were unceremoniously shifted back and forth. David, with his strong self-confidence, presented himself in a cosmopolitan manner and tried to make us believe that he knew the exact market figures for the water and sewage market in the entire USA. At some point, an impressive number was written on the bottom right of the whiteboard, David's target for the coming year. Based on this figure, Sam increased the sales to be achieved for each subsequent year by 10% and after 10 min the go-to-market strategy for the next 5 years for the entire USA was designed.

After that, the game started all over again. It was Jose's turn to work with Sam on a five-year plan for South America. Jose was generally more reserved in his demeanor and seemed more reliable and profound in his assumptions and statements. After some time, the five-year plan for Jose's region was also on paper and we had achieved the goal of the meeting. But when it came to how much budget we were going to spend and invest in go-to-market (GTM) on marketing and communications, I asked David and Jose about the relevant trade shows, events and media that we should target in order to reach the relevant customers. But when these simple questions could not be answered stringently and precisely by these experienced sales managers, my doubts increased and even more than before I questioned the entire procedure of market assessment and evaluation. I called one of my colleagues and asked him to bring me the relevant market, media, and event data for the two regions into the meeting room. It took about 20 min until Lucca appeared with the requested documents.

About 70 pages of printouts and analyses landed on my meeting room desk and I immediately realized that this would not make sense this way. I asked Sam to end the meeting at this point and ask David and Jose to go through the relevant sets of market, trade show, and media analysis. David and Jose were then asked to review their assumptions on market figures and present us with the revised, validated five-year plans at the next meeting. Sam kindly accepted my request and 3 days later we were able to finalize both sales strategies for presentation to the division management. My lesson was that I would never again go to such a meeting without the appropriately prepared, relevant, and validated information. With my responsibility for the divisional strategy and the related business development, I could not and would not support and accept such a nontransparent and non-resilient process. For me, accepting such a procedure was at the limit of compliance.

4.2.2 The Data Cube Is Created

I asked Lucca to make an appointment with me. In this meeting with Lucca, I explained my idea of a multidimensional data cube (Fig. 4.1), with which I wanted to have immediate access to any data regarding application, industry, region, and also time. As a manager, it is almost impossible to know all market figures in detail from a certain organizational size. But it must be possible to access and retrieve the relevant figures immediately, always up-to-date and validated.

Together with Lucca, I set out to develop a process model of how we could implement this data cube effectively and quickly. The process model also served to enable Lucca to gradually implement the data cube alongside its other operational activities. I structured the development process for him in accordance with the Template-based Management approach, so that he could then proceed on the basis of it. Previously, Lucca received requests for research and figures from the division on a situational basis and then outsourced these to consulting firms or analysts. That was expensive and took a long time. On average, Lucca had to wait around 3–6 weeks for such reports. Even then, this was no longer a modern way of working, and Lucca itself found it unsatisfactory. I held him in high esteem, because he was a brilliant and intelligent, highly committed, and motivated employee with an incredible ability to grasp things.

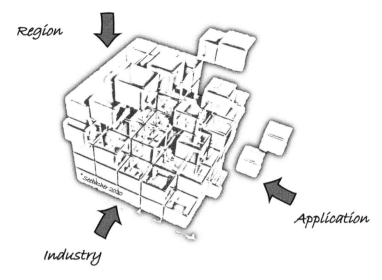

Fig. 4.1 Multidimensional data cube (Source: Own representation)

The data cube should enable us to access relevant figures, data and facts interactively and always up to date in such meetings and thus to accompany and support any assumptions and discussions with corresponding valid and verifiable information. After all, this was about investments in new markets, which we had to make very carefully and very cautiously in order not to have an unnecessary negative impact on our annual results. After just a few months, we had the first version of the multidimensional data cube (MDC) ready. Every quarter we expanded the functionalities but also the data integrated into the MDC, thus gradually developing the core of a predictive intelligence.

The PI maturity model is thus based on the stages completed in the various projects. The model reflects,

- How and above all which data is collected, aggregated, and provided.
- How, where, and when data and information are disseminated.
- How data is analyzed, evaluated, and processed.

These three categories can be used to characterize the different stages of the PI maturity model. These characteristics also define how the three target dimensions of the PI maturity model change over time.

4.3   The Three Dimensions of the PI Maturity Model

Data-driven management also means that all actions should ideally be objective, reliable, and transparently measurable. In terms of predictive intelligence, there are direct and indirect target dimensions or parameters (Fig. 4.2).

Indirect, longterm parameters

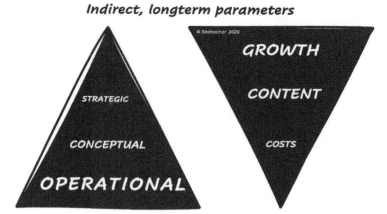

Direct, shortterm parameters

Fig. 4.2 Direct and indirect target dimensions and parameters (Source: Own representation)

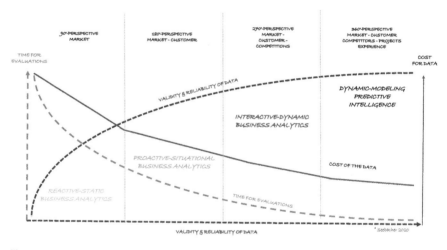

Fig. 4.3 Predictive Intelligence maturity model (Source: Own representation)

The illustration allows three essential dimensions to be derived, on the basis of which the PI maturity model is set up and which has already been introduced in Chap. 2 (Fig. 4.3):

1. Validity of the data (x-axis)
2. Time required for analyses ($y1$-axis)
3. Cost of the data ($y2$-axis)

These essential target dimensions only became apparent in the course of the various projects and studies. They are those aspects that best illustrate a stringent approach in terms of how they change over time as a PI project is implemented. For only if the path to 360° data-driven management is realized and driven by the entire organization not in a blatant but authentic and intrinsically motivated manner will these parameters also undergo a corresponding change in line with the PI maturity model. I refer to my work on the evaluation of the efficiency of quality certification (Seebacher 1996), in which it was proven that only when a topic is really and authentically addressed can the corresponding expected economic effects be realized in the long term. A half-hearted approach, which tends to focus purely on the fulfilment of an activity's duties, also demonstrably influences the savings or optimizations ultimately achieved. A decisive aspect in this context is also the support and involvement of the management.

In the following, the three dimensions of the maturity model for Predictive Intelligence are discussed.

4.3.1   Validity of the Data

It is crucial that figures, data, and facts are valid and thus provide a reliable basis for analysis, evaluation, and planning. Just as it is essential for an aircraft pilot that his weather and flight data are reliable and correct in order to be able to fly short, medium, or long distances safely and as optimally as possible, the data must also be of the highest quality for short, medium, and long-term corporate management. This circumstance applies not only to internal but also to external data.

Many different studies prove that the reliability of the data used can currently only be insufficiently evaluated. The 2020 *B2B Marketing Readiness Self-Assessment*,[1] which was conducted by the author in cooperation with marconomy,[2] has also confirmed this. Currently, only about 50% of B2B marketers are responsible for the content of market and business data, and a third of all B2B marketing managers do not even know where and by whom in their companies this important information is collected, processed, and validated. This fact per se would not pose a problem. But when 75% of marketing managers in the industry say they are contacted at least once a month about figures and data from the field of *Business Intelligence* (BI) and *Market Intelligence* (MI), this raises questions and concerns. Because these executives have to work with information that they do not even know who or what department is providing it. In addition, 34% of these managers are contacted at least once a week by their colleagues in sales with regard to corporate strategy issues, 19.8% once a week and as many as 12.6% several times a week. The fact that managers in organizations are questioned on strategic issues of corporate

---

[1]https://www.marconomy.de/welchen-entwicklungsstand-hat-ihr-marketing-a-927719/. Accessed: September 8, 2020.

[2]https://www.marconomy.de/. Accessed: September 8, 2020.

management and then provide information and assessments based on data of which they have no knowledge of the source, origin or significance, shows how explosive the situation currently is in the organizations.

This is because the opinions and expertise of the surveyed colleagues are regarded as valid and on this basis company-relevant decisions are then prepared and made. There is no doubt that business development is an important function for companies. BI deals with questions of how and where new business can be optimally developed with regard to return on sales (RoS). Currently, two-thirds of companies do not have this topic in marketing and 60% of companies do not even have it in sales. However, this contradicts the fact that 42% of B2B marketers are contacted and consulted on the subject of business development at least once a month, 14.5% once or even several times a week—although they know nothing about objectivity, reliability, or validity of the data used.

During the course of studies, students learn to deal with the phenomenon of the consequences of a miscalculation at the beginning of a process or an analysis. A small error or deviation at the beginning leads to enormous deviations in the final result. Imagine a rocket taking off on a journey of many thousands of kilometers. If this rocket is launched with only a single degree of deviation from the initially calculated course, it will never reach its defined destination and will miss it. The same applies to data-based management. If the wrong data is used, this can have fatal consequences for companies.

4.3.1.1 Therefore, Examine Whoever Binds Forever!

Within the scope of one of the projects underlying this publication in the area of implementing predictive intelligence, we used various relevant databases from external providers. This was about a very specific, narrow market for which there was and is only a very small number of database providers. For years, the company had purchased a section of the entire database every year for a high five-digit sum and used it as a basis for corporate management and also for sales control. Thus, market share increases were defined based on the current market share in order to derive the goals for the sales department or the respective sales manager in a region, but also to grow congruently with the market or even exceed an anticipated market growth. This project is interesting in two respects.

Until now, this external database was used one-dimensionally. This means that the purchased data was not linked or processed with data from other sources in any way. Through our work on predictive intelligence for Jaydee's Inc. we also developed a multidimensional data cube (MDW). In the MDW, different data sources were integrated and linked by the data field "Country." Data from the World Bank, the International Monetary Fund were used as well as data from the *International Trade Center* (ITC) and other industry and segment-specific databases of private providers. The sample of data to be used must be specifically defined on a case-by-case basis.

> **Tip:** It is not always necessary to purchase entire data stocks or databases if this does not make sense for your own company and its regional or content spectrum of activities. Most providers of databases also make it possible, if you insist long enough, to purchase even excerpts from databases. This can help to save considerable costs.

On the basis of this clear allocation and corresponding analytical evaluations, we were able to recognize that there was a calculation error in the database of a provider. Our standard processes for internal data preparation caused this error. I still remember one morning when I came into the office and my colleague asked me to talk to him.

Augusto, a Brazilian, explained what had happened and how he validated the process again. He carried out three different analyses and came to exactly the same result over and over again: there was a serious miscalculation in the database on the basis of which corporate strategy issues of the highest relevance to top management had been processed and worked out for years. As a result, the current market data was too high and thus provided a distorted picture. Through cross-sectional and comparative analyses, we were able to identify this overly positive presentation and then validate and confirm it several times in the control loops mentioned above. This was again only possible because we designed, validated, and installed the entire model of connections and algorithms ourselves step by step. If you buy data or solutions externally in the context of *cloud sourcing*, then in most cases the underlying, running calculation algorithms are not known, similar to a *black box*. This leads to the fact that the methodology and structure of data sets and the underlying calculation schemes can of course only be evaluated and validated to a very limited extent. Also, in this context, *make* offers sustainable decisive advantages compared to *buy*.

So, we contacted the database provider, whom we already knew personally by now, since we had been in contact with him again and again. In the meantime, an intensive and regular exchange with him had developed and his input certainly played an important role in the development of some algorithms of today's predictive intelligence concept. John from the external database provider was immediately in the picture and immediately recognized the error. He thanked us very much and was visibly impressed by our competence. John and his database were evergreen in the relevant market segment, and everyone knew him. He is a *grand senior* of market data and his feedback and confirmation of the validity of our statement really mattered to us. John adapted his database and corrected the error. From that point on, his database now showed correct market potential, which was critical for Jaydee's Inc. to make valid and realistic assessments of sales potential and business development.

4.3.1.2 The Profit Lies in Purchasing!

But the project also brought to light another insight that should bring sustainable benefits. Through the internal calculation and data processing processes developed by us, we were able to reproduce the mechanisms of extrapolation of externally purchased databases after a short time. This enabled us to determine the forecasts more precisely and more validly. I asked Augusto to first extrapolate the data for the various applications and regions internally to 3, 5, and 10 years without reference to the respective forecasts of the various databases. We then compared these data series with those of the database providers, most of whom only provided forecasts for periods of 3–5 years anyway. Our forecasts were always closely aligned with those of the vendors, and in addition, our internal validation algorithms were proven to be robust.

With this in mind, I immediately switched the purchasing of the relevant market data providers to a 2- or 3-year cycle, depending on how often the various database providers updated their data and how relevant the respective databases were to Jaydee's Inc. business. This process alone saved us a six-digit Euro amount in the short term, as we no longer had to purchase new data sets for all four databases every year. In terms of the overall budget for Predictive Intelligence, which did not exist per se and under this definition anyway, we were able to realize a saving of 70%, money that we could more than sensibly use for the purchase of additional new databases in industries relevant to Jaydee's Inc.

The validity of the data plays a decisive role. After all, it is a matter of operational and strategic corporate management. If you use bad data for data-driven management, then you cannot assume that you will be able to realize high-quality and reliable corporate management with it, because the basis is simply not valid. And if a building is built on sand and stands on feet of clay, this poses enormous risks for the entire organization. In the course of predictive intelligence work at another company, TRL Inc., we came across another phenomenon that is another strong argument for *make in* terms of predictive intelligence.

TRL Inc. is active in a very special segment of the food industry and there is no database provider in this area that can provide corresponding market figures. Therefore, we started to search for relevant external providers of market analysts and research. We conducted extensive research based on the relevant, industry-specific keywords and found some providers. At first glance, all providers impressed us with comprehensive references, worldwide presence, and a perfect *customer experience* (Halb and Seebacher 2020), because when the homepage was opened, a chat window opened immediately to be able to send a direct inquiry to the company.

However, it turned out that the initially perfect facade began to crumble very quickly. In fact, when we analyzed the presence of the various providers more closely, we found that most of these supposed locations were fake, since the addresses in *GoogleMaps* either showed entire street courses or run-down private homes in suburbs of well-known cities such as Portland, Singapore, Sao Paolo, or Hong Kong (Fig. 4.4). This is only one of a large number of examples. Such providers are a dime a dozen and especially small and medium-sized companies or organizations that are just at the beginning of the predictive intelligence

Our Location

Fig. 4.4 Supposed global presence of a research company (For reasons of data protection law, the naming of the domain is deliberately not mentioned in this illustration.)

development stage run the risk of falling victim to such providers and their not clean and validly researched data and analyses.

Unfortunately, we also had to realize that some of the top brands of research companies are increasingly conspicuous for their lack of detail and fuzziness in their reports and analyses. Within the scope of another project in the water management sector, we engaged one of the really most renowned companies to prepare a report for the Asia-Pacific region. The order volume was around 120,000 euros. The contract was awarded after detailed preliminary examination and many preliminary discussions. There were exact briefings and many rounds of coordination. When we received the draft version of the report after 3 months, we were almost shocked by the results. Although the company had never sold any machines in this region— neither directly nor indirectly—the report showed a market share of 33% for the Australian market only. We checked the various direct and indirect sales channels throughout the region, ran a query in the company's CRM and also evaluated the *installed base*[3] in the region but simply could not find such a high level of product inventory in Australia.

In order to be able to validate these and other statements that were not comprehensible to us, we compiled a comprehensive list of 27 questions to be clarified, which we sent to the supplier's team. Even after three rounds of voting, we were still unable to trace the derivation of the corresponding results. Against this background, we had to mark the entire report with the appropriate note regarding questionable validity and could therefore only use it in a very limited form for further analyses and reports for the company management. If we had used this amount not in the sense of

---

[3]This term is a measure of the number of units of a particular product type that have been sold and are in use.

the *Buy* but in the sense of the *Make*, we could have developed internally much more favorable and in addition more lasting results, whose validity could also have been clearly derived and presented.

In the context of the gradual development of data-driven management toward predictive intelligence, the validity of purchased data can be validated very quickly and very accurately. This, in turn, has a positive effect on purchasing conditions, since it is of course possible to address the issue of shallowness and fuzziness with database providers in price negotiations. However, for the data validity to develop as shown in the Predictive Intelligence maturity model, a clear *make-up is* required with regard to the topic. How the individual steps as part of the process model look like will be described in the chapter on the Predictive Intelligence Process Model in the further course of the book.

4.3.2   Time Required for Analyses

The $y1$ axis of the model in Fig. 4.3 shows the progression of the time required in each phase of the PI maturity model to produce analyses and reports. Especially in phase 1 "Reactive-static Business Analytics" all analyses and reports are purchased from external sources. This fact means that a short-term situational approach is not possible, since the organizations cannot maintain their own data or proven data science competence internally. It is only at the second stage of the PI maturity model that it will gradually become possible to proceed more and more situation-related but also proactively with regard to data-driven corporate management. This also has an immediate effect on the decreasing time required for analyses.

I remember a project in the metal industry. The customer was a medium-sized company with worldwide activities and headquarters in Sweden. At the beginning of the project, everything in the area of *Business Intelligence* was bought externally, from newsletter services to industry updates, market studies, and reports. The total annual costs for these external services alone were around 250,000 euros. Very promptly, I had an internal survey carried out, which was to provide information on the use and satisfaction with the purchased information and services. The result was hardly surprising. The news services were used but classified as "generic" and "also findable on the Internet," and the purchased reports were evaluated very differently in terms of quality and significance. In addition, the time factor of too much content was a problem for all respondents and was classified as "too long."

With this feedback, we ended the external news services at the next possible date and saved us about 80,000,—Euro. In return, we recruited a student co-worker and purchased the first industry-specific data sets from two database providers that we had previously analyzed in detail in terms of objectivity, reliability, and validity.

Tip: To analyze database providers in terms of their quality before purchasing data, it is helpful to receive a sample dataset. This can then be reviewed internally. Together with colleagues it can be discussed and evaluated on the basis of your own existing expertise. Setting up and developing a predictive intelligence model in an organization is inevitably a learning process. It will therefore be challenging at the beginning to be able to evaluate the validity of providers and data in detail. Against this background, it is advisable to use secondary research, but also a coordinated approach with internal stakeholders, for example, from sales, corporate development, or business development, to gain a joint picture of the respective providers. As the process progresses, it will become easier and quicker to carry out the quality check. This is another important argument for *make* in the field of predictive intelligence.

We used the remaining time until the external newsletters and industry updates expired to compile our own internal Intelligence *Updates* (IU) based on our industries, markets, and competitors and send them to our internal customers. Initially, these IUs were sent to the rapidly growing distribution list once a month. At the end of each IU, there was a link to an interactive online survey, in order to immediately obtain feedback from the recipients regarding content, length of contributions, graphic design and, above all, suggestions for optimization and ideas for further relevant content. The result was that we were able to send out timely information, news, and updates that were much more individually tailored to the needs and requirements of our internal customers and readers. And when the external news subscriptions finally expired after 3 or 6 months, no one noticed any more, because everyone was now convinced and enthusiastic about the advantages of the internal Intelligence Updates.

As soon as we had the first databases in the company, we set up an Excel table with which it was possible to filter the data according to appropriate criteria and then send it to our respective internal customers, the inquirers, in the form of specially produced PowerPoint reports. Initially, the average response time was around 2–3 weeks. After only 3 months, the average processing time was already between 5 and 7 days, so we were able to reduce the processing time by 65% in a very short time, which in turn brings enormous advantages in terms of situational, data-driven management. When we had submitted the first reports to our internal customers, and thus the stringent and consistent way of preparing the data in terms of congruence with the defined question, but also of underpinning the data with appropriate cross-references, we experienced a real rush. We neatly documented all incoming inquiries after the date of receipt and always immediately checked the satisfaction of internal customers with the analyses and reports we had prepared. Satisfaction was 93%, and in the first 6 months we produced a total of around 25 analyses. Based on previous years, we calculated an average time requirement per report of around

60 days. In comparison, we realized an average requirement of 15 days over the 6-month period, averaged in terms of the final number of pages.

This is certainly a special achievement and the result of perfect teamwork. Motivated and committed employees play a decisive role when it comes to setting up predictive intelligence in an organization. After all, the devil is in the detail but also in the coordination with internal customers and colleagues. The sooner the *black box* of data and the algorithms used can be solved, the faster the internal acceptance within the organization for the developing, data-driven management will increase. This acceptance in turn is important so that colleagues and internal customers take enough time to be available for analyzing and evaluating analyses, reports, and figures, especially at the beginning of activities. Without these coordination loops, neither the validity of the generated results nor the time required to create reports will develop so quickly into a positive result.

4.3.3 Cost of the Data

At first glance, setting up a data-driven management system always seems extremely cost-intensive and complicated. This may simply have to do with the lack of transparency with regard to the topic, the corresponding procedure and the relatively manageable low information technology effort. However, on closer inspection it becomes immediately clear how attractive the *make-economics analysis* ultimately turns out to be.

If one takes the values shown above and creates a simple profitability analysis based on them, the following picture emerges:

- Savings external news services per year: 250,000 euros
- Full costs[4] 12 months of student employees: 50,000 euros
- Calculatory costs[5] of 25 analyses: 375,000 euros
- Purchase of two databases: 75,000 euros
- Full costs of a BI employee: 80,000 euros

Based on these figures, a direct saving of 420,000 euros is calculated for the first year. This may not seem impressive in absolute terms, but it represents a percentage saving of around 67.2%, without taking into account any manpower that might still be required in the case of the *buy scenario*, but merely calculating the two cost items for external news services and for 25 analyses. Furthermore, this calculation does not take into account the fact that the purchased databases were purchased not only for 1 year, but for 2 or 3 years, and thus fall less into the cost weighting in an annual consideration.

---

[4]This refers to both wage and non-wage costs for the employer.

[5]These costs are based on an average cost rate per purchased external analysis or report of 15,000 euros calculated within the company on the basis of previous years.

Furthermore, the most essential factor was also not considered in this very direct and rudimentary view, human capital (Becker 1993). It is the investment that probably represents the largest and most important factor in the development of a company's own predictive intelligence. The investment in organizational human capital is one of the most sustainable aspects of responsible and value-added organizational development. Today I am still impressed by how Paul, the student assistant, was able to gain such a deep insight into the market in a short period of time simply by creating the Intelligence Updates internally, which enabled him to quickly identify data technical correlations and uncover inconsistencies.

Learning-on-the-job (Barron et al. 1997) is a strained term but in the context of data-driven management and its establishment this method of learning plays an essential role. The higher the internal share of added value generation in the area of predictive intelligence compared to external procurement, the higher the corporate, both operational and strategic economic advantage will be in the long run. If the internal expertise grows congruently with the scope and complexity of the predictive intelligence system, data-based corporate management can provide the greatest added value in terms of corporate development in the long term. Financial resources are not awarded to external providers on a short-term and selective basis but are invested wisely in the company's own human capital and its own predictive intelligence ecosystem.

4.4   The Predictive Intelligence Maturity Model (PIMM)

In all my articles, books, MBA courses, podcasts, TV shows, or lectures, I always try to work out a core message that is decisive for me: Every project can only be successfully implemented if the methods and structures applied are consistent and efficient in working toward a clearly defined goal that is known to all participants. Depending on whether you are working in a familiar subject area or in a new one, this goal may differ in terms of time and content.

When we started working on our first projects in the field of predictive intelligence, our goal was certainly roughly defined, but by no means concretely formulated. This was simply due to the fact that at that time we did not or could not know exactly what a Predictive Intelligence for the management could, should, or should not look like in terms of content and technology. Therefore, I defined milestones that were always aimed at facilitating our work without existing budgets and additional resources in addition to our daily business.

With this approach, it was possible to show the results of the optimization of our workflows in each stage after a short time and to present them transparently. The primary focus was always on cost efficiency and sustainability in terms of the best possible reuse of purchased data and information. However, the path of small steps also had an important motivational role, because the defined milestones were clearly defined and realizable. This meant that we were able to complete all activities within the defined timeframes. These milestones were discussed and defined together. During these discussions, we also talked very carefully about what would be possible and feasible with the available information and tools—we always and exclusively started with Microsoft Excel.

Each stage was characterized by an enormous learning process, since during the implementation of the various activities we naturally encountered problems and challenges that we had not anticipated in this way. But it was precisely this interactive and situational analysis, discussion, evaluation, and optimization that gave us a shared sense of achievement, from which an enormous, positive dynamic developed. Because we always worked closely with the needs and requirements of the various internal customer groups, we also had a continuous exchange with them. This automatically led to very interesting and enlightening discussions, which had a positive effect on both the acceptance of the solution under development and the organizational learning process regarding Predictive Intelligence.

> Tip: 90% of companies today are not consistently data driven. Against this background, the establishment of predictive intelligence for corporate management means first and foremost a change management process. The ecosystem of predictive intelligence is still a *black box* for most organizations and their executives. Never underestimate or ignore this fact when you start your journey toward Predictive Intelligence with the help of this book. So, take your organization on the journey with you. Involve them in the development and learning process, because you will all benefit from it. You, because you will receive valuable and important input, and your various internal customers, because they will become familiar with the topic, will learn how to deal with it and understand which processes and algorithms are running in the background. That's why *make* is such a crucial aspect in the context of predictive intelligence, because it means that learning and development take place together and in coordination with the entire organization. This is how a good and value-adding predictive intelligence solution in the sense of data-driven management can be created in the long term.

What we now refer to as the *Predictive Intelligence Maturity Model* (PIMM) is the result of various projects in the area of data-driven corporate management, which have been methodically and structurally analyzed, evaluated, and documented ex post. The model is both a reference framework for analyzing the respective status in the organization with regard to Predictive Intelligence, but also a concrete process model for implementing Predictive Intelligence for the management itself in the organization.

Very often I am asked where the topic of Predictive Intelligence should be located in an organization. On the basis of my experience, it is not possible to give a general answer to this question, because from the point of view of organizational etymology it is crucial that the topic is located where the corresponding starting point in terms of content, methodology, and structure is available. In the further course of the book, the subject area of the necessary competences and requirements, but also the

Fig. 4.5 QR code Predictive
Intelligence Self-Assessment

organizational nature, will be dealt with in more detail, as well as the area of possible, necessary and available IT applications and solutions on the market.

If it turns out that neither in sales, marketing, or corporate development—if there is such a department in the organization—the appropriate affinity to the topic, interest or competence is present, then the management must be willing to bring a person into the company to stringently address this topic with clear guidelines and goals. Experience has shown that the return on investment (RoI) for such an investment in the human capital of the company is between 12 and 16 months, depending on how the corresponding schedule is defined. In any case, it is a more than worthwhile investment, as the various case studies at the back of this book illustrate.

4.4.1   Stage 1: Reactive-Static Business Analytics

When you hold this book in your hands, you or your organization will most likely be found at this level of the maturity model. There are two easy ways to find out quickly:

1. You use the QR code (Fig. 4.5) to go directly to the free online self-test, which guides you through 50 questions that can be answered easily and quickly. Based on these questions, you can see directly where the relevant fields of action lie.
2. Or you can always answer the following questions with "yes":
   - In most cases, analyses, reports, and studies are purchased externally.
   - Externally purchased information is not processed in a structured way.
   - Externally purchased information is only used selectively, mainly once.
   - Market reports, news, and information on competitors, projects, and other relevant details are provided by external newsletter service providers or there are no such updates.
   - There is no central organizational unit that collects, validates, processes and, on request, specifically filters data and generates reports and analyses based on it.

If you can more or less affirm the exemplary questions, then the status quo of the relevant organization with regard to PIMM is in any case at level 1.

4.4.1.1 What Does Reactive Business Analytics Mean?

Re-active describes a type of action that takes place in response to external impulses. This means that there is no independent and dynamic action with regard to figures, data, and facts for corporate planning and control. This is not surprising in most cases, since no units or teams have yet been established in the organizations that are equipped with the necessary instruments, competencies, and resources to perform and implement business analytics per se according to the definition. This is also in line with the results of the current Freeform Dynamics Study (2020), according to which just 5% of all companies can be classified as data driven within the meaning of the definition.

The forerunner is certainly the financial sector with 10% of companies, followed by the telecommunications industry (7%) and the health and life science sector with 5%. The taillights are the mechanical engineering and plant construction sector (3%), trade (3%) but also the automotive sector (2%) and the travel and logistics sector (2%). In terms of an intra-European country comparison, England is the clear leader with already 8% of all companies that can already point to data-driven corporate management. The red lantern holds Denmark with currently no companies that already use data-based corporate management. However, since by far the largest number of companies in Denmark, namely a remarkable 65%, are classified as "data-empowered," one could assume, under the aspect of Nordic modesty, that Denmark also scores in the inner-European average, but simply the definition of data-driven corporate management is applied more narrowly and stringently and therefore the Danish self-assessment is supposedly more negative compared to the companies in the EU.

The model on which this study is based refers to the PIMM and defines four different levels of development for data maturity, similar to the PIMM:
- Lack of data (3.5%): Relatively chaotic approach to data handling, resulting in lack of transparency and higher data-related risk.
- Data-supported (45.8%): Existence of the necessary basic skills, but still incomplete and often backward-looking handling of data.
- Data-driven (46%): Good situational availability of consistent, complete, current, and predictive business-related data and information.
- Data-driven (4.8%): Continuous and often real-time insights that are proactively prepared, delivered, and shared across the enterprise.

The result is not surprising. The harsh reality is that organizations that will not manage to move from the lowest category to the next higher one in a timely manner will be at a significant competitive disadvantage. In today's fast-moving and increasingly digitally controlled contingency situation, it is no longer a question of wanting to go from "data-hungry" to "data-driven," but rather of surviving. In order to become truly data-driven, it is necessary to implement a range of technologies and

Fig. 4.6 A tool does not yet make predictive intelligence (Source: Own representation)

techniques that are actually very advanced by today's standards, regardless of location, size, or sector.

There is a great danger that a company will succumb to the temptation to buy too quickly one of the tools offered with many, at first glance impressive pictures, charts, presentations, and videos. A new IT tool from the rapidly growing Predictive Intelligence Technology Stack (PITechStack) will not lead an organization from the stage of *Reactive-Static Business Analytics* to that of *Dynamically-modeling Predictive Intelligence* as a fool with a tool still remains a fool (Fig. 4.6). There is a reason why children first have to learn mental arithmetic at school and only when they have mastered the basic mathematical rules can they use a calculator and learn how to use this instrument. It is the same with predictive intelligence: If you have not learned the subject from scratch, step by step by hand, you will not be able to handle a miracle instrument or an artificial intelligence.

At this point I also refer to the phenomenon of CRM systems, which were sold and bought everywhere in the 1990s of the twentieth century as the miracle solutions to solve all problems with dissatisfied customers. Until today these CRM systems with all their advantages and options have not found their way into the minds of many sales organizations. This is simply because these systems have been put over the organizations by top management and prescribed to them, without clearly communicating and manifesting the awareness in sales as well as the necessary, basic processes but also the monitoring in the sense of the *Single-Point-of-Truth*[6] in the organizations.

Until today, there is a lack of *organizational authenticity* with regard to such instruments or systems that are technically and factually available in companies on the basis of a pure information technology implementation, but are miles away from generating added value in the organization with regard to their content-logical dimension. The triangle of trust (Fig. 1.1) with its three pillars *authenticity*, *empathy*, and *logic* is also crucial for the successful development of Predictive Intelligence, in order to establish the field of data-driven corporate management stringently and sustainably not only technically and factually, but also in terms of content and logic in an organization.

---

[6]https://en.wikipedia.org/wiki/Single_source_of_truth. Accessed: November 18, 2020.

4.4.1.2 What Does Static Business Analytics Mean?

"Static"[7] is defined in the dictionary with the following three terms:

1. *Physics:* Concerning the equilibrium of forces
2. Remaining in the same state, unmoved, unchanged
3. *Construction*: Concerning the statics of a building

With regard to the first level of the Predictive Intelligence maturity model (PIMM), the second definition is relevant. At the first stage of the PIMM, analyses, reports, data or information are used once, i.e., selectively, in the appropriate present manner. This means that there is no further processing in the sense of further use, adaptation, or any kind of interpretative or comparative evaluation. Especially in the area of data-based business management, secondary, and tertiary analyses are of the highest relevance in order to be able to recognize and derive meta-recognitions on the basis of the operative basic information.

> **Example: If a product can be sold in two different markets with different high margins, then static analysis would be able to play this off accordingly from the CRM or ERP system.** From today's point of view in the context of reactive-static business analytics, such a report would not be processed or used stringently and automatically to find out what the reasons for the different price sensitivities in the different markets are. A dynamic modelling business analytics would use automated processes to continuously collect and aggregate this data and attempt to identify correlations using various static procedures such as correlation or regression. From this, it could then be deduced what the factors are that determine why a higher price corridor can be achieved in a country. A purely static business analytics depends on informal, interpretative-discursive derivation of findings, which is why the term "chaotic" is also used in the definition of Freeform Dynamics.

Based on the following exemplary criteria, it can be determined that the requirements of the first level of maturity for Predictive Intelligence are fulfilled:

- Relevant data sources for the core industries and core markets of the organization are identified.
- Core data are entered into an Excel table.
- A first, multidimensional data model allows the combinatorial processing of the first data.
- Based on the Excel-based data model, the first graphical preparations have been made.
- First analyses and reports have already been delivered to internal customers and feedback is being recorded and incorporated.

---

[7]https://www.wortbedeutung.info/statisch/. Accessed: September 10, 2020.

• Relevant processes for Predictive Intelligence are documented and communicated in accordance with the Template-based Management[8] approach in the form of a PI Process Library (PIPL).

4.4.2   Level 2: Proactive-Situational Business Analytics

While organizations at the first stage of the PIMM react purely *reactively* to needs in terms of numbers, data, and facts, in the course of development toward the second stage of PIMM, as competence and experience increase, more and more knowledge is built up with regard to internal and external contingency factors. As I described earlier, the first measures in the first stage of PIMM should include the gradual phasing out of all more or less generic and standardized content and information purchased from external providers for a lot of money. This means that relevant information and updates must be automatically searched and researched. This is the only way to develop an enormous amount of knowledge within the shortest possible time and, above all, the knowledge of relevant and valid, freely accessible information sources.

The subsequent processing of the collected information into company internal *news updates* or *newsletters* (Fig. 4.7) deepens this knowledge, because information must be understood, put into context, and then also brought into the respective content form with regard to expression and language. This regularly occurring process creates an enormous agility and flexibility to deal with an ever increasing and more complex amount of data and information. If, as part of the initial measures, raw data on industries and general economic figures is also purchased, with which a student co-worker then fills the first templates and Excel tables, correlations, developments in regions and markets become even more transparent and easier to recognize.

4.4.2.1 Why a Proactive Approach Is Such an Important Step?
This leads to the fact that a purely reactive action on level 1 of the PIMM now becomes a more proactive support. Proactive is defined in the dictionary as follows:
1. Business: Planning and acting early, with foresight and clarity with regard to future challenges
2. Acting in advance

This means that the increasing data agility and data flexibility inevitably leads to an ever more pronounced *associative* and *combinatorial competence* within the respective organizational unit driving the topic of PI. Against this background, developments in industries, countries, markets, or regions, but also in specific applications and special areas of focus or market participants, can be continuously observed and documented at an early stage. This knowledge can then be

---

[8]https://www.springer.com/de/book/9783030566104. Accessed: November 18, 2020.

Xylem Reports Solid Earnings Growth On Five Percent Organic Revenue Increase

Excluding the impact of restructuring and realignment, the Company delivered adjusted net income of $143 million or $0.79 per share in the quarter. Excluding the impact of foreign exchange translation, adjusted earnings per share was up 10 percent. Second quarter revenue was $1.3 billion, up 5 percent organically with revenue growth across all end markets, led by double-digit growth in the U.S. and continued solid momentum in China and India. Reported operating margin in the quarter was 12.7 percent and adjusted operating margin was 14.3 percent, up 50 basis points compared to the prior year. Xylem is updating its forecasted full-year 2019 revenue outlook to be in the range of $5.29 to $5.38 billion. On an organic basis, Xylem's revenue growth is narrowed to a range of 5 to 6 percent (2 to 3 percent on a reported basis) from previous guidance of 4 to 6 percent. Read more.

Flowserve Corporation Reports Second Quarter 2019 Results

Reported Earnings Per Share (EPS) were $0.44, and Adjusted[1] EPS of $0.54. Total bookings were $1.11 billion, up 6.5%, or 9.9% on a constant currency basis, and included approximately 1.0% negative impact related to divested businesses. Backlog as of June 30, 2019 was $2.2 billion, up 14.0% versus 2018 year-end, on 1.12 book-to-bill. Flowserve revised its 2019 guidance, including increasing its Reported and Adjusted EPS target to a range of $1.75 to $1.90 and $2.05 to $2.20, respectively. Both the Reported and the Adjusted EPS target range now include an expected revenue increase of approximately 4.0% to 5.0% year-over-year and remain based on the other previously announced assumptions. Read more.

Sulzer And Nidec Formalize Field Service Agreement In North America

Following last year's agreement for Sulzer to provide sales and technical support for Nidec medium voltage (MV) drives in North America, the two companies have now formalized the field service offering. Having completed technical training, field service teams from Sulzer are now able to offer operators of Nidec MV drives onsite support. The agreement with Nidec offers Sulzer's customers direct access to high quality MV drives that can be designed to suit each application. At the same time, Nidec customers will benefit from expert support on site as well as access to local, well equipped and modern maintenance facilities. Read more.

Biwater Wins RO Contract For Perris II Desalter In Southern California

Fig. 4.7 Company internal Industry Intelligence Update (Source: Own representation)

communicated proactively to the relevant internal target groups either directly in regular calls and meetings or indirectly via intranet-based information industry portals, newsletters, or podcasts and vodcasts. Depending on how the acceptance of the PI department increases within the entire organization, the more proactive the PI team will and can be. The PI team can thus set impulses and initiate discussions when relevant developments in relevant areas and topics are identified.

The change from a reactive to a proactive approach represents a decisive step in the direction of Predictive Intelligence, because the point is that only by being aware of the core function of Predictive Intelligence for management can this function be used correctly in an organization in the long term. It is essential to always keep the *subsidiary value* of Predictive Intelligence in mind. This means that even at the highest level of development, PI should and can only serve management as a regulatory and informational framework. Even if PI will generate ever more precise and valid analyses and reports, no company can and must switch completely to the *autopilot mode* and rely 100% only on PI.

Similar to an airline pilot, complex maneuvers such as take-off and landing, but also evasive maneuvers in thunderstorms and turbulences, are proactively performed manually by the pilot and not by the autopilot. In a figurative sense, this means that a business plan for a market entry created from the PI must ultimately be validated and analyzed by the management to ensure that the necessary means and resources are either available or can be provided on time. The move to proactive business analytics is therefore a delicate but important step in change management, as internal customers will have to deal with and get used to the fact that the PI team suddenly has more knowledge and can provide valid proof of this.

At this point I would like to point out the so often strained, but so correct and important quantity structure in the context of change management and change projects, that 20% of those affected certify an openness, 60% a neutral attitude, and the remaining 20% an absolute aversion and rejection of any change. Taking this into account, internal customers can be intuitively assigned to the different groups and thus make life much easier for themselves with regard to the PI-relevant change process.

4.4.2.2 Why Does It Have to Be Situational?

Situative is derived from the Latin "situs" in the sense of "situation" and "position" and actually means that something is or must be related to a situation. Often the term context is also used, or the contingency situation. In science, there is also the field of contingency theory, which aims to establish relationships between things and situations in relation to the relevant environment. The discipline of organizational etymology can also be found in this scientific environment, since it is based on the fact that organizational constructs, just like individuals, always develop and change in direct relation to their situational environment.

In the context of PIMM, *situational* refers to the ability to not only use external and internal content and information in its current form, but also to adapt, change, and develop it according to the situation in order to be able to work out, deal with and possibly answer specific questions more precisely and validly.

> **Example:** A sales representative receives a market analysis for a certain region. This is forwarded to the PI team. At level 1 of the PIMM, the PI team would review the report, but would not use it any further. In stage 2 of the PIMM, the report is prepared in such a way that the relevant results are incorporated into existing templates, tables, and data models. This would then be used to compare and evaluate the consistency and congruence of the data in the company's own databases. If there are any discrepancies, the PI team would try to explain them and coordinate them with the relevant sales staff. Thus, the ability of situational business analytics covers two essential elements: first, the primary gain in insight from the new report and second, the secondary gain in insight regarding data congruence and validity. The tertiary knowledge gain that may possibly take place refers to the creator of the report in question, in terms of its quality and excellence with regard to a possible future purchase of specifically relevant data.

The development from *static* to *situational* business analytics is a major step forward in terms of economic value add. This is due to the fact that the PI team is able to recognize developments on its own initiative—as proactive—and immediately relate them to its own business situation—i.e., situationally. If, for example, a competitor launches a new product in a highly profitable segment that is important for its own company, then this is crucial information from the perspective of risk management and its own business planning. The PI team can now use proactive situational business analytics to relate the various pieces of information and put them into their current context. In this way, threats, opportunities, potentials, but also risks can be recognized early and communicated to the organization.

On the other hand, this expanded, important competence will also further increase the acceptance and appreciation of the PI department. This is again an important step in terms of organizational learning. In fact, the organization gets the opportunity to become familiar with the topic of business analytics as part of predictive intelligence and to develop the ability to use it optimally for its own sustainable corporate or departmental development. As part of this development step, interactions and coordination with the various internal customers should constantly increase and become more intensive. The overriding principle in this phase must be to always meet internal customers promptly and competently in order to build trust and establish oneself as a reliable partner in the area of data-based management.

On the basis of the following exemplary criteria, one can recognize whether one has reached the second degree of maturity for Predictive Intelligence:

- External analyses and information or newsletter services are no longer or only selectively purchased.
- Market and competition data for all industries relevant to the respective organization are collected and integrated into the data model.
- First analyses are already prepared via interactive dashboards and can be accessed by specially selected key users.
- Increasing numbers of requests for analyses and reports.
- Ongoing, more intensive involvement in more and more operational and strategic issues of corporate management.
- Expansion of the internal clientele.

4.4.3   Level 3: Interactive-Dynamic Business Analytics

With increasing intensity of coordination and interaction with the various internal customers, proactive situational acting will unconsciously develop into Interactive Dynamic Business Analytics. *Interactive* in this context refers to an admitting, supporting, or related mutual reaction to each other. The PI team has thus become an integral part of all corporate thinking and acting. While in the beginning, the PI team's internal customers were primarily sales and management, it can now also provide valuable information for areas such as innovation management, research and development, or product management and marketing. From the initial 90° data perspective with external economic data, it has now become an approximately 270° data world, which now also includes information on customers and competitors. The decisive factor, however, is the attribute *dynamic*,[9] which is defined in the dictionary as follows:

1. Physics concerning the movement generated by forces
2. Full internal movement, with rapid change
3. With zest for action; full of energy to accomplish something

Regarding the third level of the PIMM, the attribute *dynamically* focuses on the ongoing and immediate adaptation of data and information, made possible by simple but powerful IT support. In concrete terms, this means that at the third level of the PIMM, a predictive intelligence portal must be made available to the entire organization 24/7, making it possible to retrieve the most interesting and relevant data and information on an individual basis and to display it in an easily readable form.

This has the enormous advantage that the PI team no longer has to extract every inquiry from the system itself as an analysis or report, prepare it and send it to the respective internal customer, as was previously the case, but that 80% of the inquiries can now be generated and retrieved by the internal customers themselves, autonomously, at any time with the help of the PI system. As a result, PI experts can now concentrate primarily on the value-adding, complex activities such as data validation, extrapolation, and evaluation, but also on direct consulting and support for internal customers on more complex issues. The case studies at the end of the book provide an overview of such more complex projects. This represents a further essential step with regard to the own further optimization of the resources used, as the

- definition of requests,
- the communication of the requests,
- possible clarifications in case of uncertainties,
- the search itself up to the. . .
- . . .preparation of the report and
- its preparation

as repetitive activities can now be handled completely automatically by internal customers, similar to the automation of repetitive activities in marketing and sales. The time savings are enormous and can be easily achieved without large investments in IT or PITechStack applications if predictive intelligence for management in the *make process* itself is implemented internally from the very beginning. The capacities released by the PI team are needed anyway to prepare the development step toward the fourth stage of the PIMM.

---

[9]https://www.wortbedeutung.info/dynamisch/. Accessed: September 10, 2020.

One can assume that one has reached the third degree of maturity for Predictive Intelligence if the following criteria are fulfilled:

- Continuous integration into various aspects of corporate management.
- 270° data perspective (Fig. 4.8) is integrated into the multidimensional data model.
- Data model is available throughout the organization via a 24/7 interactive solution.
- Data model is fully mapped via a dashboard solution that can be easily adapted to the various needs of internal customers.
- The PI team focuses on data quality, secondary and tertiary evaluations (Fig. 4.9) and also supports the various internal customers in more complex issues such as short-term optimization of sales or *working capital*, innovation management, product adjustments or developments, and even the preparation of profitability analyses for market entries or strategic issues for long-term corporate management.

4.4.4   Stage 4: Dynamic Modeling Predictive Intelligence

Completing the first three levels of the PIMM is homework in the sense of duty. Once the previously defined criteria of the third stage on Predictive Intelligence have been met, the freestyle begins. In the meantime, one is very experienced in dealing with multidimensional data and a playful lightness develops, with which one can prepare and interpret questions that arise in an increasingly creative and valid way, more and more quickly in terms of numbers and information technology. You have reached the point where you are able to enable and guarantee data-based corporate management. So, what are the differences between the third and fourth levels of the predictive intelligence maturity model?

Based on the designation in the PIMM, the word *"modeling"* is now found, which is defined as follows[10]:

1. Create a shape from a material
2. Reproduce a complex process in its essential elements
3. Create a unique specimen, which can also serve as a template for further productions

Modelling in the context of the fourth level of PI maturity refers to the forming of data models in terms of future scenarios and alternative actions. In principle, this modelling can be two-dimensional, firstly longitudinally over a period of time and

---

[10]https://www.wortbedeutung.info/modellierend/. Accessed: September 11, 2020.

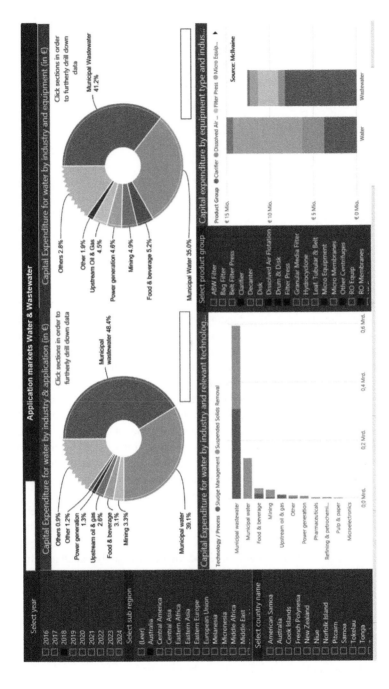

Fig. 4.8 Screenshot from internal PI portal showing dashboard for industry-specific value-chain analyses (Source: Own presentation)

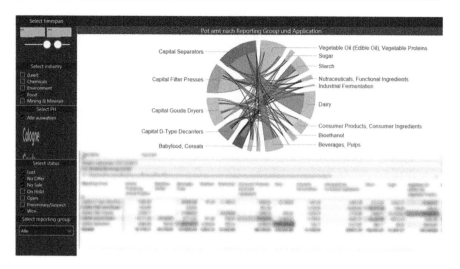

Fig. 4.9 Screenshot from internal PI portal showing dashboard for secondary and tertiary evaluations regarding product flows (Source: Own representation)

secondly horizontally with regard to options for action for a defined point in time or measure. Modeling is done by adjusting various influencing factors in order to calculate, interpret, and evaluate the resulting changes to the data model—as part of the decision-making process in the context of corporate management.

The field of artificial intelligence (AI) comes into play here in order to be able to carry out *interactive* and *real-time modeling* with correspondingly large amounts of data and to calculate interdependencies as well as probabilities and weightings. The different methods of AI are used to gain further insights from the data. The possibility or functionality of modeling can also increase the sensitivity with regard to strategic corporate development measures, because similar to a business game, a defined measure is immediately applied interactively and dynamically to the entire corporate construct of numbers. In this way, decisions can be dynamically calculated and immediately evaluated with regard to their effects.

Alternative courses of action can thus be optimized and thus the entrepreneurial risk minimized. What was previously done with the support of exquisite strategy consulting in the form of scenario analysis, which often took weeks, can now be defined, calculated, adapted in iterations, and then immediately calculated again at the push of a button on this fourth stage of the PIMM. However, this is again only possible if an organization has neatly aggregated, combined, and validated the corresponding 360° data from the relevant sources during the development through the PIMM, and thus a sufficiently large data pool is available to be able to seriously perform such modeling. The decisive factor here is that the data is not only

- longitudinally over the course of time,
- but also, horizontally, across different industries, and
- vertically, across the various applications and products,

multi-dimensionally as comprehensive as possible and mapped in the PI system. At this fourth stage, the efforts of the first three stages of the PIMM then pay off in many ways. Because the larger the available data pool is, the more valid and precise the evaluations can now be made with regard to prediction as part of *predictive intelligence.*

4.4.4.1 What Does Predictive Intelligence Mean?

More and more often, this term is found in publications, which can be traced back to the Latin verb "praedicere" in the sense of "to prophesy" and "to predict." The word is not to be confused with "praedicare," because this verb, which is to be conjugated to the A-conjugation, means "to proclaim publicly." Against this background, *predictive intelligence* thus stands for a predictive and predictive intelligence. This also corresponds to the terms that can be found in the dictionary of the German Economy[11]:

- Foreseeable
- To be seen
- Calculable
- Do not occur spontaneously(d)
- Predictable
- To be expected
- To be expected
- Imminent

The difference between the third and the fourth stage of the PIMM is thus the change in the horizon of observation, which is primarily focused on the short, medium, and long-term future perspective through the involvement of AI, in order to be able to ensure the so important *competitive advantage* in all respects through the highest possible precision. Predictive Intelligence is intended to forecast the change of one or more parameters with regard to the entire changing situation on the basis of existing data from the past into the future, in order to be able to offer various action scenarios initially. In the further course of the PI's development, the PI automatically prioritizes the various possible action alternatives with respect to the most economically sensible variant in each case, in order to be able to provide management with even better and more targeted support in the sense of data-driven corporate management.

The more intensively PI is used in the context of corporate management, the faster it will gain even more precise insights through unsupervised learning at the hidden intermediate levels of the Deep Learning System, which in turn will have a positive effect on the continuously increasing *predictive precision.* An important factor in this context is the completion of the horizontal data perspective from the 270° of the third level to the fourth level and the 360° panoramic view. This last mile refers to the behavior of direct and indirect customers, but also of relevant influencers

---

[11] https://www.dwds.de/wb/pr%C3%A4diktiv. Accessed: September 11, 2020.

Fig. 4.10 ABM dashboard of a marketing automation solution (Source: Marketo)

(Weinländer 2020). This information must be automatically collected from various data sources and fed into the multidimensional data model. To be able to close these last 90° of the data perspective, two essential aspects are required: ABM and crawler.

4.4.4.2 What Do ABM and Crawler Mean?
The abbreviation ABM stands for *Account-based Marketing*,[12] a term used in modern B2B marketing. ABM is about implementing special measures for certain customers who are important to the company in order to proactively develop such customers from a strategic point of view. Through the use of marketing automation solutions such as Marketo or Hubspot, actions of these defined customer companies can be recognized online and documented in the system. This in turn is helpful in understanding what certain employees of these defined, important customer organizations are looking for or researching on the Internet. This information, but also the level in terms of the intensity of these activities, provides valuable indications of the area of the purchasing process in which the respective customer organizations are currently located (Fig. 4.10).

---

[12]https://podcasts.apple.com/de/podcast/b2b-marketing-guidebook-for-classroom-to-boardroom/id1511875534. Accessed: 11, September 2020.

The second essential aspect is so-called *WebCrawlers*. Crawlers[13] are also often called *spiders, searchbots,* or *robots*. They are computer programs that automatically search the World Wide Web for certain defined information and analyze websites. Crawlers are mainly used by search engines to index web pages. In the context of PI, however, they are mainly used to collect web feeds, e-mail addresses, or other information, i.e., the activities of known employees of defined key accounts. It is important to note here that all these measures naturally comply with the provisions of the General Data Protection Regulation (GDPR)[14] and are completely legal. Because only through the legally prescribed, obligatory requirement of the consent of website visitors with regard to the setting and admission of cookies can the activities of interested parties and researchers be recognized and documented. In addition, no personal data is collected or recognized.

ABM and crawler in combination with *Customer Touchpoint* and *Customer Experience* insights can thus close the last remaining $90°$ of the data perspective and ensure a complete, data-technical all-round view.

4.5   What Is the Decisive Factor?

The predictive intelligence maturity model described in this chapter is an experience-based frame of reference that can be used as a guide during the implementation of predictive intelligence for data-driven business and management. The subject area of PI is complex, which is why there is no shortcut if you want to set up the subject area in a stringent, valid, and sustainable manner. Using the PIMM and the criteria and characteristics per maturity level derived from it, continuous benchmarking is possible to check at all stages whether one is on the right path and where along the path one is with one's own organization.

In the following sections, we will show what the concrete, ideal-typical process model for establishing a company-specific predictive intelligence for management looks like and which steps are required at which stage. In addition, the self-assessment tool for PI, which is based on PIMM, will be presented, which can be used to determine an indexed, exact PI maturity index easily and quickly.

Further Reading

Barron, J. M., Berger, M. C., & Black, D. A. (1997). *Introduction to on-the-job training* (S. 1–3). Kalamazoo: Upjohn Institute for Employment Research.

Becker, G. S. (1993). *Human capital—A theoretical and empirical analysis with special reference to education* (3. Auflage). Chicago: University of Chicago Press.

Freeform Dynamics Ltd. (2020). *The road to becoming a data-driven business*. Research report.

---

[13]https://en.wikipedia.org/wiki/Web_crawler. Accessed: November 18, 2020.

[14]https://en.wikipedia.org/wiki/General_Data_Protection_Regulation. Accessed: November 18. 2020.

Halb, F., & Seebacher, U. (2020). Customer experience und touchpoint management. In U. Seebacher (Hrsg.), *B2B Marketing—A guidebook for the classroom to the boardroom*. New York: Springer.

Seebacher, U. (1996). *Evaluierung der Effizienz einer Qualitätszertifizierung am Beispiel des Finanzdienstleistungsbereiches*. Dissertation an der Wirtschaftsuniversität Wien am Institut für Technologie und Produktionsmanagement.

Seebacher, U. (2020). *Template-based management—A guide for an efficient and impactful professional practice*. Cham: Springer.

Weinländer, M. (2020). Corporate influencing und thought leadership. In U. Seebacher (Hrsg.), *B2B marketing—A guidebook for the classroom to the boardroom*. Cham: Springer.

The Predictive Intelligence Self-Assessment

5

5.1 The Necessity for the PI-SA

The term PI-SA is more widely used in the field of school education and represents a test procedure to compare the educational level of a country with individual other countries, but also with the international average. PI-SA in the context of data-driven management is intended to serve a similar purpose. This orientation guide is intended to clarify in which of the relevant organizational and content-related areas what kind of preliminaries already exist in an organization. The aim is to efficiently and effectively develop and establish this topic area in and for an organizational unit of a company, however, large it may be, in a sustainable manner.

The test procedure is based on the previously discussed maturity model for predictive intelligence (PIMM) and therefore reflects the gradual requirements of the model. In this way, the test procedure can also be carried out continuously as a status analysis during the establishment of a data-driven management. Ideally, the instrument of divergence analysis is also used to optimize the validity of the collected data.[1] The PI-SA can be performed by one or more members of the project team or only by the project manager. These respondents provide a very direct but also subjective perception of the Predictive Intelligence Project, which in turn could be too positive in terms of the project. In order to identify such a possible positive deviation, a sample can be defined outside the project team in the organization from internal customers and these customers can also have the PI-SA performed. A mean value is calculated from these "external" respondents and compared to the "internal" mean value. Based on the findings of the divergence analysis, the validity of the statements is minimized the greater the divergence, i.e., the deviation, of the values or averages generated in each case. This analysis of the deviations can be carried out

---

[1] https://help.sap.com/doc/erp_sfi_addon10/1.0/de-DE/1e/db6139d6a72419e10000000a11402f/content.htm?no_cache=true. Accessed: September 21, 2020.

for the entire question sample, but also only for the individual content modules or sub-areas of the PI-SA, which will be discussed in more detail below.

The PI-SA thus shows not only where an organization stands in relation to PI, but also whether the work on predictive intelligence is also being perceived and received by internal customers in the respective unit. Once again, it should be noted here how crucial the coordination and alignment is in the context of data-driven management for enabling and ensuring the so important organizational learning process. The aim is to ensure that information and communication with, but also within, the respective organization are strictly adhered to as part of the initiative. Only if the necessary transparency and knowledge of predictive intelligence is created through intensive and proactive interaction with the organization in question can the enormous effects of PI be realized in the long term in the interest of the company.

5.2   What Are the Main Areas of the PI-SA?

The Predictive Intelligence Self-Assessment is divided into eight content elements, which are underlaid with different question complexes. The PI-SA is presented in the following overview:

1. PI Potential Index
2. Value Chain Index
3. Cost Efficiency Index
4. Structure Index
5. Strategy Index
6. Distribution Index
7. PI Infrastructure Index
8. PI Competence Index

On the basis of these eight areas, a corresponding spider chart can be generated from the answers, which shows very clearly at a glance how an American example organization is set up in terms of predictive intelligence (Fig. 5.1).

Figure 5.1 shows the status of an organization that is already very advanced in terms of PI. I have been working with this organization on the basis of the Template-based Management (TBM) approach (Seebacher 2020a, b, c) for about 3 years. The spider chart shows on the one hand how great the PI potential of this organization is (91.3%) and on the other hand how far the different index areas could be developed during the 3-year project without any specifically required budgets. In the following sections, this example evaluation will be referred to again and again in order to better illustrate and clarify the values and their meaning.

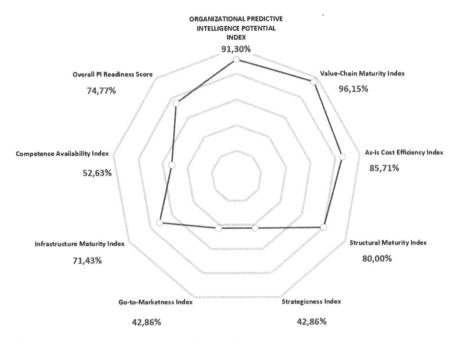

Fig. 5.1 Evaluation of a PI-SA survey (Source: Own presentation)

5.2.1   The PI Potential Index

Is it even worthwhile for an organization to invest in data-driven management or predictive intelligence? This question may seem strange to some people, but especially in times of a worldwide COVID-19 crisis and the resulting massive cuts in the entire economy, everything has to be questioned against the background of the *Remocal Economy* according to Seebacher (2020a, b, c) and the *New Green Deal* according to Rifkin (2019). The PI Potential Index (PI-PI) uses six structural questions to determine how great the potential for data-driven management of an organization is by asking how many industries, regions, or countries the unit in question is active in. In addition, the question of what number of products are offered for which applications is also important. The more heterogeneous on the one hand the offer of an organization is and on the other hand the multitude of different markets, the more important it is to act in a sustainable way very precisely on the basis of predictive intelligence. The more areas an organization is active in, the more extensive and complex the respective contingency situations become, which in turn must be mapped and analyzed on the basis of large amounts of data, i.e., *big data*.

Large amounts of data do not represent a burden at all, but on the contrary the necessary knowledge and competence, in order to be able to make more and more precise statements regarding corporate management based on it over time. In order to be able to fulfill this function or task stringently and validly, however, it is crucial to collect, validate and process the corresponding internal and external data and information in a structured manner at already an early stage. However, this requires an underlying concept with regard to structural and process organization for data-driven management and a corresponding data model. Only then is it possible to use this information to plan ahead and to evaluate and calculate upcoming business decisions.

The higher the PI-PI, the greater the potential of an organization in terms of predictive intelligence and vice versa. In any case, a company that offers only one product in one country will derive much less long-term benefit from Predictive Intelligence compared to a medium-sized company with a very disaggregated product portfolio and a global presence, as the evaluation in Fig. 5.1 shows. A value of 91.3% indicates a very high potential for the analyzed organization. A non-timely, concerted approach to establish Predictive Intelligence could be classified de facto as management negligence and in the long run these companies would get into massive difficulties regarding the Return on Sales (RoS).

Answer the following questions (Table 5.1) to determine the PI-PI for your respective organizational unit by marking the respective answer.

This index is compared with the indices 2–8 in the course of the evaluation and then results in a weighted summary of the overall degree of maturity for predictive intelligence. This means that the PI-PI is included as a weighted factor in the respective current PI maturity level and thus the overall potential of predictive intelligence determined for an organization is related.

5.2.2   The Value Chain Index

Value chains have always been an important structural element for analyzing and optimizing process structures. However, the awareness of value chains and the knowledge of their importance is too low in most organizations. So, what is a value chain? The value chain represents the stages of production as an ordered sequence of activities. These activities create value, consume resources, and are linked together in processes. The concept of the value chain as a systemic element was first published by Michael E. Porter (1986):

> Every company is a collection of activities through which its product is designed, manufactured, distributed, delivered and supported. All these activities can be represented in a value chain.

Value chain is often only used to refer to the graphic illustration in the sense of a value chain diagram. The term value chain is often also used to describe the word *service chain*. D. Harting (1994) defines these terms with the "stages of the transformation process that a product or service goes through, from raw material to final use." The standard model of the operational value chain can be found in Fig. 5.2. However, it is always forgotten that under this generic operational value chain there are others, which then map and represent the value chain of an individual department on a deeper systemic level.

Table 5.1 Questions on the Predictive Intelligence Potential Index (PI-PI)

No.	Question	Answer options						pts.
		0	1	2	3	4	5	
1	In how many industries is the organization active?	I do not know	1	2	<5	5+		
2	On how many continents is the organization active?	I do not know	1	2	3	4+		
3	In how many countries is the organization active?	I do not know	1	<10	<25	25 +		
4	How many products/ solutions does the organization offer?	I do not know	<5	<25	<50	50 +		
5	How many production sites does the organization have?	I do not know	None	<5	<15	15 +		
6	What is the percentage of fraudulent transactions?	<0.1%	0.1– 0.3%	0.3–0.5%	0.5–1%	1– 3%	3– 5%	
7	What is the current set-up in terms of marketing, product mgt./ marketing, business development, and sales?	I do not know	In one unit	2 or more in one unit	All individually			
8	What marketing strategy does the organization pursue?	B2C	B2B	B2G (Business-to-Government)				

The value chain as a methodical and sophisticated instrument allows the activities of a relevant organizational unit to be analyzed comprehensively and consistently. The value chain is thus the link between the operational and the conceptual-structural level. However, the practical handling of the value chain is fraught with a number of problems:

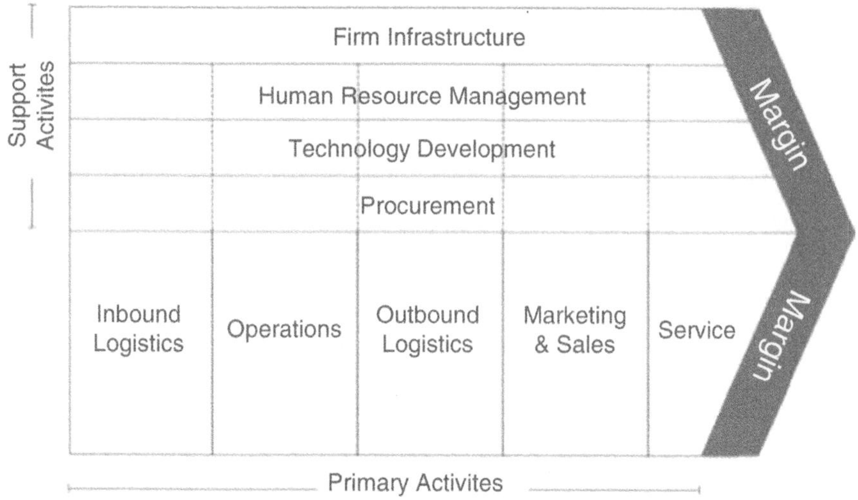

Fig. 5.2 Model of the operational value chain (Source: https://www.marketing91.com/value-chain-porter/. Accessed: November 19, 2020)

- The analysis requires a considerable amount of time.
- Working with value chains requires extensive methodological and structural competence.
- Strategic planning usually takes place through moderated working sessions with the responsible managers. A comprehensive analysis of the value chains is often too complex in this context and meets with a lack of acceptance and motivation, since in most cases the previously mentioned competencies in the area of methodology and structure are missing.

And this latent lack of methodological and structural competence (Seebacher 2020a, b, c) is the reason why the potential of working with value chains is often not used, especially in the field of conceptual corporate management. Reference is made here to the work of the Russian economic researcher Nikolai Kondratieff. The Russian scientist Nikolai Dmitrijewitsch Kondratieff (1892–1938) is the founder of the theory of long waves. In the course of his economic researches in the years 1919–1921, he found out that besides short cycles lasting up to 3 years and medium cycles lasting up to 11 years, there are also long economic waves lasting 45–60 years. In 1926, he published his findings in the German language "Archive for Social Science and Social Policy."

One of the best-known representatives of the theory of long waves and one of the most respected masterminds of the information society is Leo A. Nefiodow. He has been active in research and development since 1965 and was an advisor to the Federal Ministry of Research and Technology, several state governments, and international organizations. One of his focal points is futurology, in the context of which he also examined the causes of a lack of innovative power. He came to the conclusion that the economic systems and technologies in the sixth Kondratieff were now so far developed that the weakest link in the chain would now be man and his methodological and structural competence.

This is also proven by the many internal company projects that are neither implemented on time nor within budget. This is despite the fact that highly endowed experts with doctorates from the most renowned technical universities are working on them. The reason why these projects fail is that due to a lack of methodological and structural competence, a machine or a solution as part of a modern, automated technical sales force is primarily recognized and understood in terms of content rather than structure. As a result, the brilliant technical experts get lost in detail, but in the end the new machine or the so essential automation and enablement solution is never finished.

Experience has shown that not a single new product has been brought to market by various customers in a period of 3 years, despite a technology management or research and development budget in the millions. At another medium-sized company, a Configure-Price-Quote (CPQ) solution that could have been purchased ready to use in the market was still not consistently designed, let alone implemented, after 5 years. For these customers, I then used the Template-based Management approach (Seebacher 2020a, b, c) in order to quickly establish the necessary project management knowledge and also the ongoing project monitoring, thus minimizing costs.

5.2.2.1 The Different Markets

In the context of predictive intelligence, thinking in terms of value chains plays a very decisive role. The experiences of the first projects in the context of Predictive Intelligence have shown that the majority of companies only cover parts of industrial value chains with regard to their product portfolio. As a result, figures, data, and facts about markets and industries present a false picture. If, for example, the global mining market had a volume XA—the *absolute market*—and consisted, for example, of a three-part value chain mining (XM), transport (XT), processing (XP)—thus $XA = f_{(M + T + P)}$, then the *relevant market* XR for a supplier of submersible pumps used only in the first part of the industrial value chain "mining" would no longer be XA, but $XR = f_{(M - T - P)}$. It follows that the relevant market XR is in any case smaller and different from the absolute market XA. In this context, the relevant market again depends on the respective product portfolio of the investigated company. If one does not take into account the structure of the relevant industrial value chain, one works with wrong, too high figures, which can have fatal consequences on investment decisions, as well as evaluation of the own market share.

The question arises why the respective industrial process is not simply used as a frame of reference. Two factors are decisive for this:

- Manageability of the relevant data
- Accuracy paradoxon

With regard to the first factor, it is decisive that, on the one hand, the majority of companies do not serve just one industry, but at least two or more. This means that the volume of data to be processed is automatically many times greater in relation to just one focus industry. If, in the context of Predictive Intelligence, the operative process data of an industry were to be used or wanted to be used, the effort of data generation would be many times greater and thus more cost intensive. Subsequently, however, the data volume would also increase disproportionately.

> **Example: Imagine you should analyze a process. The process according to the quality management system (QMS) has 15 activities. You should now analyze the times for processing, transport, control, and waiting times for the entire process. The process is performed by 10 employees. This means that within the scope of analysis P, you would have to analyze a total of 15 activities with 10 employees in relation to four activities, i.e., $Pf_{(A\ =\ 15*10*4)}$. However, if the analysis is based on the value chain approach, in which this process consisting of 15 individual activities would be divided into four value chain sections, the effort of the Analysis P would be significantly reduced from $Pf_{(A\ =\ 15*10*4)}$ to $Pf_{(A\ =\ 4*10*4)}$.**

The process as a frame of reference is the valid structural level for operational optimization. However, when it comes to predictive intelligence, the process level as a frame of reference is too granular and, in the long term, can only be handled with an unjustifiable amount of effort, especially since most providers of market data do not keep information on either the process level or the value chain level anyway.

On the other hand, one must also be aware of the accuracy paradoxon. According to the[2] Pareto principle, the effort required to collect market data based on the detailed processes of an industry is disproportionate to the accuracy and significance of the data obtained. Data accuracy decreases disproportionately with increasing depth of detail, which is why the industrial value chain is used in the context of data-driven management, as it is sufficient as a construct for data processing in terms of processability as well as accuracy.

Against this background, it is fundamental to map the industries served by an organization in the form of value chains. This involves determining the annual investment in machinery and equipment (*CAPEX*) as well as in ongoing service and maintenance costs (*OPEX*) per defined section of the value chain. The second set of questions (Table 5.2) of the PI-SA, therefore, captures the degree of maturity of an organization in dealing with the relevant industrial value chains.

On the basis of these questions, the degree of maturity can be determined regarding the so important creation of value chains. The value of the example enterprise with 96.15% refers to an already very comprehensive and pronounced work with the relevant industry-specific value chains. The high value suggests that, by and large, the necessary basis for the development of predictive intelligence is

---

[2] https://de.wikipedia.org/wiki/Paretoprinzip. Accessed: September 21, 2020.

Table 5.2 Questions on the Value Chain Index (VC-I)

No.	Question	Answer options						pts.
		0	1	2	3	4	5	
9	Do you already use VC (VC is used as an abbreviation for value chain at this point for ease of reading) for the analysis, adaptation, development, planning, and structuring of industry-specific offers?	I do not know	No	Partly	Yes			
10	Does the organization have cleanly researched, consistent and valid, documented VC for all industries and segments covered?	I do not know	No	Partly	Yes			
11	How are these VC developed?	I do not know	Externally by consultants	Together with consultant	Internal			
12	How are these vC documentations updated?	I do not know	Externally by consultants	Together with consultant	Internal			
13	How often are these VC documentations updated?	I do not know	Never	Every 2 years	Annually	More often or continuously		
14	Who is responsible for the VC work?	I do not know	Other	Distribution	Prod. Mgt. / Mkt.	Marketing		
15	Who is involved in the VC work?	I do not know	Only the responsible team	Two or more teams	All relevant internal stakeholders	Situational and flexible integration depending on WSK		
16	What data is used for the VC work?	I do not know	External data only	Internal data only	Internal and external data			

available in the organization and only individual sub-areas of more complex industries, in this case the food industry, need to be completed.

5.2.3   The Cost Efficiency Index

The development of an own Predictive Intelligence infrastructure offers enormous cost advantages, as is also evident from the maturity model for Predictive Intelligence. On the basis of the various PI projects, we have compiled the questions on the Cost Efficiency Index (CE-I) in order to identify the most important cost drivers and the resulting potential. An internal, organization-own PI can, among many other effects and services, replace external information and newsletter services very quickly and easily at low cost. These significant savings can be used directly for the development of own competences or employees but also for the purchase of further industry-specific data. In order to evaluate your current cost efficiency in regard to PI, complete the answers in Table 5.3.

With these questions, it becomes apparent where the great cost potentials lie in the short and medium term, namely in the shifting of funds from external service providers to the internal provision of services as far as possible. Especially in times of high cost pressure, the focus must be on increasing internal value creation. Every Euro used to generate internal added value is many times more sustainable than one spent externally.

The value of the example organization in relation to the CE-I with 85.71% shows that more than three-quarters of the costs have already been converted from external and short-term to internal and sustainable. For example, all external newsletter service provider subscriptions were cancelled at the next possible date and immediately high six-digit Euro amounts were saved. These were used to purchase additional data from pre-selected and pre-qualified sources to expand the internal data pool for the development of time series and corresponding analyses.

Further significant savings were made possible by the more detailed selection of required data segments within database packages. However, this in turn requires expertise in terms of required data needs and relevant offerings in the market. In general, with regard to CE-I, the principle that profit lies in purchasing and that internal value creation is in any case the more cost-optimal option, in the long run, is also applicable.

5.2.4   The Structure Index

The next section of the PI-SA is dedicated to the current organizational structure. The aim is to find out in which areas of the organization the various topics and responsibilities relevant to Predictive Intelligence are located. This information can be used to determine whether competencies and responsibilities are scattered or centrally located. The more scattered the required departments and competencies are, the greater the challenge of bringing all these people and interests together. If,

Table 5.3 Questions on the Cost Efficiency Index (CE-I)

No.	Question	Answer options						pts.
		0	1	2	3	4	5	
17	What percentage of the marketing budget is currently allocated to Market/Bus. Intelligence (MI/BI)?	I do not know	<2%	2–5%	5–10%	+10%		
18	How often are updates sent to the organization in the form of an MI/BI newsletter?	I do not know	Not at all	Irregular	Regularly (e.g., ¼ annually, 2-monthly, monthly)	Monthly		
19	How many external analyses, reports, studies, etc. are purchased on average per year?	I do not know	20 and more	10–20	5–10	<5		
20	What are the average costs of these external reports per unit?	I do not know	25,000 euros or more	10,000–25,000 euros	5000–25,000 euros	Less than 5000 euros		
21	How many external service providers for data, information, newsletter/updates, etc. are currently contracted?	I do not know	5 or more	2–5	Less than 2	0		
22	What are the approximate annual costs for these service providers in euros?	I do not know	100,000 or more	50,000–100,000	25,000–50,000	Less than 25,000		
23	Which department provides the budget for this?	I do not know	Several departments	Distribution	MI/BI only	Marketing only		

however, the topics are already centrally located in one or two departments, this saves time and reduces the need for coordination. On the other hand, it will be necessary to bring these people or teams on board from the very beginning or even to leave the leadership to them.

> **Important: It is not decisive with whom or where the topic of Predictive Intelligence is located. It is essential that a stringent and committed approach is taken on the basis of a concept that shows the way forward. The situation is comparable to the question of whether sales or marketing must have the lead in the context of *Predictive Profit Marketing* (Seebacher 2020a, b, c). Years ago, I would have been inclined to assume that marketing must clearly have the lead here. Today, I see this in a more differentiated way, because in the end it is all about the fact that a manager, from whatever area, has understood the task and is committed and focused, and is starting this "journey." It is not about who that is in the sense of a function, but who in the sense of a person, because we are talking about paradigmatic change processes here. Such processes require authentic, empathic, and logical leaders, because only then can an organization based on trust jointly master such a challenging task.**

As a structural starting point for Predictive Intelligence, if such a department already exists in an organization, it can be the Market and Business Intelligence (MI/BI) team or a central department in the *corporate development* environment, often referred to as *Group Development* or *Corporate Development*. In rare cases, *Central Intelligence* (Strohmeier 2020) units already exist, but experience has shown that in most organizations either no such unit can be found or individual persons are scattered as lone fighters and not coordinated in the various parts of an organization, more or less structured to perform this task. The current study by Freeform Dynamics Ltd. (2020) confirms this stock taking, since currently about half of the companies use data in any form at all to support corporate management. As a next step, please answer the question on structural issues as shown in Table 5.4.

The value of the example organization in illustration 6.1 with 80% already refers to a pronounced structure in relation to predictive intelligence. In concrete terms, this means that the task of market and business intelligence is established and located in the area of marketing. It started with external data on the most important industry, with which about 70% of the total turnover is generated. As the "service department" for sales, the MI/BI expert generated a rapidly increasing number of analyses and market reports within the marketing team. These were received very positively and gratefully by the sales department. A lively and interactive exchange of ideas developed. Over a period of 2½ years, the company began to generate analyses of customers and products on the basis of data from its own CRM and ERP-systems. This led to marketing being able to further manifest its own position in terms of data and information as a competent contact within the organization.

Table 5.4 Questions on the Structure Index (SR-I)

No.	Question	Answer options						pts.
		0	1	2	3	4	5	
24	Is the MI/BI function located in marketing?	I do not know	No	Yes				
25	If NO, where is MI/BI currently located?	I do not know	Distribution	Other departments				
26	If YES, how often do sales ask for MI/BI support?	I do not know	Monthly	Weekly	Several times per week			
27	If YES, is MI/BI information 24/7 online, interactively available for sales?	I do not know	No	Partially	Yes			

Against this background, further data dimensions were then added step by step and in consistency with the maturity model for predictive intelligence, so that after 3 years a 360° data panorama was created. In advance, no claim was made in this organization for the MI/BI area, as this would naturally have led to resistance. The strategy was to develop trust by supporting and generating added value in the sense of valid and user-friendly analyses and market reports, and in this way to develop acceptance among the various internal customers. The formal, organizational step that the *Global Director of Marketing and Communications* was shortly afterward assigned responsibility for strategy and MI/BI as part of the adaptation of the organizational chart was the logical consequence. Change is the only constant in our lives and that means that stringency and perseverance always lead to the goal. There is no shortcut to success.

5.2.5   The Strategy Index

Building on the Structure Index (SR-I), the Strategy Index examines the extent to which the topic of corporate strategy is defined and organized. Predictive Intelligence not only focuses on short and medium-term aspects of corporate management, but also on strategic issues based on the increasingly precise and further extrapolatable multidimensional data. The section on case studies also deals with strategic projects in more detail. However, in order to develop the corresponding PI competence also with regard to strategic aspects of data-driven corporate management, it is essential to start at the operational level. Otherwise, the logical and structural on the one hand and the organizational maturity on the other hand, which is necessary to perform strategic work in a meaningful and valid way with the help of predictive intelligence, are missing. At this point, it should be pointed out that a new software will not repair or optimize processes that are poorly or

Table 5.5 Questions on the Strategy Index (SA-I)

No.	Question	Answer options						
		0	1	2	3	4	5	pts.
28	Is the topic of strategy located in marketing?	I do not know	No	Yes				
29	If NO, where is the topic currently located?	I do not know	Distribution	Other departments				
30	If YES, how often does the sales department ask for strategy support?	I do not know	Monthly	Weekly	Several times per week			

insufficiently defined. This is also the case with predictive intelligence. Only if you know the processes, interrelationships, logics, and mechanisms of data-based corporate management from the ground up can you work with it in a playful, creative and strategic way.

In this context, the preparation and establishment of predictive intelligence must therefore also take into account how the broad and important topic area of the strategy is currently set up in organizations. The strategy index is mapped and defined on the basis of the following questions from an organizational perspective (Table 5.5).

The example evaluation in Fig. 5.1 with a value of 42.86% shows that the degree of maturity with regard to predictive intelligence is not yet as high in the strategic topic area as in the other index areas described above. The current challenge is that no clear responsibility is currently defined with regard to strategic aspects of corporate management. This is simply due to leadership weaknesses in management. The management is led by a less conceptual and strongly operative leadership personality, which leads to short-term actions and thus medium and long-term aspects are neglected. Strategically, work can only be done if management also has the competence to work in this way. However, the example organization has been operating in a strategic management vacuum for about 1½ years without any real strategy, which leads to this low rating. The good thing about this evaluation is that the organization does not lie to itself and assesses itself very well on the basis of the facts.

Once again, this circumstance shows the lasting damage that actionist management can cause when working towards goal fulfillment on a purely operational level and in the short term. Even such a powerful instrument as Predictive Intelligence cannot eliminate and absorb such management weaknesses, because in the end, as in all areas of management, instruments are only enablers. Decisions must nevertheless be made by people and if, due to a lack of methodological and structural competence, managers are only co-drivers of an organization and succumb in helplessness to the

Peter principle[3] of achieving their own incompetence in relation to their own position, then even a clean and stringently applied predictive intelligence cannot solve such a situation. Peter and Hull (1972) states:

> After a certain time, each position is filled by an employee who is incapable of fulfilling his or her task.

According to Peter's theory, every member of a sufficiently complex hierarchy is promoted as long as he is successful in his position, up to the point where this manager reaches the level of his inability to successfully fill a position. In the concrete case of the example organization, however, the manager in question has already failed to successfully fill the two previous positions, so the promotion to divisional manager was all the more surprising for all those involved. The chaos was therefore perfect. The crucial point is that no matter how good an approach or instrument is, it cannot compensate for management incompetence. You have to be aware of this. In this context, you cannot blame the people or a concept like the one presented in this book on Predictive Intelligence.

5.2.6   The Distribution Index

According to management mastermind Philip Kotler (2007), distribution is the umbrella term for marketing and sales, because it is about the distribution of products or services in relevant markets. Often the term *go-to-marketness* is also used—as in Fig. 5.1—which refers to how a company's relevant services and products are marketed to the markets. The Distribution Index examines how developed this part of the corporate value chain is. No matter how good a product is, it will not be bought by customers if it does not reach the customer in terms of marketing. The area of future business development is crucial in the context of predictive intelligence. Therefore, the questions in the Distribution Index (D-I) focus on the area of *business development*, since this function must define and identify where, when, and how an organization's services and products are to be distributed in relevant markets.

It is not only about the distribution of the goods, but rather about the distribution of content in terms of marketing, in order to generate as many *inbound leads* as possible (Wenger 2020). Inbound leads are incoming inquiries for products and concrete offers generated by marketing. Such inquiries have an extremely positive effect on the respective *Return-on-Sales* (RoS), because in this way the cost- and time-intensive cold calling can be avoided. Modern industrial goods marketing can now automatically cover large parts of the sales-related value chain in order to only integrate sales when inquiries have been concretized and validated to such an extent

---

[3]https://en.wikipedia.org/wiki/Peter_principle. Accessed: November 20, 2020.

Table 5.6 Questions about the Distribution Index (D-I)

| No. | Question | Answer options | | | | | | |
		0	1	2	3	4	5	pts.
31	Is the topic of business development located in marketing?	I do not know	No	Yes				
32	If NO, where is the topic currently located?	I do not know	Distribution	Other departments				
33	If YES, how often do sales ask for business development support?	I do not know	Monthly	Weekly	Several times per week			

that the time frame, the decision maker, and the budget for the purchase decision are clearly defined.[4]

This means that sales can concentrate on the really relevant inquiries, but also on key customers. In one of our many projects, we increased the number of inbound leads generated by marketing based on predictive intelligence by 350% (!) within just 12 months, generating a sales volume of around $76 million from this, with total company sales of around $700 million. We are thus talking about more than 10% revenue that was realized through data-driven marketing within just a few months—and without additional costs (Seebacher 2020a, b, c). In this context, we are now assessing the current organizational status by answering the questions in Table 5.6.

Also, in the area of the distribution index, the sample organization does not do so well with 42.86% compared to the first indices. In the context of the establishment of predictive intelligence, it will happen very often that the Strategy as well as the Distribution Index will only increase in the further course of time, since these are downstream structures as well as more extensive activity fields. These two indices will also only rise if management has or develops the appropriate understanding and commitment to predictive intelligence or data-driven management. However, if, as mentioned above, the dilemma of the Peter Principle occurs, it will be almost impossible to perform in these two index disciplines.

In this case, it should be considered to change the unit or the company, because in the long run the meaningful establishment on the one hand and the comprehensive exploitation of the potentials of Predictive Intelligence will not succeed.

---

[4]https://anchor.fm/b2bmarketingguidebook/episodes/Next-Generation-B2B-Marketing-featuring-Joel-Harrison-Editor-in-Chief-and-Co-Founder-of-B2B-Marketing-edn1kd/a-a24ehs3.   Accessed: September 21, 2020.

5.2.7 The PI Infrastructure Index

In order to start establishing Predictive Intelligence in an organization, no special applications or tools are actually required initially. Experience has shown that anything that is too complicated at the beginning is only disturbing and distracts from the essential. In most cases, companies will not have their own, special budget for the development of a data-driven enterprise control system. Therefore, it is crucial to know ex antes which infrastructure relevant for PI is already available and thus can be used at minimum cost.

Based on the various PI projects and the common instruments and communication channels used in this context, the PI Infrastructure Index (PI-I^2) (Table 5.7) therefore determines which useful applications can be used in the establishment of PI. The higher this value is, the better and more comprehensive the PI-relevant infrastructure already existing in the organization under investigation.

In the further course of the book, the topic of the *PI-TechStack* will be discussed in detail. With 71.43%, the sample company is in the upper midfield of the PI scale. As part of the company-wide Microsoft license, the company has its own MS PowerBI system available, which is also used to design interactive, internal customer group-specific dashboards. These dashboards are played out 24/7 over the company's intranet, allowing registered users to work interactively and autonomously with the predictive intelligence solution at all times. The internal data for the PI solution is drawn from the company's own CRM and ERP system as well as from the marketing automation solution (MA) rolled out in the company. This MA solution, in turn, is linked to the lead scanning solution, creating a continuous, automated process.

The missing points result from the lack of a CPQ solution. Such a solution is a decisive factor for the end-to-end automation of the sales value chain from lead generation to the playout of offers using PI-supported *dynamic pricing*, which allows the calculation of price corridors based on the situation by means of regression and the immediate consideration of these corridors based on the stored offer data (Cummings 2013). Thus, no price ranges are gambled away ex ante and the relevant room for negotiation is given directly to the sales department on the basis of realized sales of the relevant product in the same industry or application in the target region. This example shows once again how everything in the field of predictive intelligence must work together and interlock. If one part of the mosaic does not work properly, then an important component in the sales or PI-specific value chain is missing. However, this mosaic can only be developed properly if an organization has a *master mind* for predictive intelligence that meets the following requirements (Fig. 5.3):

• Distribution competence
• Digitization competence
• Methods competence
• Structure competence
• Process competence

Table 5.7 Questions on the PI Infrastructure Index (PI-I^2)

No.	Question	Answer options							pts.
		0	1	2	3	4	5		
34	Does the organization have a worldwide available 24/7 intranet?	I do not know	No	Yes					
35	Does the organization have an organization-wide CRM system?	I do not know	No	Yes					
36	Does the organization have an organization-wide ERP system?	I do not know	No	Yes					
37	Does the organization have an organization-wide Business Intelligence system? (Common business intelligence solutions include Click, PowerBI, SAP Analytics Cloud or Tableau)	I do not know	No	Yes					
38	Does the organization have an organization-wide marketing automation system? (Popular marketing automation solutions are for example Hubspot or Marketo from Adobe)	I do not know	No	Yes					
39	Does the organization have an organization-wide lead scanning system? (https://pitchview.de/?gclid=CjwKCAjwwab7BRBAEiwAapqpTHC8z-P_cu2-5S5qxIsbiGf0o8tW1lu0foWRA4YX2CVXIYBUDA7n5hoC51cQAvD_BwE. Accessed: September 22, 2020)	I do not know	No	Yes					
40	Does the organization have an organization-wide available Configure-Price-Quote-System? (https://en.wikipedia.org/wiki/Configure,_price_and_quote. Accessed: November 22, 2020)	I do not know	No	Yes					

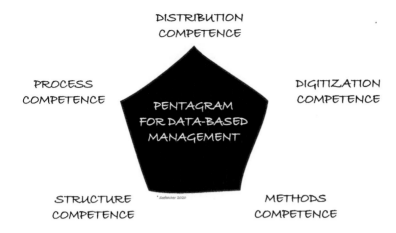

Fig. 5.3 Pentagram for data-based management (Source: Own presentation)

In addition to these competencies, which the PI mastermind of an organization must bring with it, there are also operational areas of competence that must be developed and established in the company in the medium term in order to be able to implement data-based management based on predictive intelligence. The PI Competence Index (PI-CI) is based on these additional, in part new operational competencies. The comprehensive competence model for PI is in more detailed explained in the relevant chapter of this book.

5.2.8   The PI Competence Index

The last index in the PI-SA helps to determine the current status with regard to the operational competencies already mentioned above (Table 5.8). The earlier one is aware of the necessary knowledge areas, the earlier one can begin to develop these areas internally. This approach is not only more sustainable, but also much more cost-effective, especially since many of these new areas of competence are not yet appropriately present and available on the market. This is due to the fact that Predictive Intelligence is a new field per se and therefore the entire training area naturally needs some time to develop the new or adapted curricula.

If there are any uncertainties at this point regarding the various positions or their tasks and competencies, please refer to the section in this book on the area of required PI competencies. There the individual position profiles are explained and discussed in detail.

On the basis of the evaluation of the example organization with a value of 52.63%, it has already successfully mastered half of the way with regard to the required competencies or the suspension within the organization. The major short-coming is the still poor image of marketing within the organization, although

Table 5.8 Questions on the PI Competence Index (PI-CI)

No.	Question	Answer options						
		0	1	2	3	4	5	pts.
41	Is there a Data Science Manager (DSM) in the organization?	I do not know	No	Partly	Yes			
42	Does the organization have a Content Asset Manager (CAM)?	I do not know	No	Partly	Yes			
43	Is there a Marketing Campaign Manager (MCM) in the organization?	I do not know	No	Partly	Yes			
44	Does the organization have a Marketing Operations Manager (MOM)?	I do not know	No	Partly	Yes			
45	Is there a Marketing Performance Manager (MPM) in the organization?	I do not know	No	Partly	Yes			
46	Is there a Marketing Technology Manager (MTM) in the organization?	I do not know	No	Partly	Yes			
47	At what level is the senior vice president or director of marketing or CMO positioned in relation to the board of directors?	I do not know	3 or more layers below	2 levels below	1 layer below	At Management Board level		
48	At what level is the Head of Marketing positioned in relation to the Management Board?	I do not know	3 or more layers below	2 levels below	1 layer below	At Management Board level		

considerable successes in the area of *sales enablement* in the sense of generated *inbound leads*, sales from focus campaigns but also significantly increased visibility in the relevant segments could already be realized through a successful branding campaign for the medium-sized company. Jeremy Rifkin (2019), the famous economist, has expressed this very clearly in his book that the stoicism in the sense of the resistance to change of many top managers will lead to the downfall of many renowned corporations and companies. This resistance to necessary and meaningful organizational change also exists in the area of data-driven business management as part of modern industrial goods marketing. This stoicism is also the reason why many B2B marketing teams and organizations continue to be disregarded.

Within the framework of *change management*, a rough grid is always used with regard to the willingness of organizations or the employees of these organizations to change. This grid defines the following three groups:

- 20% are open and immediate supporters of change
- 60% are initially neutral and can be inspired for the change with appropriate arguments
- 20% are the refusers who are against any change and who cannot be convinced

In the context of the *Remocal Economy* (Seebacher 2020a, b, c) and the *New Green Deal* (Rifkin 2019), 20% of today's top managers will simply be phased out because they will not recognize the signs of the times and the need to rethink and change their actions. The astonishing and dangerous thing about the current situation is that if countermeasures are taken too late, the stoicism of these phase-out managers will lead to the demise of large, traditional companies and the loss of many thousands of jobs, jobs that all economies would and will more than urgently need in a post-Corona phase.

Regardless of these circumstances, the establishment of a data-based management system also means to a large extent competence development. It is about the sustainable development of new, innovative, and interesting areas of knowledge. The opportunity for companies is to be able to attract a new, young generation of brilliant employees to the organizations, because the field of activity of predictive intelligence will not only be extremely exciting, but above all will be essential for the success of companies in the long term. Those companies that start today to invest in these skills and young employees will be the winners in a disrupted new industrial world in the long run.

5.3 The Evaluation of the PI-SA

We have now answered all segments of the Predictive Intelligence-Self-Assessment in terms of content. In the following, we will now evaluate the previously given answers. To do this, enter the points given in the second row of each answer in the various tables so that the entire rightmost column is filled with points. An example of a pre-filled table is shown here (Fig. 5.4).

No.	Question	Answer options						
		0	1	2	3	4	5	pts.
31	Is the topic of business development located in marketing?	I do not know	No	Yes				*1*
32	If NO, where is the topic currently located?	I do not know	Distribution	Other department				*2*
33	If YES, how often does sales ask for business development support?	I do not know	Monthly	Weekly	Several times per week			

Fig. 5.4 Example evaluation of the distribution index (D-I)

Table 5.9 Evaluation table index segments

Table	Table name	Achieved table score (TE)	Maximum achievable table score (TM)	Determination of index value (TE/TM)*100
6.1	PI-PI	_____	30	_____/30 _____/100%
6.2	VC-I	_____	27	_____/27 _____/100%
6.3	CE-I	_____	28	_____/28 _____/100%
6.4	SR-I	_____	8	_____/8 _____/100%
6.5	SA-I	_____	5	_____/5 _____/100%
6.6	D-I	_____	5	_____/5 _____/100%
6.7	PI-I^2	_____	14	_____/14 _____/100%
6.8	PI-CI	_____	26	_____/26 _____/100%

On the basis of the answers entered, the value "1" was taken over for the right column named "Pt." in the second line of question 31. For question 32, the value "2" was taken accordingly. This results in the table number for the D-I in this case in the value 3 and, on this basis, a percentage value of 60% in relation to the total possible maximum value of 5. The maximum value "5" results from the answer "Yes" for question 31, which is assigned the value "2", and the answer "Several times a week" for question 33—question 32 can only be answered in case of a "No" for question 31—which is assigned the value "3."

In the next step, all Tables 5.1, 5.2, 5.3, 5.4, 5.5, 5.6, 5.7, and 5.8 are to be completed with the same procedure and the respective table totals are to be transferred to Table 5.9.

To determine the *Overall PI Readiness Score*, the percentages in Tables 5.2, 5.3, 5.4, 5.5, 5.6, 5.7, and 5.8 must be added and then divided by the number 7. This

Table 5.10 Evaluation table overall PI Readiness Score (PIRS)

Table	Table name	Determination of index value (TE/TM)*100	Interim values	
6.1	PI-PI	_____/30 _____/100%		Percentage value Tables 5.2, 5.3, 5.4, 5.5,
6.2	VC-I	_____/27 _____/100%	_____/ 113	5.6, 5.7, and 5.8 divided by
6.3	CE-I	_____/28 _____/100%	_____/ 100%	Percentage value PI-PI _____
6.4	SR-I	_____/8 _____/100%		
6.5	SA-I	_____/5 _____/100%		
6.6	D-I	_____/5 _____/100%		
6.7	PI-I^2	_____/14 _____/100%		
6.8	PI-CI	_____/26 _____/100%		

determined value is then related to the value in Table 5.1. The following calculation must be performed.

In the last step of Table 5.10, the PIRS for the organization under investigation is determined, which is then entered in the corresponding field in the spider graph, just like the other index values, to complete the self-assessment for Predictive Intelligence (Fig. 5.5). Thus, the PI maturity level for the relevant organizational unit is now defined and the status quo shows where one can or must start from.

On the basis of the realized projects, a semiannual PI-Self Assessment can be helpful to reflect on one's own development. As already discussed, the involvement of internal customers is certainly also an important aspect in order to obtain a valid picture of the situation with regard to the degree of maturity for Predictive Intelligence.

5.4   Knowing Where You Are

This section describes the "PI compass" that allows you to take the right path from the beginning. Again and again, the topic of data-driven business management and even more so the new field of predictive intelligence is unnecessarily mystified. As always in life, it requires an eye for the big picture but also the appropriate basic skills in relation to the previously described pentagram on Predictive Intelligence. When we started the first projects in the context of Predictive Intelligence, we had to proceed intuitively and logically. It was not about products and systems, but about methods and structures. We were neither statisticians, nor computer scientists, nor specialists for valves or engines, but we were problem solvers who could efficiently and effectively resolve a situation into structures and thus analyze it. In this way, we

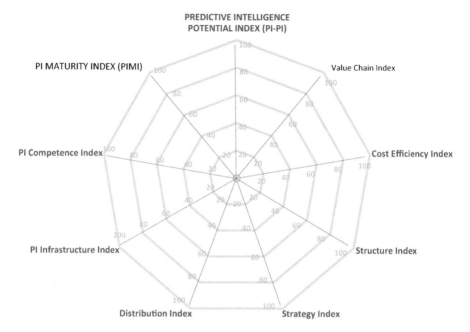

Fig. 5.5 Spider grid for PI-Self Assessment (Source: Own illustration)

were able to transfer the problem or task to be solved into a process model according to which we proceeded step by step.

It was an iterative process and when we started Predictive Intelligence out of necessity a few years ago, it was far from being predictive intelligence. It was an approach to the world of Business Intelligence and together with our internal customers we could learn and develop. We did not have more than any other company, but we dared to venture to new, unknown shores. Today, we are proud to trace our path to this fascinating topic in order to get you, the reader, on the road to data-driven business management.

We hope that with the Predictive Intelligence Self-Assessment (PI-SA), we have provided you with a simple but all the more helpful tool to deepen the necessary sensitivity with regard to relevant organizational but also instrumental and competence-theoretical factors.

Further Reading

Cummings, T. (2013). Everything you need to know about dynamic pricing. *The Christian Science Monitor*.

Freeform Dynamics Ltd. (2020). *The road to becoming a data-driven business*. Research report.

Harting, D. (1994). *Wertschöpfung auf neuen Wegen*. Beschaffung aktuell. 7/1994.

Kotler, P., et al. (2007). *Marketing-Management: Strategien für wertschaffendes Handeln* (12. Auflage). München: Pearson Studium.

Peter, L. J., & Hull, R. (1972). *Das Peter-Prinzip oder die Hierarchie der Unfähigen.* Reinbek: Rowohlt-Taschenbuch-Verlag.

Porter, M. E. (1986). *Wettbewerbsvorteile (competitive advantage). Spitzenleistungen erreichen und behaupten.* Aus dem Englischen übers. von Angelika Jaeger. Campus.

Rifkin, J. (2019). *Der globale Green New Deal: Warum die fossil befeuerte Zivilisation um 2028 kollabiert—und ein kühner ökonomischer Plan das Leben auf der Erde retten kann.* Frankfurt: Campus Verlag.

Seebacher, U. (2020a). *B2B marketing: A guidebook for the classroom to the boardroom.* Cham: Springer.

Seebacher, U. (2020b). *B2B marketing essential: How to turn your marketing from a cost into a sales engine* (2nd ed.). Graz: AQPS.

Seebacher, U. (2020c). *Template-based management—A guide for an efficient and impactful professional practice.* Cham: Springer.

Strohmeier, L. (2020). Central business intelligence. In U. Seebacher (Hrsg.), *B2B marketing—A guidebook for the classroom to the boardroom.* Cham: Springer.

Wenger, St. (2020). Erfolgreiches lead management. In U. Seebacher (Hrsg.), *B2B marketing—A guidebook for the classroom to the boardroom.* Cham: Springer.

The Process Model for Predictive Intelligence

6

6.1 Every Path Begins with the First Step

It is like always in life. Everything you do for the first time seems to be overpowering and unsolvable. It is no different in the field of data-driven management or predictive intelligence. Why it is like this is easily explained, because a new topic is comparable to a very large project. One asks oneself the question, after the "where" one should start at all. To solve this paradox, it is helpful to analyze this situation from a structural point of view in order to demystify this supposed powerlessness in relation to this new topic.

A suitable model for this is that of Kenneth Blanchard (born 1939), who developed a maturity model for situational leadership theories together with Paul Hersey. This model was developed in the early 1980s (Sturm et al. 2011) and the authors distinguish in their model between four different leadership styles. These styles have to be adapted to the context of the respective situation:

- Delegate
- Support
- Convince
- Instruction

Of central importance in Blanchard and Heyse's model is the degree of maturity of the employees managed. The manager must assess the maturity level of the employee based on his or her diagnostic skills in order to apply the appropriate management style to the situation. The maturity level of the employees is composed of the competence and the willingness to fulfill tasks (Scheer and Kasper 2011). Against this background, the manager assigns the respective employee to one of four maturity levels (Fig. 6.1).

The conclusion of this situational leadership theory is that for employees who are still inexperienced (cf. M1 and M2 in Fig. 6.1) in a certain subject area, it is crucial to define small, precisely defined, and manageable tasks. On the other hand, an

© The Author(s), under exclusive license to Springer Nature Switzerland AG 2021
U. Seebacher, *Predictive Intelligence for Data-Driven Managers*, Future of Business and Finance, https://doi.org/10.1007/978-3-030-69403-6_6

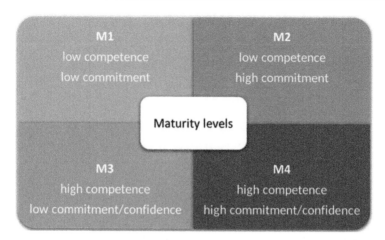

Fig. 6.1 Employee maturity levels (Source: https://granite.pressbooks.pub/ld820/chapter/10/. Accessed: November 20, 2020)

experienced and committed employee would be more frustrated by such microgranular tasks as part of a very direct management style. This means that, with regard to the new topic of Predictive Intelligence, most managers find themselves in an inexperienced stage of maturity. Therefore, the process model described in this section of the book should be used as the virtual coach to clearly structure this ex ante seemingly overpowering topic in small task steps in order to get it off the ground efficiently and pragmatically.

Against this background, all activities relating to the sustainable development of predictive intelligence within an organization must be characterized by an integrating management style, since all participants initially tend to be classified at a lower level of maturity with regard to the task at hand. This means that at the beginning of the Predictive Intelligence Journey (PIJ) the *Telling* in the sense of small and precisely defined tasks must be applied (Fig. 6.2). In the further course of the Predictive Intelligence Initiative and when the further stages of the PI maturity model are reached, a participative leadership style with *Selling*, *Participating*, and then *Delegating* can then gradually be applied to support and enable the joint development of competencies as part of organizational learning (Fig. 6.2).

6.2   The Preparation

Before starting the operation, it is useful to consider some basic aspects. It is crucial to question why you are holding this book in your hands and why you are taking the time to deal with this topic. Again, there can naturally be different reasons for this. Where did the impulse come from to qualify the topic of data-driven corporate management? Finding out about it is an important indication of possible internal customers or problems for further action. Which possibilities are there:

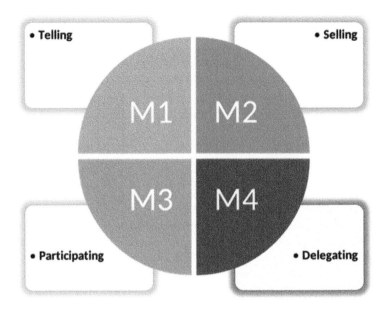

Fig. 6.2 Maturity level-related leadership styles (Source: https://granite.pressbooks.pub/ld820/chapter/10/. Accessed: November 20, 2020)

- The boss or the Board gave the order to take up the topic.
- There were requests for support regarding market figures, customer data, or similar.
- You were called into a sales meeting to quantify markets for new or existing sales representatives together with the sales department.
- You were asked to prepare a profitability analysis with regard to the development of new markets.

This exemplary list of possible situations could be continued at will. It is crucial to structurally develop an understanding of whether the need for data-driven management has become latent out of necessity, or whether one or more people in the organization concerned have put this topic on the agenda out of foresight. It is often the case that the topic of data-driven management is gaining in importance, either due to poor sales figures in a region or a product, or the failure to achieve the defined annual targets.

6.2.1 Understanding the Batch Situation

If, so to speak, the house is already on fire, then in most cases there is already a clear picture of the internal organizational interests. The management wants ambitious and valid sales plans and targets, and the sales department wants ease-to-achieve ones. Such lower sales plans will only be accepted by management, if management itself cannot prove higher market volumes based on available real market figures and data. In reality, it will not always be so black and white, but in general, stakeholders can be characterized by these points of view. In any case, in this context one can assume that a certain pressure to act already prevails, which in turn requires a stringent and efficient procedure, since the topic has obviously already reached a certain visibility.

If the house is not yet on fire and this book, for whatever reason, has found its way into your hands, then you should identify a possible first customer within the organization, with whose help you can realize so-called *quick wins* by taking the first small steps. If the question now arises as to who such an internal pilot customer could be, then you must reflect on what every economic action is all about, namely money. Against this background, everyone is a potential internal customer from whom there is money to be made, either because sales in a country or region are not on target or because a certain product is not being sold according to forecasts.

But before we start to look for the first internal customer, another consideration should be made. Who are the companions and which competencies can already be drawn on in the organization? What are the basic starting scenarios in this respect? Either one is a lone fighter in a professionally assigned topic or, as a manager, has a team around him or herself or is a member of a team. If you are part of a team, then the question of the internal team culture arises. Are topics addressed openly or does the team spirit offer more room for improvement? How do you rate the direct manager, more open to new things or not?

At this point, we make the assumption that a fundamentally positive environment prevails and therefore a new topic can be discussed in or with a team. However, for a meaningful and substantiated discussion to take place, a common knowledge base must be available. Therefore, before the next step is initiated, this book should be worked through to the end to know the goal of the Predictive Intelligence Journey. Only if this big whole is completely internalized and understood, one knows the destination coordinates. These are important to know intuitively and to have the feeling if you are on the right way or if you are already wasting time on the wrong way. Just as a pilot knows the target coordinates of his flight, every predictive intelligence professional must also be aware of the long-term goal of the development.

> **Tip: How to recognize that you have internalized and understood the goal, you can recognize by the fact that you can explain the topic of data-driven management in your own words, based on predictive intelligence, in a simple and understandable, logically comprehensible way. This also includes being able to point out and substantiate the advantages in terms of cost savings and revenue optimization, but also more precise decision preparation and the associated minimization of risk by means of examples.**

In this context, it has proven to be helpful to compile a set of slides to introduce, explain, and present the topic on occasions that arise. The compilation of such a presentation deepens one's own knowledge, offers an opportunity for reflection and reveals possible existing gaps in content. Especially at the beginning of the *Predictive Intelligence Journey* (PIJ), active communication and information is an essential component in order to develop a solid starting point in the sense of a common understanding.

6.2.2 Include the Allies

If one can fall back on one's own team, this will in any case be the hard core for the successful implementation of a Predictive Intelligence. The team can act as a sparring partner as well as a test person for presentations, analyses, and reports. If, however, you are a lone fighter in a small company, you should look for companions within the organization from the beginning in order to have sparring partners and test persons at your side.

What should be searched for? In order to answer this question, it is necessary to clarify the respective individual suspension in the organization. Because depending on the subject area from which the topic of Predictive Intelligence is taken, both the chain of argumentation and the sovereignty of content in terms of acceptance differ. This is against the background that, regardless of the respective topic, one is unconsciously confronted with a certain standing of the respective department. From an organizational-structural point of view, one speaks of an informal organizational hierarchy or organizational disparity, which, however, varies from one industry to another and from one region to another.

For example, marketing in the business-to-consumer sector (B2C) has a higher standing compared to industrial goods marketing, the business-to-business sector (B2B) (Seebacher 2020a, b, c). However, this disparity is much smaller in the Anglo-American sector compared to continental Europe. The area of finance and controlling gained importance in the late 1980s and 1990s but has not lost any of its importance but its standing within organizations, since finance and controlling has a dusty image that is oriented toward the past. Many companies use the term *Commercial* and include in the financial area also the financial and order-oriented contract management for both customer orders and external sales structures, such as agents or distributors. The enormous hype surrounding Industry 4.0 and the topics of *Internet of Things* (IoT) and *Internet of People* (IoP) have greatly benefited IT departments in terms of their standing within the organizations.

While the IT departments were a little dusty about the topics ERP and CRM, they were able to bring themselves back into the modern-day limelight in the course of digitalization, even if in most cases the IT departments are referred to behind closed doors as "overhead slingshot" and "standstill dynamics." These terms find their cause in the often too expensive and too slow internal project management. Surely not all IT departments should be lumped together, and many IT departments do an excellent job.

This by no means scientifically conceived, interpretative-prosaic execution of informal organizational hierarchies could be expanded at will and also deepened, especially with respect to regional and country-specific differences. This would go beyond the scope of this publication. But what is important is to be aware of the existence of these informal hierarchies within organizational constructs. These always go hand in hand with the responsible leader and his or her individual standing. Whatever function or position you are in, you should empathetically try to understand how the various parts of the organization perceive the topic of predictive intelligence. And in doing so, one should also question, in any case, if there is a mandate for it, from where and why it was given.

If, against this background, companions are now being sought in the organization, then these should be located in units that have a corresponding standing in the hierarchy but also an affinity for new and number-driven topics. On the other hand, internal customers, as described above, should also be found, where the proverbial "sales shoe" pinches. In this search, the basic principle of change management should not be disregarded in order not to rely on change-resistant colleagues, but to identify those who can recognize and assess the potential of the PI initiative.

Ideally, the activities relating to the *Predictive Intelligence Journey* (PIJ) are set up and implemented jointly by Marketing and Sales. In this way, the necessary activities can be started step by step in a sales-oriented manner and quick wins can be realized immediately. Based on this experience, the measures can then be scaled and expanded.

> **Tip: Predictive Intelligence is based on data. Data is the tool of modern marketing departments, as they have been working with customer data for years and plan and implement campaigns based on it. In this context it is only logical but also makes sense from an organizational point of view to start from the marketing department with the topic of data-driven management. This also ensures the highest efficiency and effectiveness, since the existing data dimensions are only expanded step by step and not first another department has to learn how to handle the data already internally available in the company in order to then expand the data focus.**

Organizations are natural constructs, and they function amoebic by changing and adapting according to the situation. Therefore, ideally the person or department that has already intuitively demonstrated a corresponding structure and data affinity in daily work and has thus been demonstrably successful should be entrusted with the Predictive Intelligence Initiative. Most of my PI projects started with one or at most two people. The distribution of roles was such that the manager brought in the big picture conceptually and a young colleague made the operational effort to implement the activities step by step. In most cases, the topic was new to all those involved, and it was all the more fascinating to see what an impressive learning curve all those involved were going through.

Once you have identified a team of three or four companions, you have already taken a big step toward the start. It is essential that you have a colleague at your side

---

JUNIOR MARKET STRATEGIST (F/M)

Your tasks:

- Strategic, active and sustainable development of the division
- Support of the Global Marketing & Communication Director in ongoing projects
- Data-driven conception of market development, penetration and selection
- Direct reporting to the Global Marketing & Communication Director

Your qualifications:

- Degree in Economics (BSc, MBA) preferably with focus on strategic marketing or company/organizational development
- 1 - 3 years professional experience in management consulting
- Very good written and spoken English skills
- Secure handling of MS Office
- Strong communication skills and intercultural competence
- Independent, structured and analytical working style
- Ability to work in a team, flexibility and resilience

Fig. 6.3 Job advertisement Junior Market Strategist (Source: Own presentation)

who typically has a high affinity for MS Excel and numbers. In this respect, such colleagues have an economic or financial background. In many of the projects, I always referred to the *onboarding of* a student employee if the organization was per se located in the medium-sized sector in terms of size. If a student employee works on a 50% contract basis at the beginning of his or her studies, then you are investing directly in your own human resources, because in the long term, this employee will be a key success factor for data-driven management. Because working with numbers in the context of the company's business, an enormous amount of structural knowledge about the business of the respective organization is created within a short time.

Recruiting such a *Junior Market Strategist* is of course no easy task, which is why a job advertisement (Fig. 6.3) that has been successfully used several times is provided as a template here. This information can be used to address and reach young, interested employees. In all the recruiting processes that were accompanied, there were sufficient inquiries from outstanding young applicants. Of course, the recruiting process itself also plays an important role in the following. Once it happened that an excellent employee had already announced that he or she would be happy to accept the position. But then, to the surprise of everyone involved, the head of the division intervened to interview the young expert in turn. This led to irritation on the part of the applicant and to a refusal after the interview with the head of department, because the latter was naturally unable to provide competent

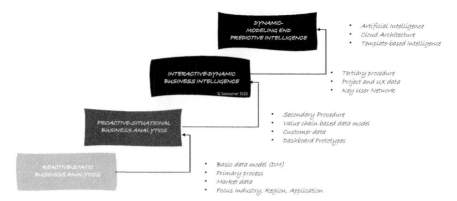

Fig. 6.4 Predictive Intelligence Maturity Model (PIMM) based on Seebacher

information regarding the position at hand. The procedure of the division manager not only led to the loss of an outstanding employee, but also to damage to the *employer branding* and the external perception of the company.

In the further course of the book, relevant competencies in the context of Predictive Intelligence are discussed in more detail. Once you have implemented these basic preparations, you can begin the first activities on your journey toward Predictive Intelligence. This journey leads along the four levels of PI maturity already introduced and described. Different core activity areas can be assigned to these four maturity levels, which are shown in Fig. 6.4 and which are now described and critically discussed in the following.

6.3   Phase 1: Reactive-Static Business Analytics

In the course of completing the first stage of the PI maturity model, three core activities are involved:

- Definition of important segments in relation to the respective organization to narrow down the initially relevant set of data to start with this selected data segment.
- Selection of valid external providers of market and economic data and, based on this, structured collection and processing of this data for internal handling of research requests.
- Definition and development of a basic data model with the help of which initial evaluations and analyses can be carried out.

These activities can be initiated and implemented without additional budgets. This is a crucial aspect, because very few managers would allocate ex ante budgets and resources to a new, little-known topic. Therefore, the entire process model presented here is designed to achieve tangible successes within a short period of time without additional costs, and thus to communicate them, so that PI activities can be expanded and extended step by step—always together and in close coordination with the entire organization.

6.3.1   Where Does the Shoe Pinch?

The classic change management theory proves that the willingness to change is greatest when the shoe pinches. In the context of the first phase of the PI journey, this means that one should look for such problem points within the organization. In this specific case, it is a matter of sales-related deviations that lead to the defined goals not being achieved and thus latent need for action. To find such areas, it is necessary to structurally deal with the sales figures of the respective organization. How can this be implemented operationally? The concrete procedure depends on the size but also on the geographical presence of the respective organization. The following criteria are relevant:

- Number of countries or regions relevant for sales
- Number of industries served

Based on these two categories, the following four scenarios can be defined as orientation guide:

- Scenario 1: National organization with one product or with focus on one industry.
- Scenario 2: Regional or international organization with one product or focus on one industry.
- Scenario 3: National organization with several products and/or with focus on several industries.
- Scenario 4: Regional or international organization with several products and/or with focus on several industries.

For all scenarios, the basic rule is that you have to create access to sales. Initially, it is crucial to assume that you will encounter headwinds immediately if you get the wrong person on board. It is always about organizational sovereignty and sensitivities. During the entire PI journey, it is therefore necessary to ensure that the standard distribution of 20% change-willing, 60% change-neutral, and 20% change-rejecting employees is taken into account. Therefore, consider who is to be classified as trustworthy in sales or also in finance. Approach this person and make an appointment. This first meeting should be a reflective discussion about how—assuming you are responsible for marketing or work in marketing—marketing can help sales to work even better for the benefit of the entire company.

During the first exchange, the possibilities of modern marketing are presented. It is about selected topics of modern (B2B) marketing such as LinkedIn focus campaigns, social selling or also lead scanning, lead nurturing (Seebacher 2020a, b, c). On the basis of these topics, it will be explained how efficiently and effectively sales can be supported in a very targeted manner on the basis of the latest, cost-minimizing technologies. Against this background, a critical discussion and dialogue should then take place in which area of sales it would be useful and necessary to provide support. In every organization, there are always certain sales areas where there is room for improvement. It is important to identify them, because the relevant product manager or the responsible sales employee will be interested in doing everything possible to optimize a weakening turnover.

> **Note: If the organization in question is in the fortunate position of not having any sales problems, the first PI project could be the introduction of a new market or a new product. Because even within the framework of such measures, correspondingly measurable and tangible results can be achieved quickly.**

One of the most recent PI projects involved a national organizational unit of an international corporation based in Northern Europe (see scenario 1). The marketing manager was responsible for Switzerland and we were looking for a PI pilot. Since the company only supplied one industry and was only responsible for Switzerland, we compared the sales development of the different regions within Switzerland. We created a ranking of the sales figures in absolute terms and in relation to the *compound average growth rate* (CAGR)[1] of recent years. We immediately recognized that the French-speaking part of Switzerland would offer the potential to launch the first PI pilot project. It played into our hands that the sales manager in charge was also a brilliant, smart, and open-minded colleague and therefore the perfect project partner.

Another customer was a globally active machine and plant manufacturer, for whom it was also necessary to define a PI pilot area (see scenario 4). In this specific case, we compared the five industries supplied by the group and realized that one industry accounted for more than 60% of sales. Against this background, we, therefore, began to develop data technology for this core industry in order to be able to make data on this industry available internally for the entire organization worldwide very quickly. This approach would also be applicable for an organization in scenario 2, since in this case, of course, this one industry is the all-important one and must therefore be available in a timely manner.

Scenario 3 appears to be the most complex in terms of defining an effective and successful approach. With regard to a sustainable approach, it would be advisable to conduct an industry analysis of the turnover. Depending upon whether in the respective organization a growth (variant 1) or, however, a penetration strategy (variant 2) would be pursued up to date, then for variant 1 an industry would be suitable, which lets corresponding growth expect and for variant 2 one with stable numbers, however, possibly an attractive margin expectation. Based on these

---

[1]https://en.wikipedia.org/wiki/Annual_growth_rate. Accessed: November 20, 2020.

considerations, it becomes clear that from the very beginning, corporate strategy considerations play a decisive role, because it is simply a matter of return and profit or their sustainable safeguarding and optimization.

On the basis of and with the help of the criteria, scenarios, and variants presented, it should be possible to identify the initially relevant data segment(s) together with the first PI companion(s) from the organization on the basis of the discussions held and the initial sales analyses. Once the segment(s) have been defined, the first step is to collect as much information as possible about them internally. In this context, it is also about the search and research within the organization for market reports, analyses, and studies that are already available internally as they have previously been purchased from external service providers. If there is a CRM system in the company, then information should be identified and extracted for the relevant data segments. In the beginning, it is a matter of expanding and deepening one's own sensitivity and competence, depending on one's already existing knowledge in dealing with numbers and data. Even if, in retrospect, an activity should turn out that de facto no new or additional knowledge could be generated, this insight also represents valuable information in the context of the measures implemented. It is this intuitive situational learning experience and the resulting learning curve that is necessary at the beginning in order to be able to set up a functioning PI environment in the long term.

> Tip: This activity has been successfully completed if a clearly defined, content-related data segment is available at the end in the context of one or more first, small PI pilot projects. This includes having identified and integrated one or more internal customers from other organizational units such as product management or sales. For the first time, the subject area of data-driven corporate management also had to be presented and explained to colleagues. These internal presentations are of great importance to develop the knowledge about it in the organization but also to sharpen and deepen the own view. Each question and each discussion automatically leads to an intrinsic reflection, which in turn contributes to the manifestation of the relevant knowledge.

6.3.2 Who Delivers What?

As soon as the first field of activity has been coordinated and narrowed down with internal customers in terms of data and turnover, the task is to compile the necessary information and data material. In most cases, this also requires purchasing or obtaining data from external database providers. In many cases, this means that either complete desperation prevails at the latest now, when, for God's sake, such data can be obtained, or panic breaks out because of the fact that it all sounds like a lot of money again. Once again, you are now confirmed in holding the right book in

Fig. 6.5 QRC to WU Vienna
for retrieving database
providers

Fig. 6.6 QRC to the
European Commission for the
retrieval of economic
databases

your hands, because for both scenarios concrete information is provided below and
helpful tips from PI projects are explained.

An overview of always up-to-date database providers is provided by many
different, freely accessible institutions, such as the Vienna University of Economics
and Business Administration, whose overview can be accessed via the following
QRC (Fig. 6.5).

But also, the European Commission offers an overview of relevant economic
databases freely accessible under the link provided in Fig. 6.6.

These are only two of many different websites that offer an overview of relevant
economic databases. In general, the following list can be used as a starting point,
regardless of focus regions or industries:

- Bureau van Dijk—Amadeus Medium Companies
- Bureau van Dijk—Amadeus Large Companies
- Bureau van Dijk—Amadeus Very Large Companies
- S&P—Compustat Executive Compensation
- S&P—Compustat Global
- S&P—Compustat Compustat North America—annual update

- S&P—Compustat Compustat North America—monthly update
- CRSP Stock Annual
- CRSP/CompuStat Merged Annual
- CRSP Indexes Annual
- Option Metrics—Ivy DB US
- MSCI ESG KLD Stats
- McIlvaine
- Global Water Intelligence
- Statista
- Technavio
- Euromonitor
- Eurostat
- APnews
- Bloomberg
- Frost & Sullivan
- Infinity Research

With this overview, you have a broad and valid starting point from which to get started. The number of database and information providers is constantly growing. It is crucial to identify the relevant one or ones, but also and above all to identify the best and most valid provider or providers. In most cases, you do not need complete databases at the beginning of PI activities, but only excerpts from them. These excerpts can represent specific applications, countries, or regions that are sufficient to implement the first, previously defined PI pilots. This fact is important, because in the course of data collection, the primary concern is to identify who is providing valid data and, above all, which data is initially relevant.

> **Tip:** When data is purchased from external providers for the first time, free temporary access to the databases helps to get an idea of the data structure and data quality. Every data provider wants to sell his data. Be direct and open, and ask for free sample data so that you can analyze and discuss it internally with your colleagues. Specify as precisely as possible, based on the previously defined PI pilot projects, which data you would need, because then you can already use this initial, free data to generate evaluations that can be shared and discussed again with internal customers.

This means that free sample data should be used in the first step and individual, relevant segments from databases in the second step. However, before data is purchased de facto, the databases, which are freely accessible free of charge by many different institutions, should be thoroughly searched for relevant data and information. After all, nothing would be worse than having to purchase data and then an internal customer or colleague accidentally notices that this data was available in another, freely accessible database. That would be fatal for the PI project. Therefore, from the very beginning, caution is the mother of the china box and homework should always be done carefully before creating facts by spending money.

6.3.3   To Be or Not to Be

Especially at the beginning of PI activities, a significant process of change is initiated with the goal of significantly increasing the degree of internal value creation in terms of business intelligence. In this context, two possible initial scenarios can be referred to:

- Scenario 1: No research and analysis activity
- Scenario 2: Already existing research and analysis activities

If you find yourself in scenario 1, there are fewer challenges at the beginning of the activities, because you start from the green field. This means that there are no ongoing activities in the area of data-driven management, whose ongoing operation must be maintained in parallel and in addition to the incipient PI activities. The only challenge that needs to be overcome is to carefully and continuously inform the organization about the new topic area of data-driven management. Strictly and permanently, aspects and benefits but also insights in the context of Predictive Intelligence must be communicated to the organization in order to continuously develop awareness and knowledge. This can be ensured through internal communication as well as through employee and management events. In one specific case, we developed our own internal focus campaign on the topic of Predictive Intelligence with news articles, podcasts, and vodcasts. Within the scope of this measure, we mixed basic information with applied findings and results from ongoing activities, which we then presented and illustrated together with the various internal customers. In this way, we gave our first internal customers an internal platform to present themselves and also managed the transfer to new customers and research needs.

If, however, an organization is to be assigned to scenario 2, then it is necessary to carefully and step by step handle the ongoing inquiries and orders for market analyses and studies more and more internally. Scenario 2 has a light and a dark side. The light side means that there are funds and budgets available for activities in the area of data-driven business management, because otherwise no external research contracts could have been awarded. In any case, these funds are available and can subsequently be used much more efficiently and sustainably within the framework of internal PI activities.

The dark side is that internal customers already have certain ideas and expectations regarding analyses and research or *industry news updates.* This circumstance must be taken into account to the extent that a step-by-step internalization of the value creation into the own organization should initially work as close as possible to the external designs, documents, and structures. After all, even if these external documents have not been very valid or generic content, they certainly represent appropriate benchmarks. Everything will be compared to them superficially and intuitively, and an abrupt deviation from the external provider's usual newsletter will inevitably lead to an outcry in the organization. Such incidents cost time and energy, and can be avoided by an empathetic and prudent approach. Because once the baby is born, a colleague will surely plead for the external newsletter service to continue to be subscribed to—even if it is generic and too expensive, because no one will take care of this detail anymore.

The instrument of internal customer surveys has also proved helpful in this context. For one customer, it was also a matter of cancelling the *Industry Update*. This item cost around 50,000 euros per year, which had to be paid for from the marketing budget of around half a million euros, as there was no separate budget for data-driven corporate management. As part of the internal customer survey, we sent the newsletter to all internal recipients and asked them about their general satisfaction, the frequency of the newsletter, but also about possible suggestions for improvement. We evaluated this data and based on the suggestions for improvement, we designed our own new and optimized newsletter. We presented it to a small user group, incorporated their feedback, and shortly after started to send out our own internal industry newsletter. This was preceded by the fact that we had already announced a relaunch of a further optimized industry newsletter as part of our internal communication.

This internal production of news and updates enabled the new student co-worker to gain a deep insight into the various industries in which the organization was active in a short period of time. This had a direct impact on the quality of the analyses and research to be produced. More and more, everything was recorded and analyzed in an appropriate context. Data and information could be immediately related and validated. We made a virtue out of necessity and created an incredible added value for the organization. This colleague is now the manager of a group-wide predictive intelligence unit that is involved in all areas of management at board level.

The example of newsletters and updates is just one area where the step from external to internal value creation needs to be planned very carefully. This is also crucial for the area of research requests. The approach in this context is based tactically and strategically on the fact that the external commissioning of research and analysis always takes a few weeks. One can play with this time window, because with increasing experience the time expenditure for analyses and searches will rapidly decrease as shown in the relevant chart regarding costs of data, validity of data, and time required for researches and reports already earlier in this book. This means that within only a short period of time, the time required will decrease in the double-digit percentage range.

If you set up a simple, standardized and, for example, MS Excel-based query monitoring with regard to the incoming research orders, then a good planning is possible, until when the different analyses, elaborations, and reports can be completed internally. At this point, a clean communication as part of the expectation management comes into play again. After the request has been received, an email is immediately returned with the reference that the request has been received and documented. The template (Fig. 6.7) for the specification of the research request is

Date (dd.mm.yyyy)	
Submitted by (Function & Name)	
Internal contact person(s) for data validation, if different from the applicant	
Deadline (by what date should the data be delivered - e.g. for a specific event that is about to happen)	
Capex and/or Opex	
Industry (specify one or more)	
Request (if relevant; optional: specific process step)	
Business decision to be made or business basis for the request *To avoid redundancies	
Scope of the data to be retrieved *please specify as detailed as possible e.g.: geographical scope, specific technologies, sub-applications, relevant time period (timeframe), required future prospects, external and/or internal data such as from CRM, customs tariff numbers, tender identification numbers, etc.	
Required format of the work to be delivered (PPT, Excel)	

Fig. 6.7 Template for submitting a research order (Source: Own representation)

automatically attached to this e-mail in order to efficiently and effectively query the demand.

With the help of this template, the time for the definition of PI requests can be minimized significantly. The feedback of the various users of such templates from different organizations also points out that these templates are very helpful in relation to the concrete use case with regard to which information is ultimately required and what information gain should be realized. Especially this reference to the objective is very helpful to define the concrete analysis requirements as exactly as possible. On the other hand, the template protects the PI team, which does not have to process insufficiently and validly defined requests.

> **Tip: The second activity field related to data is successfully completed when relevant data sources are validated and identified. Initial research queries are generated and implemented operationally. External inquiries are commissioned as a subsidiary and supporting measure. The decisive factor is a lack of resources or missing data. In addition, a standardized monitoring for incoming research requests as well as a coordinated and generally available template for ordering an analysis or a research should be installed and stringently in use (Fig. 6.8).**

After 6 Months 100 Percent Internal Research Value Creation

All research requests have been delivered by internal PI Team and no report had to be bought externally

- Increasing growth of research requests over the last 5 months (continues in May, so far 4 further requests, 15.05.2019) since PI has been established within organization

- Capacities fully occupied, additionally the market intelligence cube (MIC) has been created and is currently in the roll-out phase

- Further development of the MIC (competitor-, project- and plant data) to be undergone simultaneously throughout 2019

- Lead times for research requests are increasing due to lack of capacities

- Total requests since December: 31

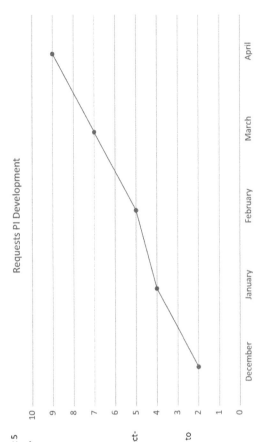

Fig. 6.8 Overview of internal value creation development

6.3.4 What a Basic Data Model Has to Achieve?

In addition to clear processes and templates, the data model as the basis for a future internal PI environment is probably the most important and, in the long term, the most decisive element. Such a data model cannot be imposed on an organization, because it must be conceived, structured, and developed gradually and carefully. Because it is the nucleus on which everything else is ultimately built. Each additional data must be integrated into the existing PI data model and linked to it. In addition, the initially static, temporally one-dimensional data model must be able to work and calculate multi-dimensionally, dynamically regressively, and extrapolatively. For this purpose, the corresponding proprietary algorithms must be integrated into the data model or stored in it. Although, from a structural point of view, existing data structures and mechanisms are always used, a PI environment can only generate maximum added value in the long term without compromise if no generic mechanisms are used, but mechanisms that are organization-specific and adapted to the needs of the target organization.

This requires that such a data model is developed step by step from the ground up and is continuously refined and expanded. A schematic prototype for such a data model is shown in Fig. 6.9. The model contains four essential areas:

- Application or segment data
- Industry data
- Geographical economic data
- Competitor data

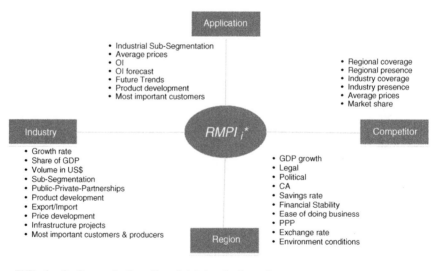

$$* RMPI_i = \beta_0 + \beta_1 \cdot Pumps_j + \beta_2 \cdot Competitor_k + \beta_3 \; industry_j + \beta_4 \cdot Geography_j + u$$
with $i \ldots Geography_i$ or $industry_i$

Fig. 6.9 Schematic representation of a PI basic data model

Such a basic data model can be efficiently mapped using a simple MS Excel spreadsheet. Experience has shown that normally such an Excel-based version can be used until the third level of PI maturity is reached.

> **Tip: It is crucial that the employee(s) working with the data model have access to powerful computers with state-of-the-art processors and large working memory. In view of the rapid developments in the IT sector, we deliberately do not provide any reference values for processors and memory from PI projects here.**

In the context of the development of the basic data model, interaction and communication with the organization are again of great importance. Not only is the topic of data-driven management as part of predictive intelligence new, a data model runs the risk of mutating into a mystery as a black box. This leads to mistrust and ultimately results in a lack of acceptance by the so important internal customers.

In the various PI projects, it has been shown that especially in the context of the development of the data model the intensive cooperation with the sales department is very valuable for all participants. Sales will naturally work intensively with the figures, data, and information from the PI. Therefore, it is necessary that the sales employees are actively involved in the various activities from the very beginning. Competence and knowledge of the relevant markets but also of the industrial value chains are essential for a valid basic data model. It is therefore recommended to work through the prototype of the basic data model with the sales department in a "Business Intelligence Workshop." The title mentioned above has also been chosen deliberately, since the term Business Intelligence has been in use for a long time and is therefore better known as Predictive Intelligence. By using a term that is already known and more in use, unnecessary confusion and uncertainty should be avoided.

The goal of the workshop is to present and discuss the data model. In most cases, the data model is a complex matter per se anyway and therefore there will be no substantial or serious objections from the sales department. Nevertheless, such coordination workshops are or will be of enormous importance and will pay off in terms of PI knowledge transfer into the organization, but also awareness and acceptance of the subject area and the enormous potential it offers. The result of the workshops should be a corresponding basic data model, as shown in Fig. 6.10. On the basis of this figure, the substantial characteristic of such a data model becomes clear. It is this a core function, which is designated in the data model with "Country Lookup," and all information from the different and in each case into the data model flowing sources with one another linked. Only thereby a multidimensional data structure and preparation becomes possible.

With this data model, first evaluations and analyses are possible. These first results are still drawn manually from the Excel sheet in order to be integrated into a presentable PowerPoint documentation. Normally, such analyses and reports will

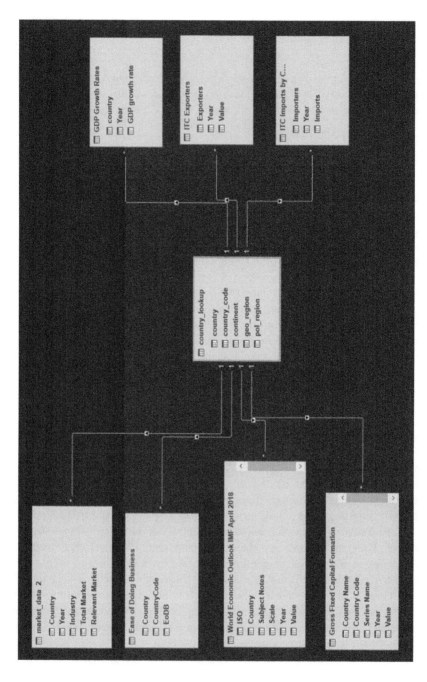

Fig. 6.10 Structural representation of a PI basic data model (Source: Own representation)

comprise between 10 and 20 pages and enable the internal customer to solve the respective task immediately.

> **Tip: Clothes make the man.** Even though the first internal analyses and reports are presented with great pride, it is essential that the greatest possible care is taken in the design and technical preparation of the documents. Even the most valid data processing will be torn apart if the design is bumbling and flawed. At this point, reference is again made to the section "To Be or Not to Be," which explains the importance of previously purchased reports and newsletters as benchmarks. Even if these documents will not have the quality of an internally produced work, they are in most cases perfectly laid out and designed. This means that, after the supposedly done data-technical work, one has to go the extra mile to put the work result into the appropriate "clothes" in terms of design. Make your baby pretty!

At this point, the most important features of good designs and presentations should be pointedly presented only as a reminder:

- No special effects for graphics or transitions
- No oversized letters, because that looks clumsy and unprofessional
- Maximum two fonts on one slide or in one report
- Strictly adhere to an existing CI of the company
- Less is more
- The following should be noted with regard to content:
  - One-page executive summary helps enormously
  - In terms of content, a stringent line (macro to micro or vice versa, but do not mix the two variants, as this will confuse)
  - One-sided conclusion with contacts, recommendations for action, etc.   You are also on the safe side if you take a look at some of the external reports you have purchased so far and analyze them structurally. If you go one step further, you take an external report previously purchased for an internal customer as a benchmark and create the first internal report based on this external report in order to make the transition from external to internal reports as "smooth" as possible.

One has completed the last major field of activity of the first stage of the PI maturity model, when one has mapped a basic data model in Excel and can therefore complete the creation of reports in a much shorter time. The data model is continuously developed and optimized by the internal elaboration of queries. The internal customers give consistently positive feedback and constructive criticism. All participants are aware of the fact that data-driven management as part of predictive intelligence does not have to be a status but a joint journey and development in the sense of organizational learning, and that this is the only way to realize it.

6.4   Phase 2: Proactive-Situational Business Analytics

After about 6–12 months, the step toward phase 2 should be taken. Here, the time span is not the decisive criterion, but rather the *authenticity of realization*. This is based on the penetration of the organization as well as the arrival of the topic in the organization. Ultimately, it is a radical change process to develop an organization, regardless of its size, into a data-driven unit. The entire structural elements described above are only the enablers and drivers of this paradigmatic, organizational realignment, because they will only be used sustainably and meaningfully if the ideas and the irrefutable necessity of such a type of corporate management really arrive in the minds of the acting persons.

This process is intrinsic to each individual colleague. Depending on how the colleagues are individually structured and trained in dealing with numbers and models, it will also take different lengths of time or require different levels of explanation in order to keep everyone at a more or less equal level of knowledge.

> Tip: Always and at regular intervals ensure feedback loops and ask what the organization thinks about the PI activities. A successful method has proven to be a continuous and short feedback loop directly linked to the transmission of work results to internal customers. Two or three short questions to the respective customer can provide valuable information on the specific report but also on the general PI status in the organization.

6.4.1   Dashboards: Let's Get Fancy!

The first step on the second level of the PIMM is a real cool and also fascinating one. In most cases, this activity will not need to be initiated separately but will be completely intuitive and automatic. Because once the basic data model is established and in place, and the first 20–40 reports to internal customers are successfully delivered, as well as the first four to five *Industry News Updates*, then an enormous portfolio of charts and graphs on markets and industries will already have been generated and thus be available.

This automatically leads to the desire not to have to create separate, manually generated graphics and tables for each research request, as this costs an unnecessary amount of time and also has impact on stringency and consistency. So, this automation, but also the subsequent replicability, will happen by itself. For the sake of simplicity, it will initially be MS Excel overviews that map various data areas as standard designs, in order to provide a clearly structured overview at a glance. A first such overview can contain, for example, the following five areas (Fig. 6.11):

- Selection area with filters for continents, regions, and individual countries, so that the contents of the other four areas can be adapted or limited to the respective requirements (far left column area).
- General market data (upper left quadrant).
- Socioeconomic data (upper right quadrant).
- Economic data (lower left quadrant).
- Trade statistics (lower right quadrant).

Based on this, the market data area (Fig. 6.12) can contain its own filter area (1) in order to filter out a certain industry (2) for a region or a country, for example, which is then displayed in the form of the entire (light) but also relevant (dark) market (3) and also displayed numerically with a mouse-over function. To improve the user experience (UX), tabular areas (4) are suitable, which in turn display the graphical comparison (2) in figures. Additional information and explanations can be displayed in separate meta-data areas (5), thus minimizing queries and interpretation possibilities.

Socioeconomic data can be presented as simple and easy to understand as shown in Fig. 6.13. This representation has proven to be practicable with the two areas of the so important *Ease-of-Doing-Business Index*[2] (1) (EoDB) and the overview of the respective population in millions of people (2). Such overviews make it easy to see how a population develops over time and with what dynamics. The EoDB Index provides an insight into the legal situation in a country and reflects legal certainty as well as, for example, the degree of corruption. For small companies, this is a good benchmark for deciding whether or not to invest there from a risk perspective, even if a country appears economically attractive as a market.

A further development of the representation of the EoDB index can be found in Fig. 6.14, where the index is displayed in color and thus easier to understand at a glance. The brighter a country is marked, the more secure it is for companies. The darker the country field is marked, the higher the risk in the respective country. The general EoDB Index is further subdivided into many more different categories in Fig. 6.14, which make up the overall EoDB Index per country:

- Duration for the foundation of a new company: Effort, time, costs, and capital required for the foundation of a company.
- Acquisition of a building permit: Effort, time, costs, and required capital for the acquisition of a building permit.
- Access to electricity: Effort, time, and cost for a reliable power supply.
- Property Registration: Effort, time, and cost to register and protect property.

---

[2]https://en.wikipedia.org/wiki/Ease_of_doing_business_index. Accessed: November 23, 2020.

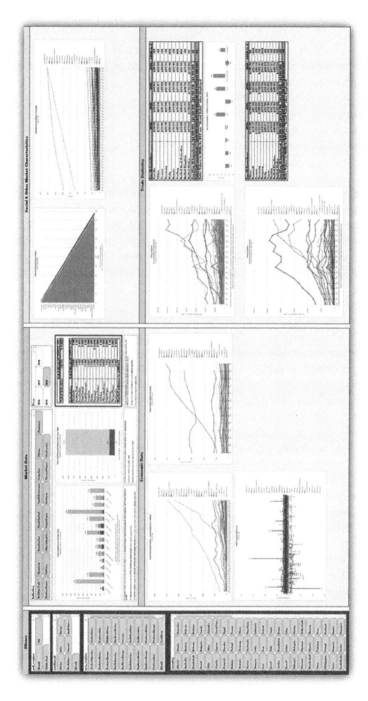

Fig. 6.11 Dashboard prototype (Source: Own representation)

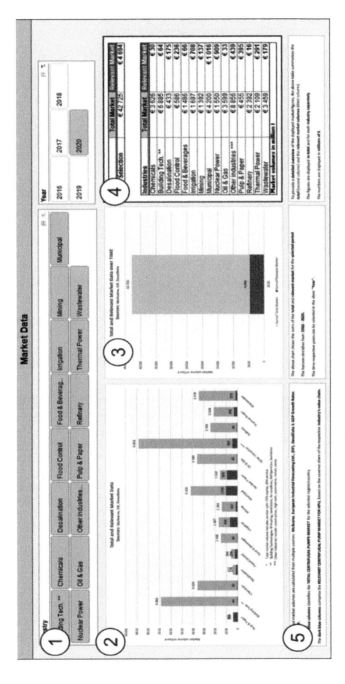

Fig. 6.12 Market data area from dashboard prototype (Source: Own presentation)

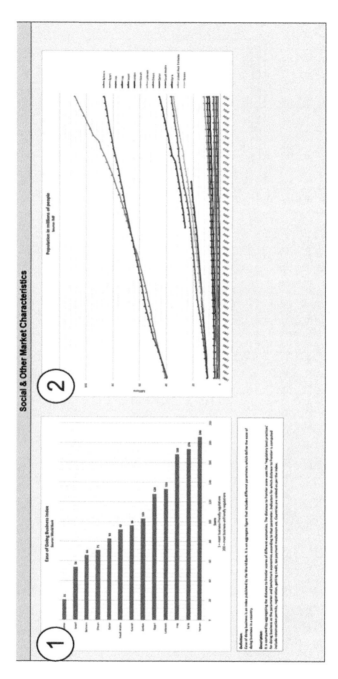

Fig. 6.13 Range of socioeconomic data from dashboard prototype (Source: Own presentation)

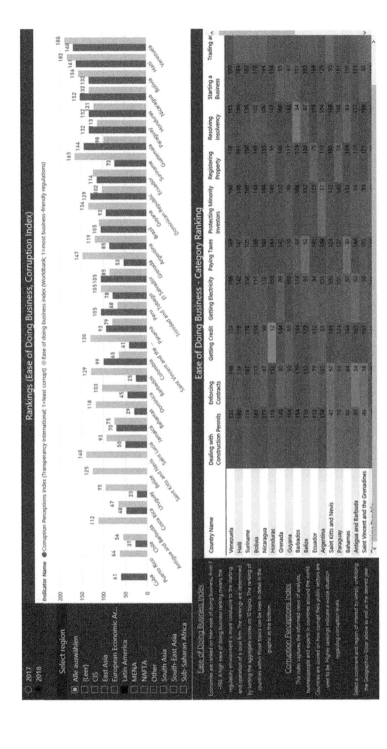

Fig. 6.14 Further development of the representation of the Ease-of-Doing-Business Index based on MS PowerBI (Source: Own representation)

- Access to credit: Effort, time, and cost to obtain a loan.
- Protection of investors: Existence of rules and laws to protect investors and minority shareholders.
- Taxes: Tax burden for companies and time required for tax returns.
- International trade: Effort, time, and costs for import and export of goods and services.
- Contract security: Existence of rules and laws to protect the interests of contractors.
- insolvency proceedings: Effort, time, and costs of insolvency proceedings and survival rate of bankrupt companies.

In a first draft (Fig. 6.15), the economic data area can contain three areas: Gross Domestic Product (1, current prices in US dollars), Gross Domestic Product (2, growth rates in %), and Gross Fixed Capital Formation (3, billion US dollars).

A further development of this field can then be extended by a further field on the basis of an MS PowerBI interface and adapted graphically accordingly. In addition, as shown in the upper left corner, a dynamic time filter can also filter out the relevant time range of interest very easily. This is shown in Fig. 6.16 once for the country Indonesia for the period from 1964 to 2018 and in Fig. 6.17 for the timeline 2010–2018.

On the basis of the further development of the views, it becomes clear that user friendliness increases enormously in the course of time. This is only possible, however, if you have a thorough command of the entire PI activity spectrum internally and are able to implement promptly received feedback to improve user-friendliness. All views and dashboards shown here in this book have been designed, implemented, and continuously optimized by only an internal workforce without any external support. In fact, they are not design masterpieces as they are used by professional providers in the market. But these dashboards have been developed within the organizations and together with them and therefore find the necessary acceptance, which in turn is crucial for the sustainable and meaningful use of PI instruments.

The fourth area of the first dashboard prototype (Fig. 6.18) can contain six areas such as:

- Import data for code HS841370 thousand US dollars (1).
- Table with the top 10 import countries of the specified selection (2).
- Bar chart showing the composite annual growth rate for these top 10 importers (3).
- Export data for code HS841370 thousand US dollars (4).
- Table with the top 10 exporting countries of the specified selection (5).
- Bar chart showing the composite annual growth rate for these top 10 exporters (6).

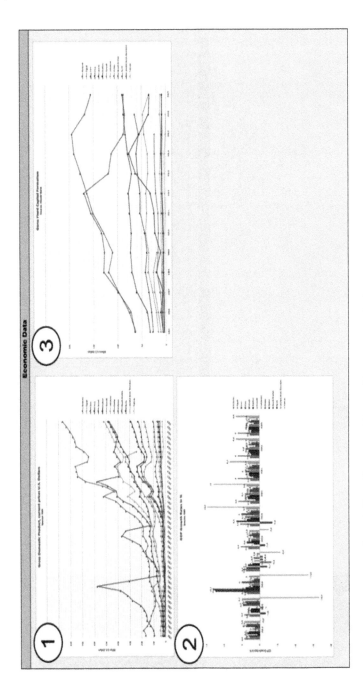

Fig. 6.15 Area of economic data from dashboard prototype (Source: Own representation)

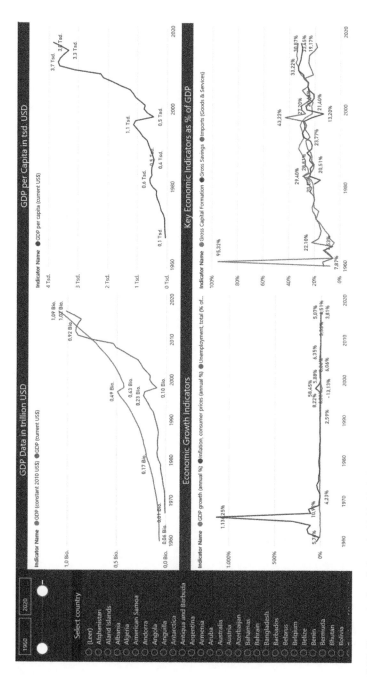

Fig. 6.16 Economic data Indonesia 1964–2018 from MS PowerBI Dashboard (Source: Own presentation)

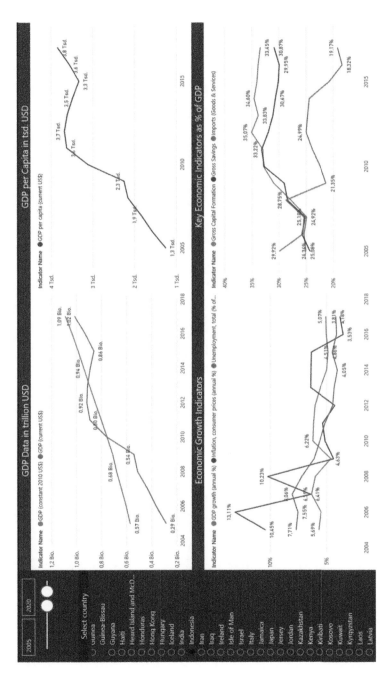

Fig. 6.17 Area Economic Data Indonesia 2005–2018 from MS PowerBI Dashboard (Source: Own presentation)

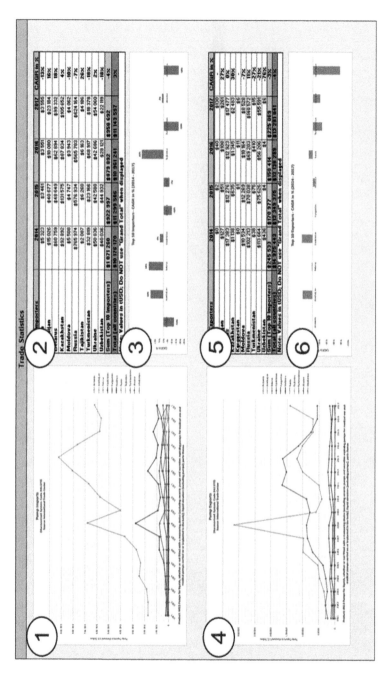

Fig. 6.18 Trade data area from dashboard prototype (Source: Own representation)

The dashboards shown above are intended as an orientation guide. From the point of view of organizational etymology, it is important that such instruments are created and developed jointly in and with the organization concerned. Such dashboards are subject to continuous change and should be so because they always reflect an organization's level of maturity in terms of how it handles data and information. If the topic of predictive intelligence is initiated and driven forward within an organization, there must also be a requirement that the entire organization concerned follows this path and develops further in this direction. And this again requires that through active use, valuable feedback can be collected continuously with regard to further user-oriented optimization.

Not every feedback should be dealt with immediately and implemented directly, because experience has shown that everyone in an organization feels obliged to give their opinion and then you run the risk of getting lost in details.

> Tip: If a corresponding corporate design specification exists in the organization concerned, it should not be ignored from the outset if possible. Even if MS Excel is not the parade instrument for sophisticated, "award-suspicious" designs, it offers sufficient leeway for at least color compliance with existing corporate design specifications.

There are basically no limits in terms of dashboard design. The important thing is that in most cases less is more. This is crucial in view of the fact that PI employees are finding more and more enthusiasm in their own activities, motivated and driven by the enormous, positive feedback from their own organization, which for the first time will receive valid and relevant data at the push of a button. In the context of this spreading enthusiasm, the focus must remain clear and deliberate. Under no circumstances should one succumb to the claim of turning data-driven corporate management into an egg-laying, milk-bearing woolly sow. Experience has shown that dashboards and reports are becoming increasingly full and therefore more confusing, because data managers always want to show everything they can provide.

Very easily and very quickly this can overwhelm internal customers. This can very quickly be interpreted as the PI teams being out of touch, which in turn can be the beginning of the end. If no countermeasures are taken, the organization slowly but surely begins to fall by the wayside.

6.4.2 It Is Time for Customer Data!

The first stage of the *Predictive Intelligence Journey* focused on the external perspective, because market and economic data are a proven means to develop or deepen the sensitivity and sensitivity with regard to data-driven business management. This is due to the fact that such data can be used to validate and verify one's own assessment of industries and markets, thus creating for the first time a valuable internal organizational discourse and reflection process. In this context, one will be surprised how exciting the next step in the PI-Journey is, namely the connection and integration of existing customer data and information.

The question arises why and for what purpose Predictive Intelligence requires customer data and information. An example from one of our PI projects will illustrate this: Certain industries and applications have relatively constant wear and tear times for certain machines or spare parts. Experience shows, for example, that in the sugar industry, certain machines or components have to be replaced every 2 years. This is simply related to the raw materials to be processed. If corresponding customer data for such applications is available from the CRM or ERP system, then marketing automation can be used to continuously run appropriate focus campaigns for foreseeable cyclical requirements, in order to be able to address the right customers directly and indirectly within the framework of *social selling* (Ermer 2020), for example, at minimum cost.

In combination with the already introduced information on industries, markets, and trade in general, further analyses for possible new investment needs of existing customers can then be determined by means of secondary procedures. Such investment needs always go hand in hand with economic growth or developments in the local currency in international comparison, up to an increase in population growth, especially when it comes to the energy sector or the food and beverage industry. The customer data can also be used to make comparisons regarding the number of sales won and lost, which in turn can be used for automated marketing campaigns to obtain the relevant background information from the customer.

6.4.2.1 Why to Start from Zero Again!

Once again it is recommended to start small. This means not rushing to the in-house IT and asking for the CRM to be connected to your own Excel or the PI system that has already been migrated to another tool. The first step begins with the internal PI team pulling data on specific customers or products from the CRM manually. This requires access to the CRM system, which is either available or not, depending on the organizational unit in which one is located. In this context, the following initial scenarios can again be derived:

- Scenario 1: CRM is not available in the organization
- Scenario 2: CRM already exists in the organization
    - Scenario 2.1: Access to the CRM system is not available
    - Scenario 2.2: Access to the CRM system is available   Scenario 2.2 is ideal, of course, because then everything is available that is needed. So, you can get started and for the first time pull data in a structured way or retrieve data from the CRM in relation to research requests to be processed, in order to be able to recognize what data is actually available in the CRM system and what is not. After a short time, we recognized that a CRM system was available at one of our customers, but that the sales figures from controlling deviated from those in the CRM system by more than 50%. What this means is that the CRM is used significantly insufficiently and is therefore not a valid data source. At this point,

management was called upon to establish CRM as a *Single-Point-of-Truth* (SPoT)[3] throughout the organization.

In the case of scenario 2.1, access to the CRM must be requested via the direct superior. Depending on which department you are in and to what extent the topic of data-driven corporate management has already been communicated as part of PI activities, you have to create the appropriate argumentation. Under normal circumstances, access to CRM should not meet with any major resistance against the background of the results and successes already achieved, because the added value of the PI project should in any case already be known within the organization.

> Tip: At this point, we would like to point out the biggest pitfall with regard to the CRM systems (Seebacher 2020a, b, c). Often, when using the term CRM, no distinction is made between the content and technical dimension of the term or system. This very often leads to further discussions regarding the sovereignty of CRM. In no way is the technical sovereignty over CRM in the context of data-driven business management intended or desired but working with data will inevitably lead to an in-depth qualitative discussion of CRM content. As a result, not only the depths and fuzziness of content but also possibilities for optimizing data quality and user-friendliness will be identified, which should then be implemented in the sense of sustainable predictive intelligence in coordination with the various interest groups.

6.4.2.2 How to Get to a CRM Quickly?

With regard to scenario 1, reference is made here to a recently realized project. A medium-sized company with a purely regional focus did not yet have its own CRM. The company was a window manufacturer, which means that the product range consisted of 1 product but about 20 product modifications. In order to be able to integrate customer data and information within the framework of data-driven management for the first time, a situational approach was adopted in order to keep costs to a minimum on the one hand and to achieve rapid success on the other. Based on the sales structure analysis, a "weakening" window model was identified and a short survey was designed for this. This survey was sent to two samples, once to customers who had recently purchased the model and once to customers who had demonstrably purchased another product from another vendor. These non-buyers were identified based on bids placed and sales not successfully completed.

A total of around 100 questionnaires were collected in this way, the information from which was incorporated into an MS Excel table. The results were processed manually and the reasons for not buying the weak product were worked out very

---

[3]https://en.wikipedia.org/wiki/Single_source_of_truth. Accessed: November 23, 2020.

transparently. The results were professionally prepared and presented to the management together with the responsible product manager. For the first time such information was made transparent and without much effort. The young colleague in marketing, who had asked me for support, was immediately commissioned to evaluate the other weakening models step by step on the basis of the presented process model.

At the same time, we began to look under the radar for a software tool that would be suitable for the small business. The tool should cover the functionalities of a CRM system and a marketing automation solution. After only 6 months, the tool was purchased, and the customer data already collected was imported into the new system. The big advantage was that the in-house ERP system could also be connected to the new tool via a one-way interface, so that customer-specific data could be imported into the new tool if required. Once again, the "homework first" principle paid off, because the management was enthusiastic about the first evaluation for product analysis. Sometimes decision makers only need a small impulse to see the big picture.

The management has to deal with many important things every day and very often there is not enough time to reflect conceptually on how the operative management practice could be made simpler, more efficient, and effective. The procedure described above brought to light a quality of product analysis that was completely new for the company management and underlined the potential of the topic but also of the young up-and-coming employee. Today, the small company is well on its way to becoming a PI benchmark and the sales figures speak for themselves, as both margins and sales figures are growing at double-digit rates on average compared to the growth rates before the start of activities in the area of data-driven management.

6.4.2.3 Why the Turbo Is Data Convergence?

The connection of external data with internal data opens up a completely new dimension of viewing. Suddenly, interdependencies can be calculated and then discussed. Product flows (Fig. 6.19) can be extracted in relation to certain applications or industries, which in turn allows to analyze why a product sells disproportionately in relation to an application and the relevant market potential. This circumstance in turn provides new insights into product characteristics, which can be further optimized in a targeted manner and then actively marketed for applications other than previously unknown *Unique Selling Proposition* (USP).

On the other hand, more complex convergence evaluations can be created with respect to absolute and relevant markets and the corresponding proportionalities (Fig. 6.20). All these dashboards were not planned as such ex ante but were created while working with the data from the different systems. These data were always first manually combined with classical lists in order to implement the effort of an IT, automated connection only when we knew exactly what should be linked to what and how. On a granular level, everything revolves around data fields and data records that have to be linked via a criterion in a multidimensional data cube (MDW). This means that it is not always necessary to transfer an entire data set, but only individual components of it in terms of criteria. If this is not considered, the

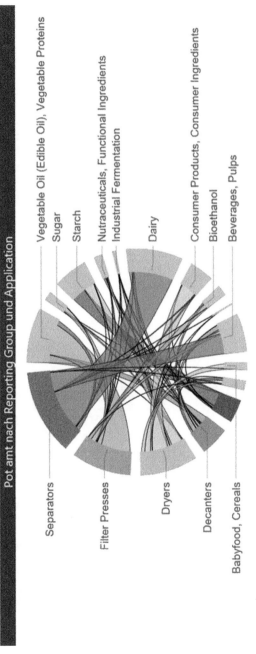

Fig. 6.19 CRM data on product flows (Source: Own presentation)

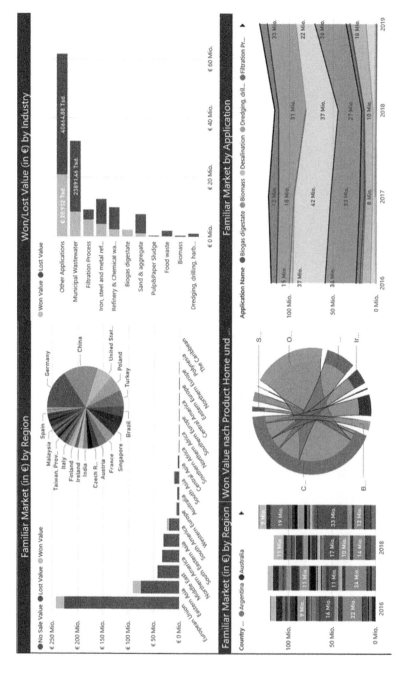

Fig. 6.20 Customer market data dashboard (Source: Own presentation)

MDW is unnecessarily inflated, which in turn reduces the performance of the MDW and thus the user friendliness.

Based on the use of data from CRM, further analyses can also be carried out, which set and evaluate first- and second-order market potentials in relation to sales/non-sales relations (Fig. 6.21). This in turn helps management to take timely countermeasures and thus minimize or avoid negative deviations. In combination with information from Marketing Automation, possible investment needs of key customers can be determined and thus directly considered in the sales activities.

6.4.3   With the Value Chain to the Relevant Market

A further important step on the second stage of the PI development model is the integration of the value chain perspective. As discussed earlier in the chapter on PI maturity in regard to the term *value chain*, this dimension must now be analyzed for the respective organization. The point is to identify which part of an industrial value chain a company can cover with its current product portfolio. Only very few companies are complete solution providers and can, for example, supply all products for an entire paper production line from a single source. In the paper industry worldwide, there is talk of a handful of companies that are such system suppliers.

Statistics show that 80% of companies can only cover between 10 and 30% of an industrial value chain. If, however, data on entire industries is used in the context of predictive intelligence, a completely wrong picture emerges, since the *absolute market* differs significantly from the *relevant market* to a company, namely the for which the respective company also has the products in its portfolio. Thus, the distinction between the absolute and the relevant market is essential with regard to the validity and precision of the data.

Value chain analyses are generally a very complex, because abstract topic—especially in the food and beverage industry there are currently only very imprecise and few figures. This is due to the fact that several different process variants with different machines and technologies exist for one and the same application or production process. Other value chains, such as those in the water industry, for example, are in turn much easier to create, since larger data sets can also be accessed.

6.4.3.1 How to Proceed?

So, what does the analysis of value chains mean? And how does this lead to the figures for the relevant market? First of all, a distinction must be made between *CAPEX* and *OPEX*. These terms define *capital expenditures* on the one hand and *operational expenditures* on the other, i.e., capital expenditure in the sense of investment in plant and machinery on the one hand, and current expenditure in terms of service, repair, and spare parts on the other. For each industry, there are also forecasts for the annual CAPEX and OPEX.

In the context of value chain analysis, industrial production processes are now divided into sections or segments because, as described earlier in this book, the division into process sections would again be too granular and paradoxically too

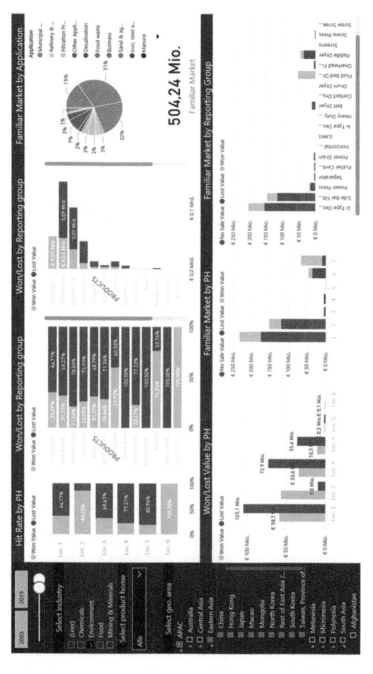

Fig. 6.21 Market success analysis per location (Source: Own presentation)

imprecise for data-driven management. On the basis of this division into sections, these segments are now allocated shares of the annual investment and service costs in the form of percentages. On the basis of this allocation, it is then possible to conclude from the absolute market to the relevant market in relation to the respective product portfolio by adding up the relevant sections of the respective value chain in relation to the current product range. A graphic elaboration of such a value chain analysis for the area of wastewater management is shown in Fig. 6.22.

Depending on the size of the organization, you can use your own employees by means of a survey for the distribution of percentages with regard to the value chain. The spread of the values must then be averaged and also used as an indicator for the validity of the information. If valid data can be accessed in the CRM and ERP systems, then this information can also be allocated to the sections of an industrial value chain to be defined and compared with the information from the employee survey.

In most projects, however, we have used external research service providers to define the relevant markets in order to evaluate the internally generated data in comparison with the externally collected information. In the long run and from the perspective of my applied research, I also hope that we will be able to use industrial swarm intelligence, by means of which we will be able to map and validate more and more industries via such value chain analyses using blockchain technology. This is the only way to ensure that the statements and predictions on CAPEX and OPEX developments in the various industries are valid and can be correlated with PI data in order to be able to extrapolate and anticipate corresponding requirements on this basis. Especially when sustainability and security of supply are considered as aspects of *Corporate Social Responsibility* (CSR), such value chain-based blockchain approaches play a role that should not be underestimated.

> **Tip:** This activity is complete when the relevant market(s) have been defined and quantified. As with the data model, the value chain perspective will be subject to constant change—and it must be, because only then can the validity of the information be continuously developed and optimized. Also important in this context is the coordination and interaction with internal stakeholders, who on the one hand have to know and accept the approach and on the other hand also the generated figures and percentages for the individual sections of the value chains.

If several industries are covered by one organization, the PARETO principle applies again. It is advisable to start with the most important industry in terms of current sales. In most cases, the largest volumes of data and information are also available for this industry. In the next step, two different paths can then be taken. Either one develops the second most important industry or—if the corporate strategy is based on growth or if the downstream industries tend to stagnate according to PI data—one

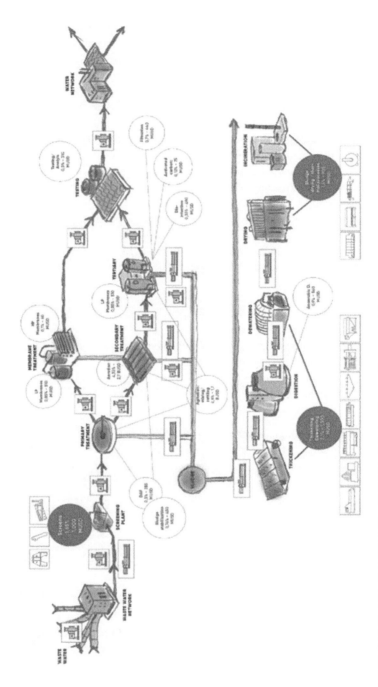

Fig. 6.22 Sample value chain illustration wastewater industry (Source: Own presentation)

consciously focuses on developing a niche industry in order to then work proactively on this industry in a targeted manner and with maximum *return on sales* (RoS).

6.4.4   How the Evaluations Are Becoming More and More Informative?

In the next step, the results of the value chain analysis described above will be integrated into the existing data model. This means that a layer is added to the external market data in order to be able to map and play out the corresponding segments of the industrial value chain in CAPEX and OPEX.

Figure 6.23 shows an industry-specific dashboard for the segment "Automation/ Control" of the value chain of the municipal wastewater management. Using the filters on the left side, the relevant market for capital investments, as opposed to the annual expenses for service and spare parts, can be played out for any region or country. On this basis, the relevant market potential can be determined immediately using the dashboard and used for further measures.

Figure 6.24 shows the same dashboard but only for the country "Argentina" selected on the left.

At this point, we would like to point out once again the necessity of internal value creation within the framework of the realization of predictive intelligence, which has already been mentioned several times, because the process model described here makes it clear how the entire structure is gradually expanding, but also becoming more complex. If you are not completely in control of the situation in this context from the beginning, then you will not be able to manage and master this in the further course of the project. Therefore, it is necessary to grow with Predictive Intelligence in terms of content and competence and to learn continuously. Only in this way can such a concept be successfully and effectively established in the long run and contribute to the company's success in the long term.

This further developed competence also concerns the field of analysis and evaluation. In most projects, the employee(s) involved were proactive in continuously optimizing not only analyses, reports, and dashboards, but also evaluations and algorithms. This is because the ongoing and continuous work with data and models automatically results in an enormous learning curve. And that is also essential, because only then is it possible for the PI team to develop and continuously deepen the required expertise and to grow with the ongoing tasks. This applied learning experience leads to new secondary evaluations in the sense of conclusive statistics and interpretative algorithms in addition to ever more diverse primary evaluations.

These are the basis for expanding, exciting discourses regarding the interpretation of data and knowledge gained, which are relevant for all areas of research and development (R&D), product management (PM), innovation management (IM), and sales. Figure 6.19 on product flow analyses shows, for example, such an evaluation based on intuitively created secondary analyses. It should be noted that in the context of predictive intelligence, the term in the *narrower sense* is used. In empirical

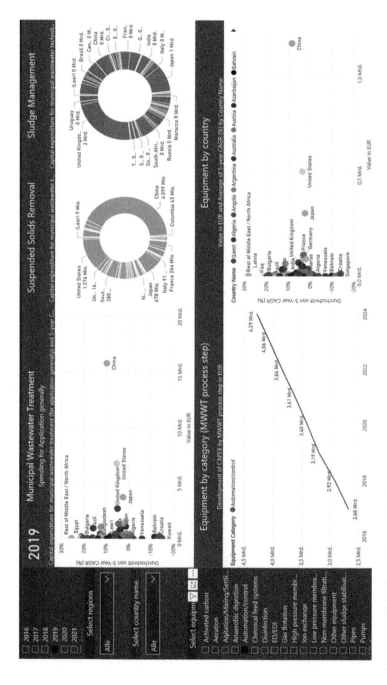

Fig. 6.23 CAPEX-dashboard for municipal wastewater management global (Source: Own presentation)

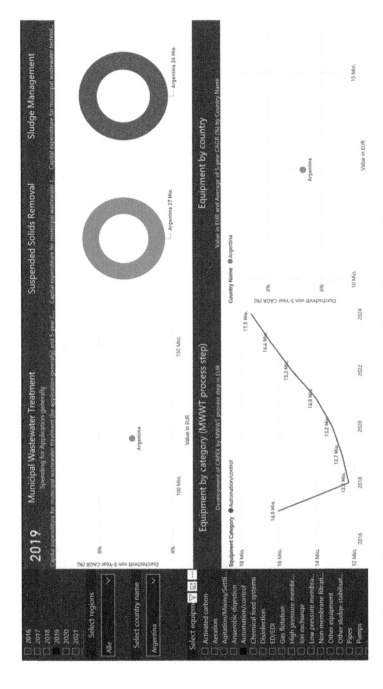

Fig. 6.24 CAPEX dashboard for municipal wastewater management Argentina (Source: Own presentation)

research, secondary analysis in a *broader sense* is the re-analysis of primary data. This is done in order to reproduce and validate old results or to answer new questions with existing data in a cost-effective way. Such secondary analyses require that data is accessible, which is achieved with the predictive intelligence data infrastructure to be developed.

Secondary analysis in the *narrower sense* and in the context of predictive intelligence refers to the further evaluation of data already obtained through primary analysis. An example of this could be a customer benefit analysis based on the product flow analysis shown above and in Fig. 6.19. Within the scope of such a customer value analysis, defined contents are played out by means of a customer journey set up together with product management and sales, which are always underlaid with one to three questions about the product or special aspects for the respective application. In return for answering the questions, the customer or interested party is given access to so-called *gated content* (Seebacher 2020a, b, c). This content helps him with regard to his work or a certain upcoming purchase process.

After a certain time, a required statistical number of answers is reached. On this basis, it is then possible to transfer correlation and regression analyses with regard to certain product characteristics, which are very positively perceived by the customer in a certain industry or application, to another industry or application or to simulate and model their transfer. This is interesting with regard to possible sales potentials and possible margins to be achieved. Secondary analyses are comparable to a further hierarchy in the context of *Deep Learning*. What *Artificial Intelligence* will do automatically and covertly in the future as part of Predictive Intelligence is still performed manually by the involved employees together with the relevant internal customers on the second stage of the PI maturity model.

This phase must be characterized by the fact that by now the entire operation with the data has been established and is perfectly mastered as a basic manual tool. This is because a creative-explorative approach at the level of secondary analyses requires that the foundation in the sense of the building block in dealing with the data has already been laid and manifested. This means that advanced and highly relevant secondary analyses are qualitatively discussed and critically debated in discourse with the various interest groups. The PI staff member(s) then only represent the interface to the already advanced data model or multidimensional data cube, which translates the spoken word into a valid algorithm and, subsequently, a prototype for a further, new dashboard, and transforms it operationally.

This prototype is then discussed, agreed and optimized with internal customers before it is "ready to go into production" globally via the interactive predictive intelligence portal, available worldwide and 24/7, in order to be able to enable data-driven innovations, optimize margins, specify products even better, and maximize sales. The data-driven, corporate blind flight should finally be history.

> **Tip:** This second stage is successfully completed when the entire organization has learned to work actively with the data from the PI team. This is accompanied by an already pronounced appreciation of the analyses, reports, data, and information from Predictive Intelligence. Over time, a common learning and development process has developed, and no one questions the subject of data-driven corporate management and the clear *make* decision associated with it in terms of the predominant internal value creation.

6.5   Phase 3: Interactive-Dynamic Business Intelligence

As the third stage of the Predictive Intelligence maturity model is reached, the comprehensive and significant added value of data-driven business management is slowly and gradually becoming more transparent. By now, all areas of the organization should have come into contact with the topic and it is crucial to see and use this exchange with internal customers as an opportunity for further optimization and adaptation of Predictive Intelligence. It is now a matter of being able to devote more attention to conceptual work in the context of data-driven corporate management and development. If this step is not successful, then there is a risk that the area of PI will not be developed stringently. Therefore, the following three areas of activity must be focused on within the third level of the PI maturity model:

- Key User Network (KUN) development.
- Integration of project data and data on customer experience (CX) or user experience (UX) (Halb and Seebacher 2020).
- Expansion of activities to include tertiary analyses.

The activities to date have led to more and more data and information being available online and adapted to specific needs. Whereas at the beginning of the activities the PI team itself had to prepare the data, extract it from the data cube and then document the findings in a report in terms of concept and content, it is now the case that 80% of information requirements can be classified as standard cases. This means that the majority of research requests do not require separate action by the PI team and its experts.

This has a very positive effect on the entire internal organizational work economy, because the information seeker no longer has to fill out the request template, forward it to the PI team and then wait for the agreed processing time to be able to process the respective question with the help of the reports and information from the PI team. Now the information seekers can access and work with the data directly online. This not only speeds up the process, but also minimizes the time and effort required throughout the entire process. To make this possible, however, the PI team must establish a network of trained users of the PI environment.

6.5.1   How a Key User Network Is Established?

A *key user network* (KUN) can be defined and set up very quickly and very effectively. The following steps have to be passed through in order to benefit from this powerful concept without any friction:

- Define criteria for key users (KU)
- Create a description of PI-KUN including goals, benefits, and tasks
- Identify and contact KU
- Define training contents for KU or KUN members
- Produce training content in the form of eLearning, podcasts, or webinars
- Implement trainings
- Activate KUN and ensure ongoing exchange and updating

In terms of predictive intelligence, a KU defines itself as someone who continuously works with internal and external data and who also needs this information. These persons should be located in the departments' Research and Development, Innovation Management, Marketing, Product Marketing, Product Management, Corporate Strategy, and Sales. In the previous projects, the first KUs were derived directly from the operative work, because they were those persons who either showed general interest since the beginning of the PI measures and were therefore involved or who had a need for information from the beginning and communicated this need in the form of research requests to the PI team.

In most cases, the KUN has thus formed itself naturally and only for a few areas or regions of the organization's potential KUs had to be proactively sought and addressed.

KUN's approach always meets with very positive feedback, because internal customers feel that they can now work independently with such valuable data and information as "responsible" experts. What can be observed again and again shortly after the start of KUN is that more and more employees want to be included in the "illustrious" circle. Therefore, it is necessary that the PI environment remains efficient in terms of access and processing times even with an increasing number of users.

However, in order to be able to handle the PI environment correctly and efficiently, it is necessary to take part in a basic training course before someone is activated for the instrument. This basic training takes place in the form of a webinar, during which the current version of the instrument is presented, discussed, and debated online. These webinars last about 30 min and are ideally conducted in groups of up to five people. After completion of the *PI Certificate Webinar*, the respective employee is activated and can immediately start using the PI environment.

Since most organizations use an available business intelligence tool such as MS PowerBI for simplicity, there is no need for extensive installations, as most companies have automatically included corresponding applications in their office software contracts. This also means that there are no additional costs for the organizations. With a basic training, a PI user is far from being a key user, because a KU is an employee who is experienced and familiar with both the subject matter and the PI environment and who, in the figurative sense, can answer simple standard queries and problems of his colleagues at a location or in his team as *first-level support*, so to speak, like a helpdesk.

This on-site and timely support function is designed to contribute to work efficiency and effectiveness and to minimize the workload for the core PI team to deal with the more complex inquiries, problems, and issues. In the further course, it is important to keep the KUN constantly informed with updates and to communicate new and possibly interesting, relevant use cases through special case study trainings. This regular exchange is also important for the ongoing query of PI usability but also for further optimization of content.

6.5.2 How the 360° Data Panorama Is Achieved?

In addition to the ongoing further development of the interactive views and designs, the last remaining data gaps are now being addressed. In line with the PI process model presented here, the only data missing are data on projects and *customer experience*, but also the digital footprints of customers and prospects. The area of projects is primarily aimed at organizations that also have to deal with long lead times in the area of large tenders and major projects. For such organizations it is and can be of enormous importance to have this information in the PI environment in order to be always up to date and also, under the aspect of account-based marketing (ABM) (Bacon 2020), to be able to provide the relevant and involved organizations and their information seeking employees with the best possible information on the right media and channels.

Figure 6.25 shows an example of a project dashboard with different overview diagrams by country and region in the upper area. In the left area, the user can filter out different types or applications in the industry that are relevant for him or her. In the central area, the entire information is then interactively displayed and linked to further information and the latest news. In the upper left area, the user can also search for the current project status. This project dashboard is especially helpful for management, because in most cases, the projects are large orders.

Also of interest in this context is the online version of the *Industry News Updates* introduced as part of the first stage of the PI maturity model. These are initially sent by e-mail to a defined internal distribution list to keep internal customers up to date. Due to the increasing automation of marketing and communication activities, it should be possible at this stage of PI activities to integrate these updates directly online and interactively into the PI environment (Fig. 6.26).

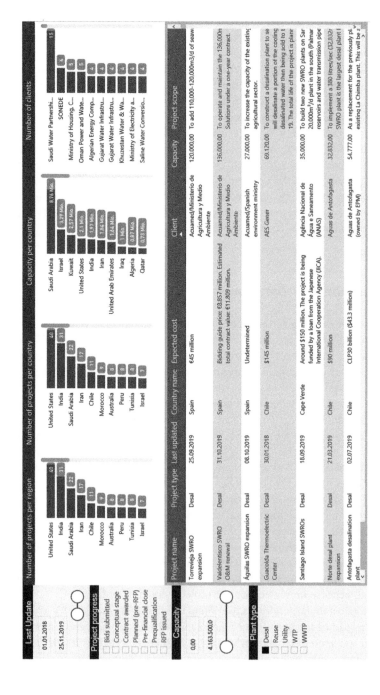

Fig. 6.25 Project dashboard for desalination projects (Source: Own presentation)

Title of Article	Segment	Subcategory	Region	Publishing Date	Link
☑ Competitors					
☐ M&A					
☐ Pumps					
☐ Technology					
☐ Environment					
☐ Food, Beverages & Bioenergy					
☐ Mining					
☐ Politics Legal Economical					
☐ Economics					
☐ Legal					
☐ Pulp & Paper					
KSB agreement links pump configurator to BIM	Competitors	Technology	Global	10.02.2020	https://...
Vensalis restarts biomass power plant at Crescentino biorefinery and expects bioethanol production later this year	Food, Beverages & Bioenergy	Bioenergy	Europe	10.02.2020	https://...
Turning sugar into Hydrogen	Food, Beverages & Bioenergy	Bioenergy	Global	08.02.2020	https://...
Bank of India, State Bank cut interest rates	Politics Legal Economical	Economics	India	07.02.2020	https://...
Paper firm UPM will spend $600 million to make chemicals from wood	Pulp & Paper	Biochemicals	Europe	07.02.2020	https://...
Flygt releases MAS 801 pump monitoring system	Competitors	Technology	Global	06.02.2020	https://...
Tsurumi acquires British dealer Obart Pumps	Competitors	M&A	Europe	05.02.2020	https://...
Grundfos opens digital showroom in Dubai	Competitors	Technology	Middle East	02.02.2020	https://...
ACCIONA to build, operate Hong Kong desalination plant	Environment	Desalination	Asia	30.01.2020	https://...
Worst drought in years pushes Anglo to sign water deal with Codelco	Mining	Copper	Latin America	26.01.2020	https://...

CONTENT

The one year MCLR comes down to 7.85% p.a from 7.90% p.a. with effect from 10th February 2020. A day after the Reserve Bank of India (RBI) announced measures to ease interest rates, the State Bank of India (SBI) and the Bank of India (BoI) have reduced their lending rates by cutting the marginal cost of fund-based lending rate (MCLR). The SBI has reduced the MCLR by 5 bps across all maturities. The one-year MCLR will become 7.85% with effect from February 10. The country's largest lender indicated that the lending rates would come down further. "The impact of the recent RBI policy measures and the reduction in deposit rates will be reflected in the next review of MCLR," the SBI said.

The BoI, another state-run lender, reduced MCLR by 10 bps for maturities up to 6 months. Additionally, the bank has reduced interest rates on the housing loan, which will now be available from 8.00% and vehicle loan at 8.50%. The SBI also lowered the deposit rates, in view of the 'surplus liquidity' in the system. The bank lowered term deposits rates by 10-50 bps in the retail segment (less than ₹2 crore) and 25-50 bps in the bulk segment (₹2 crore and above).

Fig. 6.26 Example dashboard industry news (Source: Own representation)

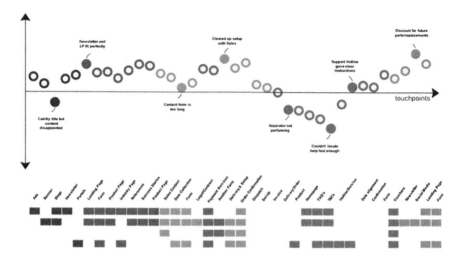

Fig. 6.27 Customer experience evaluation dashboard (Source: Own representation)

6.5.3 With Tertiary Processes into a Completely New Dimension

In addition to the project data, the social breadcrumbs of interested parties and customers should also be integrated into the PI environment in this phase at the latest. In this way, a 360° view can be achieved, and this information can be integrated into the overall PI analysis. This data is comparable to that from, for example, the *account-based marketing* (ABM) application of Marketo (see Fig. 4.10), which makes it possible to document user behavior on the basis of a once allocated IP address in strict compliance with the General Data Protection Ordinance (GDPR).[4] This information is essential in order to be able to draw conclusions about the urgency of a possible investment based on the activity level on the one hand, and to be able to see which content is consumed for how long and via which channel through the so-called *Interesting Moments* on the other hand. On the basis of these evaluations, not only the sales department can recognize where it should become active, but also marketing can see which content in which form at what time of day in which region is better and which is less successful via which channel.

If now this right area of Fig. 4.10 is aggregated and analyzed for several customers by means of secondary analysis, then a user experience curve (Fig. 6.27) is generated, which shows the performance of each individual customer contact point in relation to the others. This performance value can then be evaluated and processed in the *tertiary analysis*, either weighted or unweighted. This results in

---

[4]https://en.wikipedia.org/wiki/General_Data_Protection_Regulation.   Accessed: November 23, 2020.

two progression curves, which can be evaluated and processed with respect to criteria such as

- Cost per contact point.
- Retention time per contact point.
- Valence of the contact point in relation to possible purchase decision by means of secondary analysis to contact point behavior purchase decision correlation analyses.

Providing information on the functioning of the customer contact point itself. Another very advanced tertiary analysis in this context has been applied in some recent PI projects. In addition to the purely operational analysis of the contact points described above, the content dimension at each contact point was dynamically integrated and the measured customer behavior was directly correlated with the *content asset* used or consumed. In this way, the classic A/B testing (Seebacher 2020a, b, c) was dynamically transformed into multidimensional testing, because this procedure directly analyzes the respective content asset not only selectively in relation to the respective contact point, but also evaluates it dynamically in comparison to the other available contact points. Thus, a relational content asset value structure is created, which shows on which content in which form at which time of the day and via which channel the focus should be on, in order to be able to focus more and more on the strongest sales-promoting content assets in the sense of predictive intelligence.

Tip: The third stage of the PI maturity model is successfully completed when 80% of the inquiries are conducted online by the inquirers themselves and the key user network is established as a guarantee for timely and valuable on-site support and as an ambassador for predictive intelligence throughout the organization. In addition, the project data—if relevant—and necessary instruments and tools such as web crawlers[5] are established in order to automatically and dynamically track the entire relevant project landscape and the entire customer and user behavior and to document them in an integrated manner in the PI environment. Based on the already existing expertise in primary and secondary analysis, further development toward creative-explorative tertiary analysis is taking place, which opens up a completely new dimension for the organization and takes data-driven corporate management to a completely new level.

---

[5]https://en.wikipedia.org/wiki/Web_crawler. Accessed: November 23, 2020.

6.6   Phase 4: Dynamic-Modeling Predictive Intelligence

First of all: By reaching this fourth level, the most difficult part has already been successfully mastered, because now only the freestyle is left. However, it is essential to have fully understood and internalized the steps and activities described above, because the activities that lie ahead now require comprehensive expertise in all existing PI structures, processes, and connections. In concrete terms, the focus is now on three areas:

- Extension of the PI environment with Template-based Intelligence (TBI).
- Implementation or validation of a PI cloud architecture.
- Integration of artificial intelligence (AI) in the PI environment.

In continuation of the increasing automation of PI processes, more extensive tasks can now be gradually outsourced to internal customers using template-based intelligence at this stage of the PI maturity model. Template-based Intelligence (TBI) is based on the Template-based Management (TBM) approach (Seebacher 2020a, b, c) and enables, for example, the automated creation or generation of a comprehensive profitability analysis in the form of a PI-supported workflow. In concrete terms, this means that the respective employee is guided step by step through the process of creating such a profitability analysis by having to fill predefined templates and Predictive Intelligence pulls the relevant information from the various data sources in the background, and then creates a finished document from this. The case study in the last part of the book on the topic of medium-term predictive intelligence applications describes one such case of Template-based Intelligence (TBI).

6.6.1   How Template-Based Intelligence Saves the Consultant?

TBI combines pre-structured information collection with predefined data transfer to prepare and enable scenario-based decisions by means of template-based entry of targets or certain required information. It is in the nature of things that such TBI-based documents are merely a valid basis for decision-making, so that management can conduct a data-driven discourse. Predictive Intelligence does not replace management competence and logic but should contribute to better and more valid decision-making.

TBI can be used, for example, for the following applications:

- Market entry studies
- Product diversification analyses
- Dynamic pricing analyses
- Innovation management program planning
- Procurement-Intelligence Calculations
- Product launch planning
- R&D program planning

These are just a few of the possible use cases of PI projects in past years. Ultimately, any process in the sense of a workflow that is used at a certain regularity can be handled by TBI with Predictive Intelligence and fed from it in terms of data technology.

6.6.2   With AI It Goes into the Cloud

As the amount of data and the number of algorithms increases, each system will reach its limits. Even complex TBI-based PI workflows will require corresponding computer capacities, which is why, from the perspective of data security, risk management, and the performance of predictive intelligence, a sustainable, modern PI system architecture should be considered together with the company's own IT departments.

In this context, strategic as well as operational IT aspects have to be considered, similar to the *MarTech* and *SalesTech* (Seebacher 2020a, b, c). A precise analysis of the IT framework conditions is crucial with regard to the ERP and CRM systems used. In addition, the long-term IT strategy of the organization must be taken into account. Especially when it comes to the integration of Artificial Intelligence (AI) in the last step, a PI cloud infrastructure cannot be avoided, because AI requires enormous computer capacities and also the necessary security. At this point, we will not go into great detail about the individual activities, because at this point in the PI Journey a distinct organizational PI identity could already be developed. Therefore, compared to the first steps of this process model, a narrow frame of reference is no longer necessary for this advanced stage of a company's own predictive intelligence.

The all-important aspect in the context of the last, fourth stage of the PI maturity model is prediction, i.e., forecasting. What was initially calculated time-dynamically with the primary, secondary, and tertiary analyses will now be leveraged through the integration of artificial intelligence to a totally new level in terms of *flexibility*, *modularity*, and also *scenarioability*, as the ability to work in scenarios. While up to now extrapolations based on the method of trendline calculations have been dynamically modified by parameter inputs at certain points, the integration of AI enables multidimensional and sensitivistic extrapolations, which can calculate and play out different scenarios with different variables simultaneously.

With regard to TBI, this means that an R&D program can be automatically played out of PI in several scenarios based on clearly defined input requirements such as the annual R&D budget and an ex ante defined profit margin to be achieved by new products coming from R&D over time in several scenarios. The PI even goes one step further in order to compare the various R&D scenarios in a ranking that is relevant for the organization, from which the PI clearly defines the R&D program that appears to make the most economic sense.

There are no more limits to creativity. For the first time, data-driven corporate management will then be able to take place at such a valid level through AI-supported predictive intelligence, which stringently enables the risk-minimizing but also profit-maximizing pursuit of the essential basic economic principles discussed at the beginning of this publication.

6.7   What the Quintessence Is?

In this chapter, a pragmatic and step-by-step guide was given to set up a predictive intelligence environment for sustainable and up-to-date data-driven corporate management in an organization of any size. The concrete milestone results were defined for each of the four phases, so that it is possible to immediately recognize the achievement of objectives. In combination with the previously discussed maturity model and the self-test procedure for Predictive Intelligence, it is also possible to dynamically and continuously evaluate one's own status very accurately.

Further Reading

Bacon, A. (2020). Account-based marketing. In U. Seebacher (Hrsg.), *B2B marketing—A guide-book for the classroom to the boardroom*. Cham: Springer.

Ermer, B. (2020). Social Selling im B2B Marketing. In U. Seebacher (Ed.), *B2B marketing—A guidebook for the classroom to the boardroom*. Cham: Springer.

Halb, F., & Seebacher, U. (2020). Customer experience und touchpoint management. In U. Seebacher (Hrsg.), *B2B Marketing—A guidebook for the classroom to the boardroom*. New York: Springer.

Scheer, P., & Kasper, H. (2011). *Leadership und soziale Kompetenz*. München: Linde Verlag.

Seebacher, U. (2020a). *B2B marketing: A guidebook for the classroom to the boardroom*. Cham: Springer.

Seebacher, U. (2020b). *B2B marketing essential: How to turn your marketing from a cost into a sales engine* (2nd ed.). Graz: AQPS.

Seebacher, U. (2020c). *Template-based management—A guide for an efficient and impactful professional practice*. Cham: Springer.

Sturm, A., Opferbeck, I., & Gurt, J. (2011). *Organisationspsychologie*. Wiesbaden: VS Verlag für Sozialwissenschaften.

The Predictive Intelligence TechStack (PITechStack)

7

7.1 Is Predictive Intelligence an IT Topic?

Like everything else in our modern working and professional world, the area of data-driven business management is a subject area that in the long run cannot develop and exist without an appropriate information technology infrastructure. In the course of many different conversations with customers, colleagues in practice but also in applied research, it has become clear that it will be crucial in the context of this publication to also address the topic area of the PITechStack for the first time. So far, the synonym to MarTech and SalesTech as such has not been mentioned or introduced in the corresponding scientific or practice-relevant literature. A corresponding Google search in October 2020 for the term "PITechStack" yields a sobering result (Fig. 7.1).[1]

The first result leads to the author's homepage as he introduced this term in the German version of this management book. Neither of the two remaining hits represents a relevant result. This fact is deceptive, because of course countless providers have already discovered this highly attractive business area for themselves and offer corresponding products and solutions in the area of PI. From today's perspective, it can be assumed that we will experience a highly dynamic development of PI-relevant offerings and products in the coming years—similar to the MarTechStack (Fig. 7.2), which has grown by more than 5000% (Fig. 7.3) from 150 to more than 8000 available products in the last few years.

Against this background, it is already all the more important to group products and solutions on the basis of current providers and products. This is because a structural scheme that has remained relatively constant from the very beginning has also continued in the MarTech sector over the years, with the help of which corresponding products and solutions could be well classified. And such a resilient frame of reference is essential in order to maintain an overview in the thicket of the

---

[1] www.google.com. Accessed: November 24, 2020.

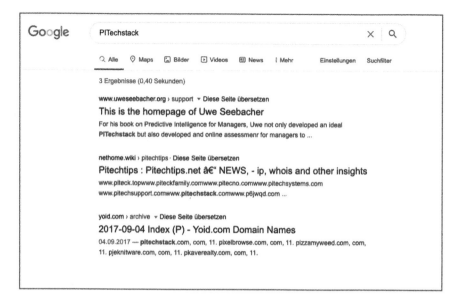

Fig. 7.1 Screenshot of the Google search for "PITechStack"

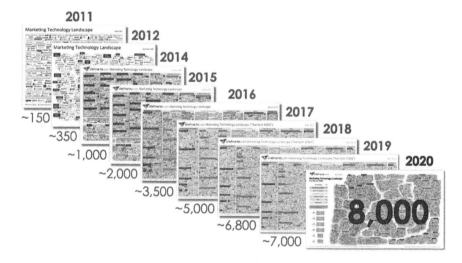

Fig. 7.2 MarTech landscape development 2011–2020 (Source: Chiefmartec.com)

rapidly growing PITech landscape as users and buyers, whether and how a possible solution can support in the current situation.

The impression should by no means be created here that data-driven management necessarily has to be a marketing issue. Ultimately, it is not relevant which department is driving this important topic forward, but rather that it is a department that has the necessary structures and competencies, and, above all, that has a manager with

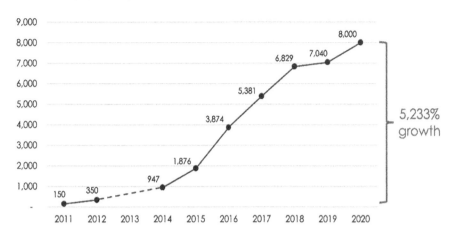

Fig. 7.3 MarTech landscape growth curve (Source: Chiefmartec.com)

the necessary conceptual and methodological experience to successfully implement this topic, which is crucial for sustainable corporate survival. However, in order to be able to discuss and structure the PITechStack in a valid and well-founded way, the developments in the MarTech and SalesTech landscapes are used as a frame of reference and experience. This is done in the context of the assumption that many developments in these two areas can also be transferred to the area of the PITechStack and will take place similarly.

7.2   IT: Quo Vadis?

If one proceeds on the basis of the procedure model for Predictive Intelligence described in this publication, then one must also think about or be aware of developments in the area of information technology in general. Because just as MarTech and SalesTech must always develop within the guidelines of a corporate IT strategy and integrate themselves into it in the best possible way, the PITech must also fit into such a strategic frame of reference. Such organizational IT strategies, like everything else, are subject to the basic principles of organizational etymology. This means that they do not develop in isolation from the environment, but always in coordination and in relation to it.

So where is the journey in the IT sector heading? From the perspective of the year 2020, the following three topics will be addressed in the field of IT:

- Edge Computing
- Blockchain
- Software-based virtualization

Edge Computing is a combination of the English term "edge," meaning border, and computer. In contrast to *Cloud Computing*,[2] Edge Computing describes the decentralized processing of data and information at the edge of a network. Applications, data, and services are thus shifted away from central data centers to the outer areas of a network. The aim here is to process data streams in a resource-conserving manner, either wholly or partially on-site, such as directly at an end device or within a production facility.

7.2.1   What Are the Benefits of Edge Computing?

However, edge computing can still benefit from the advantages of *cloud computing*, in which, technically speaking, IT infrastructures are made available via a computer network without having to be installed on a local end device. Edge computing requires the use of resources that do not have to be permanently connected to an IT network, such as controllers, notebooks, or sensors. However, this also means that such decentralized components must be made *smart*. Edge computing uses numerous technologies such as sensor networks, mobile data acquisition, mobile signature analysis, peer-to-peer and ad hoc networking, and can therefore also be used as an architectural concept for *Internet of Things* (IoT) or *Internet of People* (IoP).

After the Blockchain technology (Iansiti and Lakhani 2017) was somewhat affected by the media in the crypto sector, a change in public perception is slowly taking place. This technology, in which a continuously expandable list of data sets, the blocks, are concatenated with each other using cryptographic methods, is gradually becoming mature for many other use cases. Especially the entry into mainstream areas such as health care is leading to an enormous push for this technology with, for example, universal patient records or the pharmaceutical *chain of custody processes*, in the sense of processes for chronological documentation of evidence.

The increasing validation of the blockchain and the associated non-erasable processes by such new use cases will strongly promote the further spread of this technology. This will also lead to a major change in society's attitude toward blockchain technology, which will result in more and more industries, in addition to the financial industry, making use of the technology. This will contribute to a new dimension of performance, encouraging companies to invest in new and additional ledgers,[3] new general ledgers, to create new and different applications, and to work together on critical, sensitive data sets.

---

[2] https://en.wikipedia.org/wiki/Cloud_computing. November 23, 2020.

[3] https://en.wikipedia.org/wiki/Distributed_ledger. Accessed: November 23, 2020.

7.2.2   With the Blockchain to the PI-Portal

Based on various projects in the area of predictive intelligence and the use of industrial value chains to be able to validly realize the step from absolute to relevant markets, blockchain technology certainly represents a possible alternative. Blockchain, in fact, enables increasingly precise statements about CAPEX and OPEX per section of the respective value chain of interest by means of swarm intelligence. This would enable companies to identify even more precisely how large the de facto relevant and thus accessible market is for an application or product in a country or region.

In contrast to the current situation, where the few pioneers of data-driven management are each individually analyzing and validating the relevant industrial value chains with regard to CAPEX and OPEX, such blockchain-based value chain calculations could be much more effective, dynamic, and, above all, continuously updated and validated at any time for the benefit of all. Thus, not only the providers of data, but also the users and processors of original data would be able to profit enormously from the swarm intelligence. However, the question arises whether companies would be willing to make their unique industry expertise available as part of the swarm intelligence. At first glance, probably not. However, if one considers the general development in the context of the *Sharing Economy* (Frey et al. 2019), such an approach presents itself in a completely different light.

Imagine an institution of a chamber of commerce, whose causal interest lies in the promotion and support of its own member companies in its own country. If such an institution were to make a *predictive intelligence portal available* to its members as part of the member services as *gated content* (Seebacher 2020a, b, c), then one possibility would be to make extended areas of such a portal available free of charge in return for the provision of CAPEX and OPEX values for one or more industrial value chains relevant to the member company.

The social motive of giving and taking and its functioning can be seen more than clear in the area of marketing and the generation of customer inquiries. Potential customers are more than ever ready to give away certain information if they receive something in return. Many *Customer Journeys* (Negovan 2020) in B2B marketing are based on this mechanism and deliver impressive results.

7.2.3   Software-Based Virtualization Is on the Rise

The short to medium term developments described above are also related to the infrastructure, because the continuous improvement in the performance of conventional hardware, software-based virtualization, and micro-service software architectures will eliminate the previous advantage of proprietary, hardware-based *composable architectures*, i.e., IT architectures assembled using hardware. Although a hardware-based, composite architecture is still very often mentioned as the next level of hyper-convergent infrastructures, it will not be able to assert itself against software-based virtualization in the long term due to the slow pace of standardization. This is also against the background of the fact that software-based storage virtualization in combination with concepts and products for software-based and hardware-accelerating computing and network virtualization is just as flexible as that of composite architectures, but at significantly lower costs and with significantly higher performance.

This means that the entire field of IT is characterized by an ever-faster development with regard to the increase of processing and transmission capacities. In this context, it will be important to design any TechStack as early as possible in relation to the expected strategic-conceptual, organization-specific IT development. Conversely, this does not mean purchasing one or more PI solutions as early as possible, as this would involve unnecessary risks. There are two reasons for this: Firstly, at the beginning of the data-driven corporate management measures, the future, own PI-relevant IT requirements can only be defined insufficiently and imprecisely, if at all. Secondly, based on the various project experiences, it will take at least about 2–3 years until a real investment in one or more PI applications will be required. During this period, not only the IT of your own organization will develop significantly, but also the offer or the entire PITechStack. An unnecessarily premature purchase decision in the area of the PITechStack not only burns money, but also involves unnecessary risks that could have an adverse effect on the entire project.

7.3   Where IT Stands in 2030

At this point, we do not want to open the IT Pandora box, as this would go beyond the scope of this publication. However, given that the development of a company's own predictive intelligence is a long-term and strategic project, a look into the distant future of IT should at least provide and ensure the necessary basic knowledge after considering the short to medium-term IT development. In this context, the further comments on the PITechStack can then also be discussed and interpreted.

In the long term, experts anticipate the following significant changes that will shape and change the field of IT and technology:

- From global to local and personal
- From hierarchies and devices to networks and networked people
- From fixed assets to exchangeable, replaceable assets
- From Big Data to algorithmic business
- From resources to intelligent materials

On closer inspection, these trends are obvious. The concept of the *Remocal Economy* (Seebacher 2020a, b, c) and the associated restrengthening of local and regional products and supply chains have experienced an enormous dynamic, especially due to the COVID19 pandemic. However, this emerging return to the local is also due to digitalization, because, paradoxically, it actually makes the world smaller rather than larger.

7.3.1   The Sale Is Dead, Because It Is About H2H

Is not it true that increasing digitalization means that we can access information and data 24/7 almost anywhere in the world? Even small companies can establish a global presence virtually and digitally with few resources and very quickly. Customers of large machine and equipment manufacturers no longer have to wait weeks for a spare part because customers become manufacturers themselves by using 3D printing to produce the spare parts themselves. Many top managers in the old cumbersome industries are still unaware of the enormous pace of change. But can we know that Amazon is not already working on a worldwide network of 3D printing and shipping centers to deliver a replacement part to customers within hours of a need arising? Such a network would disrupt the industry's entire service business, which is so important and high margin, in one fell swoop.

"Technical sales is dead," says the worldwide acknowledged and famous scientist Waldemar Pförtsch in a current episode of the internationally leading B2B marketing podcast,[4] "because the purchase is in reality only a click." In the future, it will be crucial to promote and ensure the transfer of knowledge to the customer, but also and especially to the potential buyer. Only in this way can the trust and relationship with the potential customer be built up and deepened with existing customers under the aspect of Human-to-Human Marketing (H2H) according to Kotler and Pförtsch (2021). In a disruptive world, in which *competitive advantages* are being eliminated ever more quickly and products are being copied ever faster and better, relationship management will experience an enormous renaissance. In the context of a *Remocal Economy*, virtual relationship management will be one of the success factors in a completely changed role of today's technical sales.

This also means that large, conservative, and traditional companies in particular need to be more agile in order to be able to act globally but still have an authentic and stringent local presence. To this end, a simplification and streamlining of organizational structures must take place in the context of eliminating hierarchies in order to be able to act and produce more quickly in a network. The customer no longer wants to wait unnecessarily long for a spare part, as this costs time and money. Also, against the background of *Predictive Service* and *Predictive Maintenance*, the requirements for timely services and delivery will continue to increase.

7.3.2   More Agile with Networks

These changes in terms of organizational structures will also have an impact on IT in 2030, as this area is also undergoing a shift from hierarchical to network structures. The rise of *Peer-to-Peer* (P2P) means that we are moving away from rigid relationships to fluid systems and data markets. Architectures, organizations, and

---

[4]https://podcasts.apple.com/de/podcast/b2b-marketing-guidebook-for-classroom-to-boardroom/id1511875534. Accessed: October 8, 2020.

information will become flattened in terms of complexity, offering more agility and choice. In such P2P networks, all computers and devices have equal rights and can use services bidirectionally but also make them available to others.

P2P networks can be divided into unstructured and structured P2P systems. By 2030, a standard in the sense of a platform technology will have developed and established itself, such as JXTA,[5] which is supported by Sun Microsystems and is open source. On this basis, such networks can exhibit a high degree of heterogeneity and be self-organizing (Steinmetz and Wehrle 2006). This will also be necessary because not only devices and machines will be networked, but also people, whether in fixed or agile structures, will be connected. The *Internet of People* (IoP) thus represents the last mile, which will be stringently closed, since even in the context of the triumphal procession of artificial intelligence it is assumed that ultimately, humans will continue to make decisions and initiate measures.

Nevertheless, the networking of machines, that is, currently taking place will continue in the networking of people. However, just as one or more standards for networking and communication will then be required on the technical level, a uniform, common and generally valid, and understandable level of interaction between networked people will also be necessary, such as Template-based Management (TBM, Seebacher 2020a, b, c). This is because the increasing virtuality of all actions and the elimination of personal interaction will make the standardization of information transfer more important in order to ensure the corresponding information and communication efficiency and effectiveness.

7.3.3   Full Speed Ahead into the Netflix Economy

The omnipresence of data and information will be introduced in line with the increasing networking of machines and people. This brings with it a completely new value in terms of data and information, because it is no longer the machines that represent the important assets as asset components, but the associated data and information. It is less about owning a product or a machine, but rather about being able to benefit from it without a large investment. What began in car leasing at the end of the old millennium is now spilling over to the industry, where machines are no longer purchased but are paid for as a service depending on the respective capacity utilization.

The *Netflix economy* (Müller 2019) is characterized by borrowing everything possible and not buying anything more. Products are interchangeable. In this environment, trust and reputation can be replaced by social recommendations and prestige. Not having to buy products any more brings many decisive advantages for all those involved. For about 5 years now, the "as-a-service" industry (AAS) has increasingly been part of the strategic discussions even in large companies. Originally from the telecommunications industry, where cell phones were no longer sold

---

[5]https://en.wikipedia.org/wiki/JXTA. Accessed: November 23, 2020.

but given away as "freebies" under a 24-month contract, "Software-as-a-Service" (SaaS) emerged and is now spilling over into many other industries. The Netflix economy thrives on customer data, which can be used as the basis for proposing new series and films. Amazon and Google use our data and our intelligence to make a billion dollar business—directly by recommending other products to us, which in most cases are bought, and indirectly because this data is sold to other companies for a lot of money. As the amount of data increases, predictive intelligence and its precision is also improving.

Customer loyalty is the magic word in the context of Human-to-Human (H2H). Instead of selling a cell phone as an individual item, the customer is bound to the company for 24 months. On the other hand, we see a similar development as in the first years of company and company car leasing. Customers no longer need to buy company cars for their employees. Leasing is plannable, involves less administrative effort and is also much better for the company cash flow from a financial point of view. Finally, the car manufacturer extended its value chain by also making money through the leasing business, and customers optimized their cash flow by not having to buy the cars. So why not lease out large machines and equipment? Figure 7.4 schematically shows a model for the "leasing model" of the automotive industry transferred to the industry—*Equipment-as-a-Service* (EaaS).

EaaS brings tremendous benefits to all parties involved in the Netflix industry, to the end customers of the products (end user), the product manufacturer (PM) of the end product, and the machine and equipment builder (EM). The advantages for the end customers can be summarized as follows:

- No delays in delivery of the end product due to minimized or even eliminated PM downtime.
- Higher, better, and more consistent quality level of the final product due to PM's optimally maintained systems and machines.

The advantages for the product manufacturer can be summarized as follows:

- Optimized cash flow and balance sheet as the machines and the equipment do not have to be paid at once in one big lump sum.
- Possibility to adjust production capacity timelier and flexibly in regard to market demand and needs.
- Depending on service agreement with EM, 24/7 monitoring and remote monitoring of all machines, ensuring comprehensive risk management and coverage of the entire machine, predictable service intervals based on intelligent and proactive service, resulting in lower service and repair costs
- Continuously optimized plant efficiency and performance made possible through interactive, extensive data acquisition by EM and related cluster analysis and deviation evaluation, which means that relevant plant parameters can be adjusted not only for specific machines but for the entire plant value chain in order to always achieve the best output of the production process, thus reducing energy consumption and extending the service life of the machines in use.

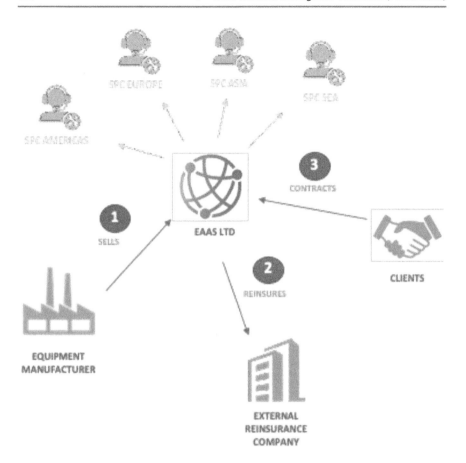

Fig. 7.4 Structure of the EaaS business model (Source: Own presentation)

And last but not least, the advantages for the machine and plant manufacturer are to be listed. We consider EaaS only in the narrowest sense, where the machine and plant manufacturer does not conduct the financing business itself, although it is a substantially good new business model:

- The machine and plant manufacturer can increase sales even in difficult times, because the product manufacturers only have to raise the monthly payments, which are much smaller than the large lump sum payments for the purchase of such equipment.
- Within the framework of the warranty agreements, the machine and plant manufacturer is given 24/7 access to the devices and data, which enables him to use the data to continuously work on the optimization and further development of the systems.
- The machine and plant manufacturer is transformed into a partner instead of being a mere seller of machines, which helps to create trust and a long-term customer

relationship, which also has a positive effect on the customer experience and customer loyalty.

All in all, this entire EaaS model is a great benefit for all the players involved. But it requires in-depth knowledge of the specific systems and machines, and the various application areas and their implications. In 2030, networked people and machines will use and pay for data and information as well as machines and devices depending on their performance with a network-based, agile and flexible IT. As a result, the entire economic activity will experience a new dimension of dynamism, as large investments will be replaced by many, small and ongoing payments, and capacities can be increased or minimized depending on the situation.

7.3.4   From Big Data to Smart Data

This increasing networking of machines and people inevitably means that enormous amounts of data must be collected, processed, and stored. In the future, the challenge will shift from quantity to quality. *Big Data* as a buzzword has found its way into all areas, but it distorts the picture because it implies that the largest possible amount of data is to be considered desirable, which in fact has only limited validity in the context of predictive intelligence.

Because with billions of connected devices and things, the analysis of the huge amounts of information is becoming more and more crucial, and above all the ex ante identification of relevant information. Such differentiation can make large amounts of data more efficient and effective to process. Organizations and people will ask themselves who has access to which data and how it is used. As has been discussed several times before, it is crucial that all parties involved know where the data comes from, how it is prepared and processed, so that it can be understood and interpreted correctly. This can only be achieved through a gradual process, in which such an environment is created on the basis of the procedural model for Predictive Intelligence. After all, a transparent and coordinated understanding of the data is crucial when the level of artificial intelligence is added, which then turns Big Data into *Smart Data.*

Smart Data (Wierse and Riedel 2017) are data that are extracted from large amounts of data using algorithms according to specific structures. Artificial algorithms then build on these natural algorithms to make increasingly precise multivariate predictions. In this way, data-driven companies will be the first to build their business success on predictive-algorithmic business. In turn, this is only possible if the required historical data from the various data sources and systems are available in sufficient quality and quantity to enable extrapolations and predictions based on it.

7.3.5   From Resources to Smart Materials

But not only data become intelligent, but also the production factors in terms of the materials used. Completely new types of materials with intelligent substances, storage materials, graphene, polymers, and nanocomposites will be created, which will also generate and contribute data and information to enable further developments. This is where materials science is becoming increasingly important. The combination of Smart Data and Smart Materials will also create *Smart Value Chains*, which in the context of the *New Green Deal* according to Rifkin and the *Remocal Economy* according to Seebacher will contribute more and more to a *Smart Economy*. Intelligent value chains are constantly optimizing themselves in terms of process and material production inputs. Smart sensor networks will gradually move toward quantified self-analysis and thus operate continuous input and output optimization.

In this way, economic activity is continuously developed by integrating smart infrastructures and information technologies. In the economy and the new workforces of 2030, the most successful companies will stringently and sustainably optimize the use of all their resources, both human and machine, for a competitive advantage. However, an increasingly large proportion of the workforce will not be human. But although machines are better than human workforces in terms of consistency, performance, predictability, efficiency, and safety, they will still be unable to match human capabilities in terms of ingenuity, novelty, art, creativity, emotion, variability, and context in 2030.

In 2030, access to data from different sources will be virtually unlimited and *digital ethics* will be the key to success. As everything is interconnected and there are billions of intelligent machines, the opportunities to do the wrong thing will increase rapidly and will be far too easy to do with just a few clicks.

7.4   What We Can Learn from the MarTechstack?

In most cases, looking beyond the horizon opens up new perspectives. In order to be able to discuss and evaluate possible developments in the area of the PITechStack, one comes across the rapidly developing area of the MarTechStack in the course of the search for reference models. The IT landscape in marketing, just like that of the PITechStack, is closely linked to a rapid increase in available data. If, in the area of marketing, the various dimensions of internal and external information on the *buyer journey* are used to quantify and qualify relevant needs and requirements, the PITechStack presents a very similar picture—only the areas of markets and production processes are added as additional data dimensions.

Because in the area of the PITechStack, the subject area of *Procurement Intelligence* must also be covered in order to be able to predict the business in the best possible way using predictive algorithms. On the basis of the rapidly developing IT landscape for Business Analytics and Business Intelligence that has begun to develop in recent years, it can be assumed that the enormous market potential in

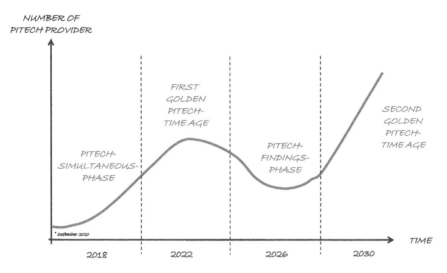

Fig. 7.5 Development of the PITechStack (Source: Own representation based on Scott Brinker, www.chiefmartec.com)

the area of the PITechStack will not remain hidden from current and many new providers. Since 2018, we have been in the first phase of the four-step process for the development of the PITechStack (Fig. 7.5). Gradually, more and more suppliers with PI-relevant applications and products are being found. As already described in the chapter on the PI ecosystem, this phase is characterized by many different, inconsistent terms and designations. The different providers try to achieve everything that can be found in the market by using as much term agility as possible, which can be found in inexperienced, but trial-and-error interested parties and thus potential customers. The first providers are already internally engaged in the revision and evaluation of their own strategy in order to be able to adapt to the new market conditions.

The problem or rather the challenge that *first mover* providers face is that dashboard solutions are developing like sand on the sea and therefore an important aspect of the preparation of data and information can be realized more and more cost efficiently and easily. In addition, data is also becoming available 24/7 more quickly, which in turn has a positive effect on the time and effort required for analysis and research, as everything can be found much more quickly and easily.

7.4.1   Why the Consulting Industry Is Disrupted?

Many of the first PITechStack providers were consulting and analysis companies. Many changes are per se underway in the area of these companies. The big shifts and upheavals began when the *Cyber Economy* and the *Cyber Commerce* emerged. The large, well-established and very conservative consulting brands felt the first shock waves that sent the many 20-year-old entrepreneurs and their dot.coms soaring into the economic stratosphere. The tried and tested techniques used by these analyses and consulting firms began to feel outdated, as the web pushed business models and thinking in new directions for which old methods had no contingency plan.

New consulting firms and consultants appeared to fill the vacuum in the consulting industry. The sheer size and organizational structure of the more conservative brand consulting firms made rapid changes and adjustments almost impossible. Today, even the former large consulting firms have mutated into workbenches and earn their money primarily as IT implementation partners.

> Management consulting is a 250 billion dollar industry. It is big. It is growing. It is highly profitable. And it's about to be disrupted.[6]

Soren Kaplan,[7] one of the leading management thought leaders, summed it up when he analyzed the consulting industry. He predicted that any mature industry would be disrupted, and as management consulting reached a mature status, it became vulnerable. Kaplan identifies vulnerabilities within the industry that will bring down the entire industry of analysts, consultants and consultants. He identifies five major flaws in the consulting business that are causing this decline:

- Consulting is a business with human beings and therefore labor intensive.
- The Consulting business model uses billable time to maximize revenue.
- The advisory industry does not offer products, but people, and the fees for consultants are often an incredible multiple of what they earn themselves, which makes consultants an undesirable evil, since everyone in the client company knows the man-day rates charged for these "juniors."
- The ever-faster dynamism of our world leads to a decreasing half-life of knowledge, facts, and figures, which means that analysts and consultants must deliver more timely results, which affects quality and validity, in an increasingly complex and demanding environment.
- The *Remocal Economy* also drives the dissemination and democratization of knowledge and simply everything else, which means that the previously well-guarded consulting secrets such as models, templates, and tools are now accessible around the clock and everyone can apply best practices themselves.

New, disruptive companies and business models are characterized by offering better and more convenient solutions at a much lower price or even for free, as Erik Brynjolfsson and Avinash Collins (2020) recently pointed out in their Harvard Business Manager paper "The Value of the Digital Economy." They introduce a

---

[6]https://www.inc.com/soren-kaplan/the-business-consulting-industry-is-booming-and-it.html. Accessed: 9 June 2020.

[7]https://en.wikipedia.org/wiki/Soren_Kaplan. Accessed: 9 June 2020.

new parameter, the GDP-B,[8] as an alternative measure that also evaluates the benefits of digital free products. Their hypothesis is that for services such as the search engine Google or the online encyclopedia Wikipedia, individuals would normally be willing to pay a monthly fee instead of not being able to use these tools. Their research has shown that search engines are the most valuable services, followed by e-mail programs and online maps.

7.4.2 What MarTech and SalesTech Teach Us?

There are three major developments that are currently changing the field of MarTech. They will terminate the end of the "first golden age of Martech" and in the following period of reflection they will lay the foundation for a second golden age, which will offer enormous potential but will probably look completely different. The future of Martech from 2022 onwards will be as follows:

- *Ecosystems*: Instead of talking about *cloud suites* and *best-of-breed* point solutions, the best of both worlds will be available in congruence with the major developments in IT described above: open platforms that serve as a stable base and are extended by large ecosystems of specialized third-party applications, but which are more deeply integrated.
- *Experts*: The distinction between software vendors and professional consulting firms will become blurred. Software companies will start to offer more expert services and analysis and consulting firms will automate their expertise and map it into software.
- *Engineers*: In the context of the major changes in IT discussed earlier, the omnipresence of data and information and increasing digitalization, any company, however, industrial, will inevitably become a software company. Against this background, these organizations will develop and launch their own commercial platforms with customized applications for customers and products, in most cases in-house with their own employees or their own IT department.

These are exactly the same trends that can already be observed in the context of the PITechStack. This is despite the fact that the development of the PITechStack is estimated to be 5–8 years behind that of the MarTechStack. The origins of the PITechSTack can be found in today's Business Intelligence IT solutions. However, the PITech area benefits from the knowledge and experience of MarTech and, above all, from the general developments in the entire IT industry, which are currently primarily concerned with IT structural aspects.

In the context of the already described and introduced process model for Predictive Intelligence, this is based on the IT and PITech-related contingency situation. It is essential to delay the point in time for PITech-relevant decisions as much as

---

[8]Gross Domestic Product Benefit.

possible until on the one hand the first mature phase of the PITech landscape is consolidated by the necessary first clean-up and on the other hand one's own organizational PI competence has matured enough to be able to make a sustainable, correct decision in this context. The adjustment leads to a higher transparency of the truly value-adding products and solutions in the area of PI and the resulting own knowledge helps to develop a profound PITech landscape in the context of the subject area but also the company's own IT strategy.

7.4.3   Away from the "Or" to the "And," and Yet Less Is More!

Whoever buys too early loses. If you look at the development of the MarTech over time, it turns out that everything becomes easier and cheaper if you take your time regarding the development of the MarTechStack. Like a jigsaw puzzle, all the pieces fit together beautifully to form a large whole. This is also due to the increasing sensitivity and sensitivity to the subject area of modern marketing, which automatically arises during the course of the project.

At the beginning of a PI project, many of the customers have only an insufficiently deep understanding of the relevant topic area, which is why a company's own "PI identity" in the sense of its own PI understanding should first be developed in order to be able to make the right decision regarding one or more PI products, at least in the long term. For a long time, it was the "either-or" in the MarTech field, but today's MarTech landscape is characterized by an "and," because the flexibility and agility of the many different MarTech products have increased enormously and almost everything is possible, networkable, and combinable. In addition, the advantage is that with regard to the PITechStack, it has become clear that much smaller ecosystems are required and ideal compared to the MarTech and SalesTech. On the basis of a schematic SalesTech-Blueprint (Fig. 7.6), it is easy to see how complex and extensive a sales IT landscape can look.

How an ideal B2B-MarTech should look like and how it can be set up is described in detail in the B2B Marketing Guidebook (Seebacher 2020a, b, c). However, this important process is discussed and outlined from a structural and contingency-theoretical perspective, because there is no one right MarTechStack. It is crucial that such an IT structure grows congruently with the topic-specific maturity level of the organization concerned, because only then can the blueprint be meaningfully integrated into an existing one and successfully connected to an existing IT infrastructure. If you search the Internet under the keyword "MarTech Blueprint" in the hope of finding such a structural diagram, you will not find what you are looking for. The different graphics naturally depict the facts from different perspectives. A very well functionally structured representation is that of Scott Brinker (Fig. 7.7), which dates from 2018 and precisely for this reason still provides a very clear overview.

In recent years, the entire MarTechStack has grown rapidly, as has already been explained several times, with the result that even proven MarTech experts easily lose track of the situation. The challenge with regard to the definition and establishment of a meaningful PITechStack is that the relevant subject area "data" (Fig. 7.8), as one

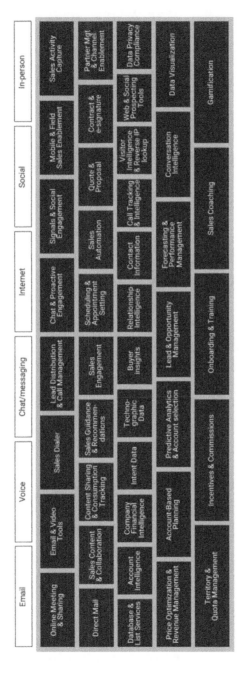

Fig. 7.6 Structural representation of SalesTechStack (Source: https://www.saleshacker.com/salestech-landscape-2019/)

Fig. 7.7 MarTechStack Blueprint (Source: https://chiefmartec.com/2018/04/martech-enabled-marketing-operations-invisible-roads-bridges/)

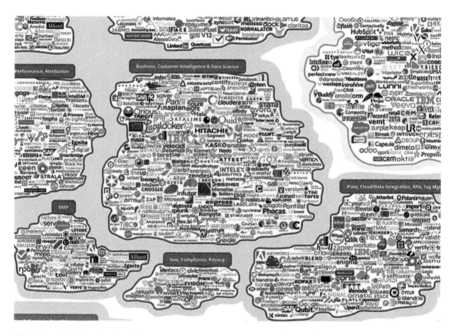

Fig. 7.8 Solutions in the field of "Intelligence & Data" (Business and Customer Intelligence and Data Science) in MarTech (Source: https://cdn.chiefmartec.com/wp-content/uploads/2020/04/martech-landscape-2020-martech5000-slide.jpg)

of six subject areas of the MarTech landscape, has grown most strongly since 2019, at 25.5%. Currently, more than 1200 relevant products and solutions fall into this area. The red lantern with a growth rate of only 4.1% is carried by the subject area "Advertising & Promotion." However, all these changes are currently taking place in

MarTech, i.e., the marketing IT-related environment per se, and not in the PITech landscape.

And it is not only that "Intelligence & Data" relevant applications can be found in the MarTech landscape, because there is also a "Sales Intelligence" area in the environment of the SalesTech, mapping sales and sales-oriented IT solutions (Fig. 7.9).

In the area of SalesTech, the company DiscoverOrg has established itself as one of the players in the field of Sales Intelligence with the acquisition of RainKing and Zoominfo. In addition, two new clusters have emerged in the SalesTech, namely the providers of *Intent Data* (Fig. 7.10) and *Relationship Intelligence*, which were previously grouped together under the topic areas of *Account Intelligence* and *Buyer Insights*. Intent Data as information on purchase intentions but also on certain behavioral patterns have become an important aspect of account-based approaches and to support the prioritization of sales efforts. While *social selling* continues to grow in importance, most companies still have problems with it, as LinkedIn inboxes are clogged with irrelevant messages and inquiries from strangers. In this context, contact initiation by a mutual acquaintance is regaining importance and with it the field of *relationship intelligence* solutions (Fig. 7.11).

But not everything that has "Intelligence" in the name automatically falls within the scope of the PITechStack, which becomes very clear from the *Sales Intelligence* area (Fig. 7.12) of the SalesTech landscape.

On the basis of the different illustrations, it becomes clear that there is de facto one or many different corresponding IT solutions for basically everything. It also becomes transparent that the respective, topic-specific offer is subject to an enormous dynamism, which leads to a rapid increase in the number of possible alternatives. Conversely, this means that those responsible for PI have to delve even deeper into the subject matter of PI in order to separate the wheat from the chaff and thus distinguish between what is useful and what is superfluous.

7.5   The Three Phases of the PITechStack

The art is to make life as easy as possible and always know just enough to be dangerous. In the figurative sense and in connection with the PITechStack, this means that one should be able to start working on the topic without additional resources and budgets if possible, then show first successes and results, and only then be able to validly prepare and make necessary investment decisions based on the professional knowledge that has arisen. After all, the earlier you acquire a relevant application in the sense of a PI-IT solution, the greater the risk of not making the right choice.

It is similar to buying a wardrobe for an infant, where you are forced to buy one in the knowledge that within a very short time the garment you are buying will be too small again. Or as a novice in white sports, tennis. If you immediately decide on a beginner's racquet, then in 2 years at the most, the change to a better, but less

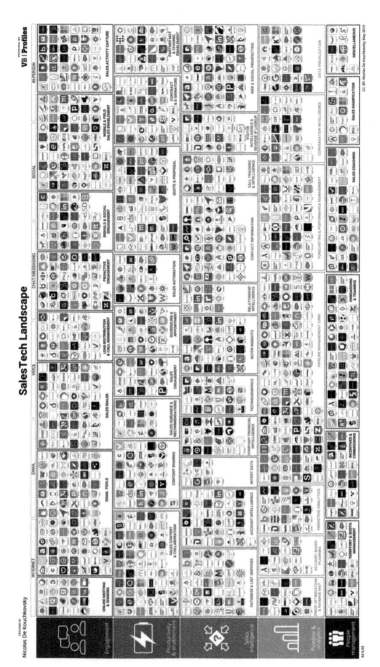

Fig. 7.9 SalesTech Overview om "Intelligence" solutions 2019 (Source: https://www.saleshacker.com/salestech-landscape-2019/)

Fig. 7.10 Provider "Intent Data" (Source: https://www.saleshacker.com/salestech-landscape-2019/)

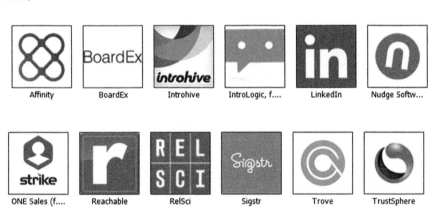

Fig. 7.11 Provider "Relationship Intelligence" (Source: https://www.saleshacker.com/salestech-landscape-2019/)

forgiving racquet for advanced players will be on the agenda. This is a normal process of development.

You will also go through this process if you develop and establish the subject area for an organization based on the process model for Predictive Intelligence. Because by taking the initiative, one does not mutate into a co-driver of PITechStack providers, but into a mature and competent PITechStack manager and in this context into a competent acquirer of a sensible and relevant application from the current PITechStack landscape. In this way, IT becomes an enabler, and one is and remains the driver of Predictive Intelligence, even with a possible small PI team.

This also means, however, that you should remain independent of IT for as long as possible in order not to waste your own powder in terms of your budget at an early stage. Hopefully, the examples from everyday life have made it clear that an

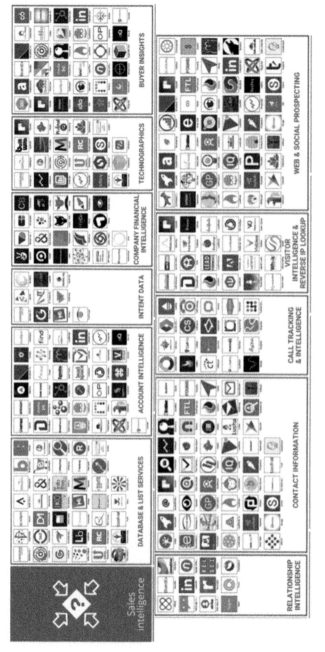

Fig. 7.12 Provider Sales Intelligence (Source: https://www.saleshacker.com/salestech-landscape-2019/)

unnecessarily early decision can lead to the recognition of having made the wrong purchase or suddenly finding oneself in an unnecessary dependency (Shapiro and Varian 1998). Against this background and the many different PI projects, the three-step concept described below was developed, which is in congruence with the PI procedure model and can therefore be applied jointly.

This procedural concept is by no means the blueprint for an ideal PITechStack, but rather a "template" for a goal and resource-oriented approach for the best possible, sustainable development of the understanding of and meaningful establishment of an organization-specific, ideal PITechStack. The following three phases can be defined:

- Excelling
- Connecting
- Shopping

These three phases are briefly described in more detail below and it is also defined how to recognize that one has successfully completed a phase.

7.5.1 The Excelling

The term is derived from the common Microsoft spreadsheet solution *Excel*. Because in this first phase of the PITechStack, it is only about learning the PI-technical "walking" on a small scale with existing software. It is about understanding data and structures. In addition, the first internal or external data must be recorded or manually entered from other source systems. After the acquisition, the focus should be on an initial data model. In the context of such a, by no means, easy task, everything that has to be learned additionally in the sense of a software solution is an unnecessary complication. Even though MS Excel may seem familiar, experience from many different PI projects has shown that even experienced Excel experts can achieve an impressive learning curve in dealing with Excel and the first data sets to be processed.

It is about questions how to connect data or which function can be used to determine the expected result. In this way, multilayered learning steps take place, the structural characteristics of which can be directly transferred to any further application purchased in the third "shopping" phase.

The Excelling phase is thus about taking the first steps toward business analytics and intelligence in a familiar application environment. For these first activities, de facto no additional IT applications are required, as it can be assumed that every company today uses one of the common data and word processing systems. Based on the activities described in the section "Where does the shoe pinch?" as part of Phase 1 in the previous chapter, the first tables are easily created and refined. Depending on the situation, one starts with a geographical region or country, as shown in Figs. 7.13 and 7.14.

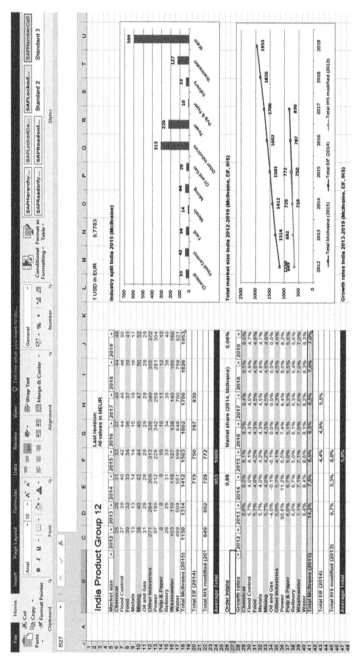

Fig. 7.13 Example of a simple country sheet (Source: Own representation)

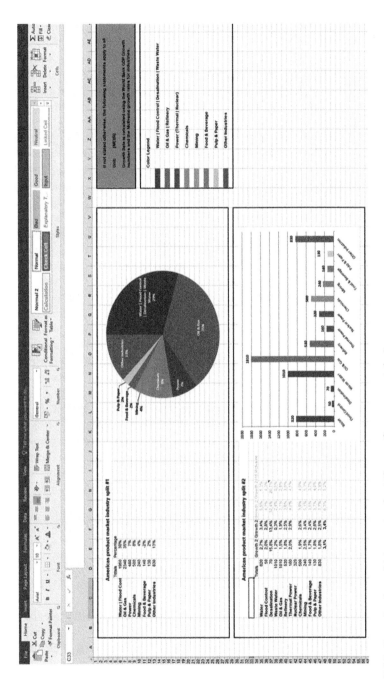

Fig. 7.14 Example of a multiple country sheet (Source: Own representation)

Step by step, a more comprehensive spreadsheet will then be created, which will include more and more dimensions. Formulas will be used as well as filter functions to automatically develop the user experience further (Fig. 7.15). It becomes clear that this is not rocket science, but rather back-breaking work. However, this is unavoidable at the beginning, since only in this way can the necessary basic knowledge be built and developed within the team. In the beginning, it is only a matter of learning or deepening the handling of data with existing applications. The focus must be uncompromisingly placed on this in order to be able to proceed efficiently and effectively.

As country segment tables grow, countries can be grouped into geographical regions, which can be stored and displayed in separate sheets within the respective file (Fig. 7.16). The decisive factor is that this is a creative-iterative process that is required to authentically develop the subject area of business analytics as part of organizational predictive intelligence. If in this phase the fatal mistake is made to have such tables created by external experts, the essential basis is missing. Even if the certainly competent, external expert can provide a wonderful introduction to the created Excel spreadsheet, it is no longer original, own work results, but external secondary ones. The difference is comparable to the situation of telling someone how it feels to burn and when someone burns himself once. The own, intrinsic learning experience has a different value and sustainability.

The *Excelling* phase also includes the careful selection of relevant external data providers. Step by step, the first sample data are to be incorporated into the Excel tableau and evaluated. The first activities for combining data from different data sources are also included in this phase, as is the initial graphical preparation of elaborated information. This graphic work should not be underestimated, since in this way the sensitivity with respect to data, dimension, and creation of a consistent and simple presentation can be trained and optimized on-the-job. If such graphics are purchased, then again, this important step of insight and learning, which is so important in the long run, is missing. However, this step is crucial when it comes to the efficient and effective design of user group-specific, interactive dashboards. Valid data is only one side of the coin, because a quickly understandable and clear preparation of information is at least as important in order to be able to provide internal customers with the best possible service.

The *Excelling* phase is successfully completed when the following criteria are met:

- First tables are created and graphically prepared.
- First external data are selected, possibly partially purchased, manually integrated, processed, and integrated.
- First analyses and reports to internal customers were played out and feedback was incorporated.
- The number of inquiries is slowly increasing and the awareness of the data issue in the organization is developing positively.

Country split	Detailed region split	Region split	Main region split	Water 2014	Flood Control 20..	Desalination 2..	Waste water 201..	Food & Beverage 201..	Pulp & Paper 2014	Mining 201..	Oil & Gas 201..	Refinery 201..
Germany	Western Europe	Europe	EMEA	264.0	13.6	0.0	370.5	82.6	25.6	23.5	9.2	35.0
France	Western Europe	Europe	EMEA	127.6	5.6	0.0	184.2	35.3	7.5	3.2	5.0	24.5
Italy	Western Europe	Europe	EMEA	77.4	3.9	1.1	163.4	18.3	4.3	0.5	6.7	24.0
Switzerland	Western Europe	Europe	EMEA	29.1	1.6	0.0	48.3	4.3	2.2	4.6	0.7	1.8
Austria	Western Europe	Europe	EMEA	22.2	1.0	0.0	40.1	9.4	4.6	0.9	3.0	2.0
Western Europe	Benelux	Europe	EMEA	540	26	1	806	150	44	33	25	87
Netherlands	Benelux	Europe	EMEA	28.7	1.0	0.0	45.1	12.2	1.6	2.1	9.7	10.7
Luxembourg	Benelux	Europe	EMEA	1.7	0.1	0.0	1.1	0.2	0.1	0.0	0.0	0.0
Belgium	Benelux	Europe	EMEA	20.5	0.7	0.0	28.0	8.5	2.3	2.5	0.0	8.2
Benelux	Nordic Countries	Europe	EMEA	49	2	0	74	21	4	5	10	19
Sweden	Nordic Countries	Europe	EMEA	29.9	1.1	0.0	35.0	7.5	21.5	24.2	0.0	10.3
Norway	Nordic Countries	Europe	EMEA	10.2	0.6	0.0	11.1	2.8	2.1	1.5	76.7	4.7
Denmark	Nordic Countries	Europe	EMEA	34.7	0.7	0.0	43.5	15.1	0.8	5.7	10.9	8.7
Finland	Nordic Countries	Europe	EMEA	12.0	0.5	0.0	20.2	3.3	10.0	2.4	0.0	3.2
Iceland	Nordic Countries	Europe	EMEA	1.0	0.0	0.0	0.6	0.1	0.0	0.0	0.0	0.0
Nordic Countries	Spain & Portugal	Europe	EMEA	86	2.3	2.2	110	29	24	34	88	27
Spain	Spain & Portugal	Europe	EMEA	46.4	2.1	2.2	58.6	13.4	4.6	3.7	0.4	11.5
Portugal	Spain & Portugal	Europe	EMEA	5.9	0.3	0.0	7.5	2.6	1.6	1.3	1.0	2.4
Spain & Portugal	UK & Ireland	Europe	EMEA	52	2	2	66	16	6	6	1	14
United Kingdom	UK & Ireland	Europe	EMEA	97.0	4.3	0.0	174.9	29.4	5.7	2.5	40.6	21.7
Ireland	UK & Ireland	Europe	EMEA	8.0	0.3	0.0	10.5	2.2	0.2	2.1	1.7	0.6
UK & Ireland	Eastern Europe	Europe	EMEA	105	5	0	185	32	6	5	42	22
Poland	Eastern Europe	Europe	EMEA	34.8	1.3	0.0	33.5	5.4	2.5	14.6	5.5	6.8
Czech Republic	Eastern Europe	Europe	EMEA	9.7	0.4	0.0	21.9	3.6	0.9	1.3	0.4	3.7
Slovak Republic	Eastern Europe	Europe	EMEA	3.1	0.2	0.0	6.9	0.5	0.8	0.0	0.0	0.5
Georgia	Eastern Europe	Europe	EMEA	0.4	0.0	0.0	0.1	0.1	0.1	0.1	0.1	0.2
Lithuania	Eastern Europe	Europe	EMEA	1.2	0.1	0.0	0.2	0.2	0.1	0.1	0.3	0.6
Latvia	Eastern Europe	Europe	EMEA	0.8	0.1	0.0	0.1	0.1	0.0	0.1	0.2	0.4
Estonia	Eastern Europe	Europe	EMEA	0.7	0.1	0.0	0.1	0.1	0.0	0.1	0.2	0.4
Eastern Europe	SEE	Europe	EMEA	81	2	1.7	63	10	4	16	1	13
Turkey	SEE	Europe	EMEA	60.0	3.7	1.7	53.3	12.3	2.2	1.1	2.3	17.0
Greece	SEE	Europe	EMEA	7.8	0.5	0.0	11.4	1.8	0.2	1.1	0.0	3.8
Romania	SEE	Europe	EMEA	8.6	0.2	0.0	27.2	1.9	1.7	1.2	9.2	2.8
Hungary	SEE	Europe	EMEA	9.0	0.3	0.0	12.2	4.5	0.6	3.0	7.8	3.4
Bulgaria	SEE	Europe	EMEA	4.3	0.2	0.0	8.1	0.4	1.3	1.2	3.7	1.2
Slovenia	SEE	Europe	EMEA	1.3	0.1	0.0	0.2	0.2	0.1	0.1	0.4	0.7
Serbia	SEE	Europe	EMEA	1.2	0.1	0.0	0.2	0.2	0.1	0.1	0.3	0.6
Croatia	SEE	Europe	EMEA	1.6	0.2	0.0	0.2	0.3	0.1	0.1	0.5	0.8
Cyprus	SEE	Europe	EMEA	0.5	0.1	0.8	0.2	0.1	0.1	0.0	0.2	0.3
Bosnia and Herzegovina	SEE	Europe	EMEA	0.5	0.0	0.0	0.1	0.1	0.0	0.0	0.1	0.3

Fig. 7.15 Example of a country segment table (Source: Own representation)

Fig. 7.16 Example of an outline of a market-region table (Source: Own representation)

7.5.2 The Connecting

The focus of the second phase *Connecting* in the context of the development of a PITechStack lies in the development and, subsequently, the automation of the connection of the various relevant data sources to the PI data model. While in the first phase the main focus was on manually performing all activities, the understanding and basis for automated integration of the first data supply systems should be available by now.

Ideally, you start with systems that are already in place in the organization, such as the CRM and ERP systems. These systems can provide essential information regarding customers, which means that we are already at the second stage with regard to the Predictive Intelligence Maturity Model (Fig. 6.4). The *Proactive-situational Business Analytics* stage is characterized by an increase in the speed of reaction but also in the significantly more comprehensive data volumes. Anything that therefore no longer needs to be processed manually will continue to save time and thus increase PI efficiency and effectiveness.

On the basis of experience, it has been shown that, in addition to the connection of internal data sources, the first external databases have also been connected to PI infrastructures by means of automatic interfaces or data crawlers. This is mostly the case in larger organizations where global markets are involved and it is already clear at an early stage of predictive intelligence which are the relevant and valid database providers, from whom up-to-date data is required on a continuous basis anyway.

Some core industries have been extensively developed in various projects and on this basis, different sets of possible, relevant database providers for these industries crystallized, which are presented in Table 7.1.

Particularly with external data sources, the company's own IT department must be selectively involved in the second phase at the latest when it comes to automatic interfaces and data integration, where company firewalls must be overcome. This means that a bigger wheel has to be turned and that questions about the necessity of such a step may suddenly be expected from various departments. This makes it all the more important in this context to be already deeply rooted in the matter and to have a very precise knowledge of what data is really needed for what purpose.

Once again, the authentic and stringent development of the relevant topic area has a positive effect, since against this background one can always provide competent and objective information and take a stand. If you are not able to do so, there is a danger that the topic becomes an exchange between the in-house IT department and the external data provider(s) and you yourself are only the co-driver of the topic.

This second phase can be considered completed if the following criteria are met:

• The organization's CRM system is connected to the PI data model.

Table 7.1 Overview of selected database providers

Automotive	Construction	Chemicals	Processing	Oil and Gas	General
Auto.com	American Chemical Society	AdhesivesMag	BSRIA	American Chemical Society	Bloomberg
Automotive.com	ChemArc	American Chemical Society	China Construction Machinery	Argus Media	Capital IQ
Automotive Insight#	Chemical Weekly	Colin Houston	Construction Week Online	Bloomberg NEF	Factset
Automotive Industry Today	Colin Houston	ChemArc	Data Group Asia	Chemical Weekly	IMF
Automotive News	Drug Master File	Chemical Weekly	Elevator and Escalator	Clarksons Platou	Industry Association
Automotive World	Euromonitor International	CESIO	Euroconstruct	Clipper Data	Lexis Nexis
Business Online	European Food Safety Authority	Construction Week	European Lift Association	EIA	Naviga
China Construction Index	Food and Drug Administration	Coatings World	IHS Global Insight	Energy Aspects	Orbis
Data Group Asia	ICIS	Drug Master File	McIlvaine	Energy Intelligence	US National Institute of Health
JD Power	IHS Markit	ERASM	Navigant	Euromonitor International	World Bank
Just.auto.com	Nexant	Euromonitor International	Project Today	Evaluate Energy	
McGraw Hill Construction	Pharma Compass	European Food Safety Authority		ICIS	
PMR	Platts	Food and Drug Administration		IEA	
Prnewswire	PubChem	ICIS		IHS Markit	
Project Today	Teknon Orbichem	IHS Markit		Industrial Info Resources	
The Construction Index		Nexant		JLC	
TheCarConnection.com		OMCIS International		JODI	
Wards Auto		PCI		Kpler	
		PharmaCompas		Nexant	
		PubChem		Oil and Gas Journal	
		Teknon Orbichem		Oilytics	
				OPEC	
				Oxford Institute of Energy Studies	
				Platts	
				Poten	
				PubChem	
				Rystad Energy	
				Wood Mackenzie	

Source: Own presentation

- Automatically defined data and information on customers can also be migrated from the ERP system to the PI data model.
- Data from external, validated, and selected providers, which are needed regularly and always up to date, are connected to the PI data model via automated interfaces (API).
- The main part of the activities shifts from identifying, selecting, and aggregating data to processing and evaluating the information and editing and elaborating more complex and extensive analyses, reports, profitability studies, and strategy papers.

7.5.3   The Shopping

If the criteria described above are met, then the homework is done. The necessary knowledge of data modeling and data processing is available, as is the relevant competence to classify and evaluate products and providers in the field of predictive intelligence, the PITechStack landscape. In the meantime, the PI data model has also become a powerful and extremely valuable instrument, which also makes appropriate precautionary measures appear sensible from an IT perspective. In this context, aspects of the system's performance must also be taken into consideration.

At this point, it makes sense to think about relevant investments with regard to the PITechStack. On the one hand, the Sturm-und-Drang time has now passed in the development of the PITech landscape and one can assume that there is a mature offering of really valid and functioning PITech solutions. On the other hand, one can refer to an organization-inherent PI identity, against whose background possible decisions regarding new, additional PITech products can be made seriously and with a view to their sustainability.

The PI-TechStack does not necessarily have to consist solely of its own applications but can also make sense by using or being linked to solutions from existing SalesTech and MarTech infrastructures. In this way, redundancies can be avoided, and meta-information can be generated. A further area that has become particularly important in more complex and international projects was the topic of *Procurement Intelligence*, which deals with the responsible optimization of supply chains in the context of the *New Green Deal* and the *Remocal Economy*. Intelligent operational procurement teams must consider the far-reaching consequences of the request before taking action. In most cases, it concerns three decision factors, which an intelligent procurement must regard regarding the selection of suppliers and the order criterion. In consideration of these three decisive criteria then the correct decision can be found in each case regarding the supplier which can be selected:

- Delivery time
- Material properties or special production process
- Price

However, in order for such a procedure to be possible, *Procurement Intelligence* must ideally have multidimensional access to all relevant supplier data, ideally 24/7, even in the past. This also leads to or requires the development of a network of possible suppliers over time. It is often the case that companies know far too few suppliers, because suppliers are only searched for and researched selectively and in specific situations. The knowledge is documented and stored, however, not lastingly in the sense of a data-driven management, so that with further projects again the before collected supplier information could be fallen back to. Predictive Intelligence means to set up thus also areas such as the procurement system according to the criteria defined in the context of this publication, in order to be able to use in the long run in the so important range of the procurement, whereas well-known still the profit lies, also accordingly all potentials.

7.6   The PITechStack-Blueprint at a Glance

In order to have the necessary view of the big picture in the context of the third phase mentioned above, an attempt will be made at this point to depict the appearance of a sustainable operable PITechStack in the form of a generic structural representation (Fig. 7.17). It becomes clear that the secret of efficient and effective Predictive Intelligence as part of a data-driven enterprise management is certainly not a

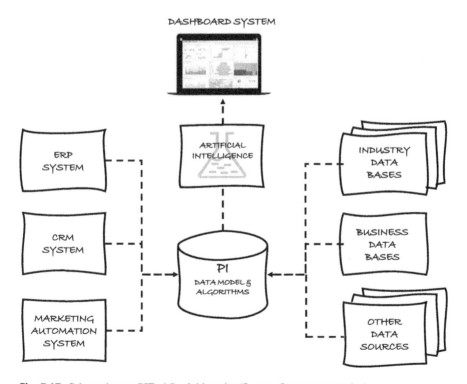

Fig. 7.17   Schematic core PITechStack blueprint (Source: Own representation)

complex IT architecture, but rather a well-thought-out and smart algorithmic, naturally matured in and with the respective organization.

Even if you could maybe buy an expensive sports car, you would never get everything out of such a vehicle like David Hamilton would. No matter how expensive a polo pony is, it will never turn a beginner into Adolfo Cambiaso, the world's best polo player for years. When you establish predictive intelligence for an organization, it only makes sense if there is a congruent development process that also focuses on the organizational learning process and actively takes it into account. Many projects have shown that less is often more and that in the early years of a predictive intelligence initiative, more should be invested in data than in systems and products.

The important aspects of a modern and sustainable PITechStack are the connection to the CRM-, the ERP-, and the marketing automation system. These three systems cover the entire customer history and perspective, because a marketing automation solution per se, can track information about customer behavior in the external area in relation to all customer contact points but also his queries and research activities. Especially in the area of larger projects the area of account-based marketing (ABM) plays an important role.

In order to keep an eye on the market, general economic developments, but also relevant large projects and the associated tenders, and to be able to work and calculate with this data, the second large area of the PITechStack (shown in the right-hand area in Fig. 7.17) is the external data area. This includes relevant and validated databases for the respective industries of an organization, as well as general and generic business and enterprise databases but also industry-specific project and investment platforms. A small selection of such databases or their providers is shown in Table 7.1.

Only when these two areas have been developed in terms of data technology and thus a 360° data perspective is represented in Predictive Intelligence, does it make sense to think about artificial intelligence. Because along with this now complete data image, the basic algorithms have also matured to such an extent that an additional artificial intelligence and the results and findings generated from it can be interpreted and validated in their meaningfulness and thus meaningfully integrated into a data-driven business practice. Artificial intelligence partly works with so-called hidden layers and procedures, in which different levels of data processing in the system of artificial intelligence are hidden from the viewer or user. This means that some processes run like in a black box. If, however, the basic competence for data-driven business management is missing and thus many interrelationships but also the corresponding sensitivity in dealing with data and algorithms are not available, AI in combination with lack of competence becomes a dangerous cocktail. This can lead to wrong conclusions and risky business decisions.

The illustrated PITechStack blueprint offers many different advantages:

- Cost minimal
- Realizable step by step
- No serious information technology interventions in existing structures

- Applicable for all possible, organization-specific IT strategies
- Greatest possible independence from external solutions
- Greatest possible, long-lasting adaptability with regard to the course of the project

With this information technology reference framework, one should be able to prepare and implement the right steps and decisions from the perspective of a future PI system environment. For a responsible manager who takes on the topic of predictive intelligence, this must also be an obligation to his own organization or management, namely, to act resource consciously. Against this background, the introduced PITechStack blueprint also allows the integration or networking of further peripheral systems, such as applications from *Event Media Intelligence, Sales Intelligence, Procurement Intelligence* or even *Engineering Intelligence, as* well as an automated system for configuration, pricing, and automatic quotation, as shown in Fig. 7.18 with CPQ-System.

Such a connection always requires ex ante an exact specification of relevant data fields in order not to unnecessarily inflate predictive intelligence while at the same time making the best possible use of data. In this step, too, an authentic internal PI project pays off once again, because only then is it possible to recognize the relevant and meaningful information in each additional peripheral system at the first attempt. In the context of the connections and interfaces that have already been implemented,

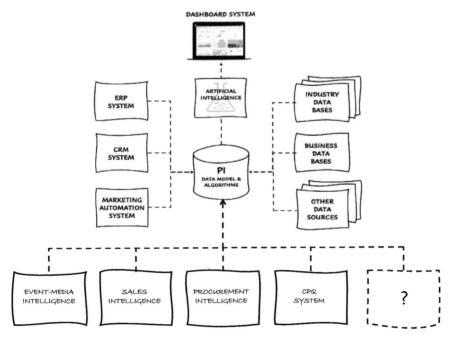

Fig. 7.18 Schematic extended PITechStack blueprint (Source: Own representation)

the further technical connection of a *sales intelligence* for the transfer of certain defined data fields should no longer pose a major challenge.

Based on the PITechStack blueprint, the following final section of this chapter will now go into more detail about the most important clusters of providers in the area of predictive intelligence. This grouping should serve to be able to classify possible inquiries very quickly, in the sense of an orientation aid. We currently distinguish four different providers or product groups:

- Data and Information
- Visualization and preparation
- Integration and evaluation
- Consultant and AdHoc Support

7.6.1　What Do Data and Information Applications Do?

The first group of providers provide various forms of data and prepared information. Freely accessible data is often prepared graphically and then offered as a service in the form of predefined dashboards. Additional offers include subscription models for newsletters or industry updates, which are regularly and automatically sent to a predefined distribution list.

Experience has shown that on closer analysis the information played out is generic and therefore not sufficiently relevant to the target group. In almost all PI projects, such information and newsletter subscriptions were terminated after a short time, because the information and news updates generated on the basis of primary and pure data providers could be designed and played out in a much more target group-specific and thus more useful way.

If the organization does not have a proven data competence, it is also difficult to analyze such offerings in terms of their quality and validity. Many offers and dashboards make a very professional and profound impression at first glance, but in most cases, they lose their luster very quickly when analyzed by an expert. The most common weaknesses are incorrect data, which can only be detected with the appropriate industry-relevant data sensitivity. Another common weakness is that such purchased dashboards contain and provide only a few perfectly programmed generic views, which cannot be adapted to an organization's various internal customers on a situational and dynamic basis.

As part of a sustainable, proprietary PI environment, ultimately only data from primary vendors with whom you will develop a good relationship over time is required. Providers of secondary data or newsletter services are de facto not required, since the resulting industry-specific data competence and sensitivity allows for a much more cost-effective, agile, and target group-specific approach. Many providers forget that within the companies not only one customer group, but several different ones must be serviced, which in turn must be reflected in different information needs and thus many different PI dashboards.

7.6.2   Visualization and Processing Applications

The second cluster of PI providers focuses on the playout and processing of data and information. In the context of freely accessible solutions such as Microsoft PowerBI, there is no need to purchase these products and services. In any case, the all-decisive basis is the validity of the data. Especially in the technical-industrial environment, the graphic preparation is of little importance. No matter how professionally the graphics are created, success leads to the acceptance of the data via a transparent procedure regarding data source, data preparation, and data processing based on the known algorithms defined together with the organization and the internal clients.

The projects have also shown that the initial, manual preparation of data, and reports contributes significantly to the organizational learning process. Through this work, the team develops a feeling for how certain forms of data need to be prepared so that they can be grasped at a glance and interpreted correctly. In this context, interaction with and feedback from the organization is crucial. External preparation of data is rather obstructive to such a learning process and should therefore be avoided.

7.6.3   Integration and Evaluation Applications

This group of providers has only established itself in the last 2 years, as it was recognized that many different systems exist in companies, which predictive intelligence must access in a meaningful way in order to avoid redundant structures.

Such applications in themselves represent an extreme added value, but they also carry a certain risk, because once the decision for such a provider has been made, one is exposed to the lock-in syndrome (Shapiro and Varian 1998). Moreover, in most cases, all generated and aggregated data is located outside the corporate network in the cloud. In this context, the question of congruence with the IT strategy of the own company also arises.

Some providers also offer their applications immediately with artificial and predictive intelligence, which is certainly an interesting approach. But once again, the question arises whether such a solution is necessary or makes sense from the very beginning, especially in the context of the data stocks of companies criticized in many current studies. Predictive intelligence in combination with artificial intelligence requires a sufficient and valid data stock, because otherwise insufficient and incorrect data will be used to prepare decisions of insufficient quality for the management, which in turn can have a lasting negative effect.

In the predictive intelligence environment, too, IT is only an enabler and not a driver. The predictive intelligence of an organization will only ever be as good as its masterminds. The purchase of a PI solution can possibly eliminate latent PI competence deficits in the short term, but in the long term it will not be possible to be a free rider of a PI IT solution, no matter how stylishly and professionally designed it is.

7.6.4   AdHoc Consultants

The fourth group of providers is sometimes very difficult to identify, as they very often also come up with dashboards and perfectly prepared, customer-specific adapted websites or news updates. Inexperienced users are then often mistaken for a provider in the category "Visualization and Preparation," which is not the case de facto.

Because the work results shown are actually only examples of consulting projects that were commissioned on a selective basis, either in the form of an analysis, research, or, for example, an industry update or newsletter. The contingency situation of the analysis and consulting industry has already been discussed in more detail. In this context, the extended offers and services of the AdHoc Consultants, who work with large armies of employees in low-wage countries in order to be able to operate cost-effectively in the market, should also be seen in this context. In certain industries, it is currently not yet possible to avoid buying in certain research and analyses from outside. Especially in complex and disaggregated value chains, such as those in the food and beverage sector, there are currently no providers of comprehensive, global market data for certain applications and products. In this case, AdHoc Consultants can provide excellent services, but once again it is necessary to identify reputable and valid providers on the basis of internally available data competence and sensitivity in order to obtain reliable results.

7.7   What Is The Environment of an Effective PITechStack?

In this chapter, we have attempted to define and discuss an ideal-typical structural plan for a company's own predictive intelligence at a very early stage in the development of a completely new generation of data-driven management systems. For IT fans, the resulting structural plan will be a disappointment, because it is a logically deductively derived, lean but pragmatic and operable approach without frills and special features. And indeed, many different projects have confirmed that there is no need for expensive tools and applications, but only a small group of authentic and committed employees whose motivation is based on being able to sustainably get something decisive for their own organization off the ground.

IT will only play an important role in the further course of the PI initiative, which will then provide the corresponding stable and secure framework for the entire topic, in order to be able to practice valid and serious, data-driven corporate management based on it. An instrument or a tool, is and remains only a tool. Even the biggest fool will remain a fool with the best PITechStack, if the basis for generating added value from such an infrastructure is not available in the form of experience, competence, and know-how.

Less is more when the path is taken toward Predictive Intelligence and when it comes to applications and products from the PITech landscape. Success lies primarily in human brilliance and intelligence, which forms the foundation for predictive intelligence based on it and equipped with artificial intelligence. If children today were to learn to calculate with a calculator right from the start, they would not be able to learn the basic skills of mathematics. Only when these have been acquired and learned can children begin to use pocket calculators to accelerate and support the calculation processes. And it is exactly the same in the context of predictive intelligence. First, the basic skills must be learned and acquired, both individually and organizationally. Only then is it meaningful and purposeful to buy the "calculator" and start using it. If this basic rule, which has apparently been used successfully for generations by our children in mathematics, is not observed, predictive intelligence will not be established and mastered meaningfully in the long run, because, in a figurative sense, one has neglected to learn mental arithmetic.

Further Reading

Brynjolfsson, E., & Collis, A. (2020, April). Der Wert der digitalen Wirtschaft. *Harvard Business Manager*, S. 50–58.

Frey, A., Trenz, M., & Veit, D. (2019). A service-dominant logic perspective on the roles of technology in service innovation: Uncovering four archetypes in the sharing economy. *Journal of Business Economics, 89*(8–9), 1149–1189. https://doi.org/10.1007/s11573-019-00948-z.

Iansiti, M., & Lakhani, K. R. (2017, January/February). Technology: The truth about blockchain. *HBR.org.*

Kotler, P., Pfoertsch, W., & Sponholz, U. (2021). *H2H Marketing—The genesis of human-to-human marketing.* Cham: Springer.

Müller, E. (2019, Juli). Die Netflix-Industrie. *Manage Magazin*, Seite 95–97.

Negovan, M. (2020). 365 tage marketing turnaround. In U. Seebacher (Hrsg.), *B2B marketing—A guidebook for the classroom to the boardroom.* Cham: Springer.

Seebacher, U. (2020a). *B2B marketing: A guidebook for the classroom to the boardroom.* Cham: Springer.

Seebacher, U. (2020b). *B2B marketing essential: How to turn your marketing from a cost into a sales engine* (2nd ed.). Graz: AQPS.

Seebacher, U. (2020c). *Template-based management—A guide for an efficient and impactful professional practice.* Cham: Springer.

Shapiro, C., & Varian, H. R. (1998). *Information rule: A strategic guide to the network economy.* Boston: Harvard Business School Press.

Steinmetz, R., & Wehrle, K. (2006). Peer-to-peer-networking & -computing. Aktuelles Schlagwort. In *Informatik Spektrum* (pp. 51–54). Heidelberg: Springer. 27.2004,1.

Wierse, A., & Riedel, T. (2017). *Smart data analytics* (englisch). Berlin: De Gruyter Oldenbourg.

The Predictive Intelligence Team

8

8.1 Is Predictive Intelligence Also a Cathedral?

Douglas McDowell, CEO of SolidQ North America has said a much-quoted phrase:

> Business Intelligence is a cathedral. And each team member plays a crucial role in its strength, majesty and beauty. Or can contribute to their failure. A BI team that has a clear vision and focuses on that vision in all its tasks will work with a synergy, enthusiasm and creativity that can never be fostered in a dispersed group of individuals, regardless of their talent and experience.

At the beginning of this book, the conceptual relationship between Business Intelligence and Predictive Intelligence was discussed and presented in the context of the ecosystem for Predictive Intelligence. In fact, there is something magical and fascinating about data-driven management, because conversations, meetings, and management meetings suddenly take place in a very focused and substantiated way on the basis of the large amount of data and information. Everything suddenly gets a grip and practically every business issue can be substantiated with data and on this basis can be discussed and interpreted on a completely new level of content.

However, such a paradigmatic change will only take place if the topic of Predictive Intelligence is implemented independently and authentically in and for an organization as described in this book. Because only then will the necessary human potential also develop step by step and congruently within the organization, in order to be able to handle and use the ever more complex and valid data meaningfully and in the sense of the business development added value-creating.

Such a development will also create the necessary knowledge and competence areas in the organization and thus automatically create a team of PI experts. In this context, the PI Key User Network (KUN) plays a role that should not be underestimated, because it can also be used to establish an important aspect of knowledge transfer in the organization and ensure its continuous and sustainable

© The Author(s), under exclusive license to Springer Nature Switzerland AG 2021   209
U. Seebacher, *Predictive Intelligence for Data-Driven Managers*, Future of Business and Finance, https://doi.org/10.1007/978-3-030-69403-6_8

development. Nevertheless, it is important to know right from the start what skills will be required over time to successfully set up PI.

Against this background, this chapter looks at the subject area of predictive intelligence from the perspective of personnel management. It deals with aspects such as roles and responsibilities as well as fields of competence, skills, and the corresponding behavioral anchors. The goal must be to be the mastermind as a business partner of HR, so that the company's own HR department can work in the best possible way if necessary. It is not the task of the HR department to always have the corresponding watertight *job descriptions* and competencies for new topics.

Within the framework of many different projects, we were only able to recruit the PI heads that were brilliant in the long term and ex post when we, for our part, on the part of the business departments, had revised and optimized the job advertisements and tenders predefined by HR against in the context of and based on our PI expertise. And it is precisely this synergy that holds enormous potential, because there are currently no graduates and candidates on the job market who have been specially trained for PI. It is therefore necessary to define so-called original competencies and to focus on these and on the professional and interest-related affinities of potential candidates in the recruiting process.

So, what is the ideal approach from the point of view of skills and resources to build the *Cathedral of Predictive Intelligence*?

8.2   What Managers Need to Know

Most of the buzzwords introduced in the ecosystem for predictive intelligence are on everyone's lips. More and more companies are already building business analytics teams and departments. This creates an important basic prerequisite in terms of skills and expertise with regard to the further development towards predictive intelligence. In most cases, however, all projects have one thing in common, because successful projects in the field of business analytics and predictive intelligence are not driven by so-called *data scientists*, but by far-sighted and prudent managers. They are the ones who make the connection to business and corporate management.

As described in the section on the Predictive Intelligence Self-Assessment (PI-SA), the PI Competence Index (PI-CI) is used to determine the presence of data scientists in the organization concerned. Data Scientists currently cover the requirements for starting a PI initiative in an almost ideal way. Therefore, if such an expert is already available in the organization in question, he or she should be consulted in the context of PI. However, one must also be aware of the fact that the competency-technical perspective will rapidly refine in the course of the PI initiative with regard to the following PI competency fields described later in the chapter.

From a content perspective, the following existing competence typologies are integrated into PI projects in this context:

• Data Engineers: Collecting and preparing data

- Big Data Architects: Building and operating the technical infrastructure
- Statisticians and machine learning engineers: Development of prediction models
- Software Developer: Integration of the models into business solutions

Managers must act as an active interface to the organization, as described in the Predictive Intelligence process model. In this function as interpreters, they must impart stringent knowledge and establish and ensure a connection to operational practice by recording the requirements and goals of a company and translating these into questions and problems of the PI, which are subsequently solved by the PI team. Through these link functions, they create understanding and acceptance for data-driven corporate management, because without transparency, acceptance, or trust, the results will not be used in day-to-day business. While day-to-day business in sales usually revolves around issues such as increasing sales or generating new leads, for many data scientists issues such as data quality or the choice of the right algorithm are important.

In this context, four essential areas of competence for managers can be defined, which they must be aware of in order to establish Predictive Intelligence successfully in their own organization in the long term:

- Living Predictive Intelligence
- Managing data as a strategic resource
- Establishing data-driven management
- Building competitive advantages through Predictive Intelligence

8.2.1 What Does It Mean to Live Predictive Intelligence?

In order to be able to provide the necessary management support for all activities right from the start, it is necessary to be solidly grounded in predictive intelligence. It is not about knowing everything exactly, but about dealing authentically with one's own knowledge. The goal is not to teach the rest of the organization, but to enable the necessary knowledge transfer at eye level. For all of us together, the successful establishment of PI is a growth path with many small steps. Only if every step of success can be climbed together will it lead to long-term success.

As a manager, it is therefore necessary to act as an ambassador for Predictive Intelligence. The goal should be to always be one step ahead in knowledge in order to be able to develop the organization further. You do not become a proven PI expert overnight, because the process requires persistence and patience. A major issue in this context of living and speaking PI is also uncertainty, fear but also rejection, because "it has worked very well up to now without Big Data, Machine Learning and Predictive Intelligence." However, this overlooks what was said at the very beginning of the book with regard to the contingency situation of a disruptive industry.

In this context, the aim is to create transparency through continuous and steady information and to gradually expand the network of PI ambassadors by interacting with the organization through pilot projects and pilot studies, so that the topic can also be communicated into the organization through informal channels.

A helpful and important instrument or model in this context is the triangle of trust, which was already mentioned at the beginning of this book and which makes it possible to create lasting trust through authentic, empathic, and logical behavior in order to consolidate a complex and protracted topic such as data-driven management in an organization.

Authenticity is closely linked to appearance and perception in the sense of a certain quality of perceptual content. Such content can be related to things or objects, people, events, or even and especially to human actions. Authenticity presupposes the congruence of appearance and reality. In case of a conscious or unconscious inconsistency of appearance and reality, this means a possibility of deception and falsification. Content can be considered authentic if both dimensions of perception are assumed to be consistent and congruent. The deviation of the "really real" and authentic from the "fake" or "supposed" real is interpreted in social behavioral sciences as a meta-level competence of humans with regard to contingency and self-awareness. Whereby this statement is also a statement to be critically questioned, because it is assumed that animals have a much more pronounced competence to distinguish authentic from simulated behavior.

Authenticity is a complex, intrapersonal growth process. One must be ready, prepared, and mature for this journey. Experts attest that this also requires the appropriate people around you to facilitate and support this growth process. And only authentic leaders can and will be able to transform an organization or team into an equally authentic one. An authentic organization is a structural construct in the sense of what the renowned Novartis Professor of Leadership and Management at Harvard Business School, Amy C. Edmondson, describes as a "fearless organization."[1] And this is where the big difference between managers and leaders comes into play. Managers in the sense of *leaders* can ignite the fire in people because they are authentic. They also accept failure every now and then and let their people fail and take such opportunities to let employees learn and grow from them. Managers are technocratic and manage through pressure and fear. Yes, leaders also exert pressure on their employees, as this promotes growth. Yes, *leaders* also use KPIs, but the setting of these performance targets is a collaborative process, and this makes leaders' employees know *why* they are doing *what* they are doing (Fig. 8.1).

Can we measure authenticity? Not really, but to prove authenticity, very far-reaching techniques have been developed that attempt to define and establish a set of criteria for authenticity in a normative way, at least for a certain area of the object.[2]

---

[1]Edmondson, A. C.: "The Fearless Organization—Creating Psychological Security in the Workplace for Learning, Innovation and Growth" Wiley, 2018.

[2]https://en.wikipedia.org/wiki/Normative: Accessed: June 8, 2020.

Fig. 8.1 Difference between managers and executives/leaders

MANAGERS   LEADERS

ignite a fire   *ignite a fire*
under   **in**
their people   *their people*

The second pillar of the triangle of trust is *empathy*,[3] derived from the Greek word ἐμπάθεια, which means "physical affection or passion." The main part of the word is "pathos" in the sense of "passion," but also "suffering." In a virtual, *remocal* world, this ability will play an increasingly important role, enabling people in business environments not only to be empathetic, but even more so to do so from a distance and virtually.

Many definitions of empathy are used with many different emotional states such as cognitive, emotional or affective, and somatic empathy.[4] What they all have in common is that empathy is about the authentic effort and desire to help and care for someone and to eliminate the difference between the "I" and the "other." With this ability, one is enabled to experience feelings and emotions that correspond to the emotions of another person. Martin Hoffmann, an American psychologist, has done a lot of research on the development of empathy, and according to him, every human being is born with the ability to experience empathy.[5] Empathy is divided into three categories:

1. *Affective empathy* or emotional empathy in the sense of the ability to respond to the state of mind of another person with the appropriate emotion.
2. *Cognitive empathy* describes the ability to understand the mental state or emotions of any other individual.
3. *Somatic empathy* is used in the sense of physical reactions—where otherwise the latter are mental reactions—which are based on the reflection of neuron reactions triggered by the somatic nervous system.[6]

Many top managers have great problems with empathy because they are very analytical and logical thinkers who get bored very quickly. The fact that their colleagues or direct superiors are not as fast as they are makes them impatient.

---

[3]https://en.wikipedia.org/wiki/Empathy. Accessed: June 8, 2020.

[4]Rothschild, B. (with Rand, M. L.): "Helping the Helper: The Psychophysiology of Compassionate Fatigue and Vicarious Trauma." University Press, 2006.

[5]Hoffman, Martin L.: Empathy and moral development: Implications for Care and Justice. Cambridge: Cambridge University Press, 2000.

[6]Rothschild, B. (with Rand, M. L.): "Helping the Helper: The Psychophysiology of Compassionate Fatigue and Vicarious Trauma". University Press, 2006.

This in turn is perceived by their colleagues as ignorant and not empathetic. But people strive for recognition in their innermost being, and if they cannot expect this kind of psychological state from their boss, it leads to insecurity, psychological misconduct, and mistrust.

The third area of the triangle is the *logic*. The word is derived from the Greek word λογική, which means "to be in possession of logical thinking, intellect, dialectic and argumentation." Despite many and extensive researches and debates, the philosophy of logic[7] conclusively uses so far only the following three criteria as a basis for a common understanding:

- Classification of arguments
- Systemic representation of logical forms
- Validity and robustness of deductive reasoning

If a manager has a problem with the topic of logic, this is considered a leadership weakness. After all, if the manager is not convinced by his ideas, why should the others follow him? This means that all three skills are essential for creating a sustainable and successful leadership environment based on trust as part of a data-driven organization where collaboration is a continuous learning process for both the individual and the organization.

> **Tip:** Living Predictive Intelligence can be compared in a figurative sense to the classic *walk-the-talk*. Even a topic as important as predictive intelligence can only be established in an organization in the long term if the manager or managers or the management team want to promote and operate authentic and stringent data-driven management in the long term.

8.2.2   How Can Data Be Managed as a Strategic Resource?

Data is the new gold. In the future, it will no longer be about products or machines, but about the relevant data and information about these machines. The race for this last mile towards the plants and machines has long since begun. All this goes hand in hand with the development of these disruptive "as-a-service" business models, which aim to collect and aggregate ever more and larger amounts of data 24/7. However, especially in the initial phase, with around 80 percent of the effort of PI projects, the preparation, and processing of this data is usually the most important part of the project. Only in the further course of PI initiatives can this effort be

---

[7]Quine, Willard VanOrman *(1986) [1970]*. Philosophy of logic (2nd ed.). Cambridge, MA: Harvard University Press. S. 1–14, 61–75.

significantly reduced by automatic interfaces and connections to the relevant data sources.

Data engineering is therefore mandatory and only if this homework is completed stringently and consistently can the development of predictive models be a free choice. However, especially in the early stages of predictive intelligence projects, the sensitivity in many departments for data engineering is very low, especially since these activities take place hidden in the background. Against this background, from the very beginning, the primary goal must be to be able to demonstrate immediate and rapid success with generated data on the basis of small pilot projects. These results can and should again flow into the first competence field "Living PI" from a content point of view and be communicated to the organization personally but also virtually in the form of internal podcasts or vodcasts but also PI webinars. Such proactive communication can be used to motivate other internal customers to profit from PI on the basis of project results and to manifest the value of data and information on a meta-level.

Managers must be familiar with basic organizational and technical issues in order to be able to assess in advance how data, once collected, can be effectively used in different contexts. With this knowledge, further *economies of scale* can be realized, since already prepared data can be used for other pilot projects. As an executive, it is also necessary to have not only an overview of common predictive intelligence infrastructures and applications, but also an understanding of data management and data quality.

In order to be able to manage data as strategic resources, the template-based creation of profitability analyses has also proven to be helpful in various projects. For this purpose, an attempt must be made from the outset to record and document savings in the area of data acquisition and processing on the one hand and sales-oriented evaluation of the use of the data on the other. The better this combination of cost minimization and revenue optimization is achieved through data and predictive intelligence, the faster the organization will change in terms of how it views data as strategic resources.

8.2.3 How Do You Build a Data-Driven Management System?

Structure-theoretically this question has already been comprehensively dealt with using the procedure model for Predictive Intelligence. While many companies have successfully implemented first PI prototypes, many fail to systematically integrate them into their organization. Especially in large companies, where one of several divisions as a data technology pioneer very successfully establishes a predictive intelligence unit, desires soon arise at other points in the overall organization. Based on our experience, the following scenarios have emerged:

- *Best Case Scenario*: Based on the pioneering work of the pioneer unit or division, the topic is then rolled out by this division to all other divisions and, in a next step, raised globally to the Group level. Such units are called "Group Intelligence" or "Corporate Central Intelligence," for example, and report to a Group Data Officer. This will result in enormous savings, since databases for the entire Group will be purchased, prepared, and processed centrally with discounts of over 60%. In addition, this unit is developing into a separate internal service department, which provides data and information across divisions and increasingly also provides conceptual and advisory support.
- *Neutral Case Scenario*: The managers acting in each case agree informally to coordinate and jointly drive forward the predictive intelligence activities on the basis of a "*shared service* approach" without official specifications.
- *Worst-Case Scenario*: No organizational changes are initiated by the official side, which is why each division develops a predictive intelligence unit on its own, continues to purchase data autonomously, establishes, and also uses its own systems and resources for complex data preparation and processing, and thus the critical dimensions and the corresponding learning curve cannot be realized in order to be able to operate PI in a timely, optimally efficient and effective manner.

In order to be able to proceed in a resource-optimized manner from an organizational perspective, companies must design an overarching predictive intelligence strategy and create appropriate organizational structures for the transfer of a prototype unit, as described above, into a regular operation based on the overall organization. Pioneers in the field of business analytics are companies such as ZF Friedrichshafen, Volkswagen or Festo, which have installed so-called *Analytics Labs*. These units are used to turn project ideas into functional prototypes in the shortest possible time. Even if these examples are based on products, this approach can also be used as an example for predictive intelligence prototypes in the sense of analyses, reports, and studies, with a view to a development or expansion into business in the sense of data-driven management. Ivo Blohm[8] states in this context:

> But building data-driven organizations is not just about building scalable prototyping factories. Rather, it often involves the systematic redesign of decision-making and business processes and accompanying change management. A recent survey by the management consultancy McKinsey shows that leading companies spend around 50 percent of their analytics budgets on the organizational integration of the solutions they develop—more than twice as much as the rest.

This means that, in addition to the content-structural implementation of the predictive intelligence process model, organizational change management is at least as important for establishing data as a driver for corporate management and control in the long term.

---

[8]https://www.zoe-online.org/meldungen/was-manager-ueber-business-analytics-wissen-muessen/.
Accessed: October 14, 2020.

8.2.4   How to Create Competitive Advantages Through Predictive Intelligence

Jeremy Rifkin brilliantly sums it up in his current book "The New Green Deal" (2019), in which he attests that the unwillingness of many top managers in the industry to change will lead to the disappearance of many international and global corporations. Managers must learn to understand the rapidly changing rules of the digital and data-driven world. It is up to them to deduce how their own products, services, and processes need to be adapted.

But this per se is also a paradigm shift, because up to now, products have sold themselves because you knew or could know your own customers personally. In order to be able to initiate and go through this change process, managers are needed who start on a small scale with predictive intelligence to solve short-term business situations and to show immediately how *competitive advantage* could be realized. Competitive advantage tends to be generically-conceptually proven, but a very operational competitive advantage can be realized and proven in many small, different measures through data-driven management. At this point, I would like to refer to the various PI case studies in the further course of this publication.

It is also helpful to look at the findings of analytics in the area of product development. Data-based adjustments of products are usually associated with high risks and it is often unclear whether and if so, which specific customer needs can be met with innovative data-based solutions. It is much more difficult to recognize or estimate ex ante whether customers are generally willing to pay for additional services generated on the basis of data. In order to solve this data paradoxon, many companies therefore consistently rely on agile innovation development methods, such as *design thinking, canvasing, template-based management, lean startup,* or *prototyping*. This is expected to identify and evaluate possible application potentials for Predictive Intelligence and to prepare them for further development, so that the business can evaluate the strategic benefit and the PI team the feasibility of such a data-based innovation.

What you can learn from this is that it is once again the path of small steps that leads to success. It is crucial to carry out applied research and development as part of an authentic, empathetic, and logical organizational learning process. It is up to the managers to pull the various threads and, above all, to link and interlink them so that a stringent and coherent predictive intelligence story emerges. If such a foundation is lived and laid by management as part of a fearless organization according to Amy C. Edmondson (2018), then from an operational point of view predictive intelligence can be set up very quickly and effectively for a data-driven enterprise.

8.3   What the Perfect PI Team Looks Like

Right at the beginning, it must be noted that the perfect PI team as such does not and cannot exist. The many different projects in the field of predictive intelligence have made it clear that, in the context of organizational etymology and contingency theory, the relevant success criterion for a sustainably successful PI organization is the gradual development and building process. It is therefore more about the "how" and only secondarily about the "what." This "how" is based on *process authenticity* and is defined by the focused but predominantly natural emergence of PI competence.

Only when a team-internal *predictive intelligence identity is* created on the basis of this process authenticity, can information and communication be coordinated and consistent externally, towards the various customers and interest groups. As in the area of industrial goods marketing, which is currently undergoing an enormous change process (Seebacher 2020a, b, c), team-internal authenticity is the decisive factor in the new topic area of data-driven corporate management in order to be able to initiate and implement the necessary organizational change process efficiently and effectively.

8.3.1   What Humanontogenetics Teaches Us

Organizations are comparable to individuals in terms of the way they work. In the organizational construct, the various organizational units represent what the limbs of an individual human being are in the human body. The arms and legs are the divisions or business units. The forearm and the upper arm are comparable to different departments, which are to a certain extent interdependent in terms of value creation but nevertheless act independently in principle. The individual fingers, on one hand, are comparable to departments, which in turn are attached to the forearm department and thus work towards it. The brain is the management of the company, which either rather, based on the theories and insights of the two different halves of the brain, acts rationally or emotionally.

The central and all-connecting systems, such as the blood vessels and the nervous system, are comparable to the regulations, guidelines, and generally applicable standards in force in the organization. Existing information and reporting systems are also part of the central information systems, which—similar to the human body—can be faulty and impaired in their functioning.

Besides these physical parallels between organizations and human beings, the much more impressive element is their mental-somatic comparability. For, just as with humans, *humanontogenetics* (Wessel 1998) as a system of statements about the holistic development and structure of the individual requires both *physical* and *mental* health. The basic premises of humanontogenetics are, firstly, the possibility of lifelong development from conception to death and, secondly, the existence of the individual as a biopsychosocial unit. In this context, organizations are also subject to a process of development and learning during their entire life cycle and represent a unity of formal and informal—conscious and unconscious—structures and behaviors.

A basic thesis of humanontogenetics defines that a human being can only exist in a sustainable, system-preserving manner in the sense of both physical and mental, if the state of an *authentic-strong identity* can be achieved. Following the theory that organizations and individuals are basically comparable system complexes, this means that an organization can only exist "healthy" in the long term if the state of such an authentic-stringent organizational identity is achieved. In such a state, short-term limitations of individual subsystems can be eradicated by the common unifying element and thus a return to the holistic functioning of the system can be realized.

Humanontogenetics combines elements of systems theory, developmental psychology and behavioral biology into a uniform model and thus provides an ideal reference and validation framework for the field of organizational development. This is because humanontogenetics, like modern organizational development, is based on the theses of lifelong development, the system of competencies, and the model of sensitive and critical phases. This means that the laws of humanontogenetics also appear to be applicable to organizational constructs at all levels.

What we can therefore derive from the comparison with the human system for a PI team, but also of course for any other team, is the realization that a purely technocratic establishment of PI-relevant competencies is by no means the sole criterion for success. Rather, it is essential to deepen knowledge on the basis of joint action and communication, thereby gradually developing a natural common understanding of predictive intelligence in order to establish team authenticity on this basis. Only when this team authenticity has been created can it be assumed that the subject area will develop congruently and stringently into an organization and continue to develop together with it. This PI team authenticity is also the seedbed for the creativity and perseverance needed to develop such an exciting but complex construct of predictive intelligence for data-driven corporate management.

In addition to this team dimension, the reference to the previously discussed tasks, competencies, and roles that managers must fulfill within the framework of predictive intelligence as part of the manager dimension should not be missing at this point. Ultimately, only this interaction will make efficient and effective PI establishment possible.

> **Tip:** If no new resources with PI-related skills are available or can be brought on board right from the start, this should not be a knockout criterion for PI. Many projects have started exclusively with already existing employees from the areas of controlling, marketing, or product management, and only after about 8–12 months were subject-specific, student employees brought on board for reinforcement.

8.3.2   Why the Good Is so Obvious

A good PI team must also have the ambition from the beginning to set itself up according to the dimension in terms of the size of its own organization. The approach often found in conservative structures of defining one's own meaning and importance based on the number of employees assigned to a manager contradicts the ideology that a manager acting in the interests of the company should display. This size-specific awareness should characterize PI activities from the very beginning.

Every early demand for additional resources and budgets offers unnecessary conflict potentials and increases the pressure for provable and valid results. Furthermore, such requests for resources and money tend to make bigger waves, which creates the unnecessary need for clarification and demand. Inevitably, discussions and talks have to be held in the management circle and thus, without comprehensive information, questions have to be answered at an early stage.

All this costs time, which could be used much better for joint discussion and idea gathering in the PI team and for operational work. It has been shown that the longer activities get along with existing or available resources, the steeper the learning curve is after a short time and also in the long run. This is easily explained by the fact that only content aspects are discussed and nobody in the organization associates this new topic with additional costs or employees. Through this intensive work with various internal customers, who are also part of the original PI team in a broader sense, the understanding of the topic itself and the value of data as a strategic resource in the organization is slowly beginning to establish itself.

Such a resource-minimizing approach gives you time to slowly approach the topic "under the radar." You get valuable and unfiltered feedback in direct talks with the various internal customers. Only when results are available and something can be presented does the "official" communication begin, not with the aim of applying for new resources and funds, but only with the focus on PI activities and communicating tangible and measurable, presentable results.

On the basis of various projects, a size-related reference framework has emerged, which should make it possible to estimate and estimate the required team size. No matter how large the organization is, it is possible to start with an internally available resource. This is because the number of requests for analyses and reports is usually low in the initial phase. It is important to carefully select the first PI team member. This potential PI pioneer should have completed either a master's degree in business administration or economics. In addition, the candidate should have a strong affinity for Excel, so that he or she can easily get into the depths of tables and models. Such a profile is not characterized by initially brilliant slides and presentation, as the focus is clearly on data collection, aggregation, but also on data selection.

In any case, the employee must have a basic understanding of business in order to be able to argue and communicate with internal customers competently and in the context of their own business during the initial pilot research. Managers who carry out this internal selection process in a far-sighted and prudent manner will also talk very openly with the candidates about their motivation and, above all, their prospects for the next 5 years. Based on these interviews, empathic managers can immediately identify the right colleague(s). When this employee starts the first activities based on the PI procedure model, this should be sufficient in terms of resources for the following 6–8 months.

8.3.3   Demand Determines the Dynamics

After these first few months, the number of inquiries will increase—depending on the initial results, the satisfaction of internal customers and subsequent internal word of mouth, and ultimately management communication. On average, after the first year, the PI pioneer organizations in question have already been granted their own PI budgets, which vary in size but are nevertheless explicit. On average, this distribution was very similar across all sizes, with two-thirds for data acquisition and one-third for resource expansion.

The expansion of resources in the form of student employees has proven to be ideal, since they already have a basic knowledge and can support PI activities for 20 or 30 h per week, depending on availability and budget, at the beginning of their studies and thus invest more than cost-optimally in future human potential. Such student co-workers can be found in the new study programs in Data Science or Business Analytics. In the context of these studies, content is taught in the areas of machine learning, in-depth mathematical and statistical basics, optimization methods, preparation, and processing of large amounts of data, and visual and explorative data science.

> It is noticeable that the known fields of study and training have so far focused on product and process topics and dimensions. The transfer to a *Management Data Science* or *Data Science for Corporate Management* with a stringent focus on the optimization of existing markets and the early identification and quantification of new markets does not seem to have arrived in reality so far. This must and will change in the near future, since in times of digitalization and artificial intelligence it is no longer necessary for companies to risk both entrepreneurial and individual existence by intuitively acting on global markets in a data-less blind flight.

This is due to the fact that most of these topic-relevant fields of study are either at chairs of statistics or in the field of computer science. Even though the curricula are designed and implemented in cooperation with several, different disciplines and departments, the transfer of topics into management practice has not yet been mapped and offered in terms of training sufficiently. This can easily be proven by a Google search for the keyword "Management Data Science Course," which does not find any corresponding educational offers (Fig. 8.2).[9]

There are a few programs that use the keywords "Management & Data Science" in their titles, but only a too small proportion of their content covers the areas of organization, innovation, and strategy. Here it would be important to work through

---

[9]https://www.google.com/search?client=firefox-b-e&q=lehrgang+management+data+science. Accessed: 15 October 2020.

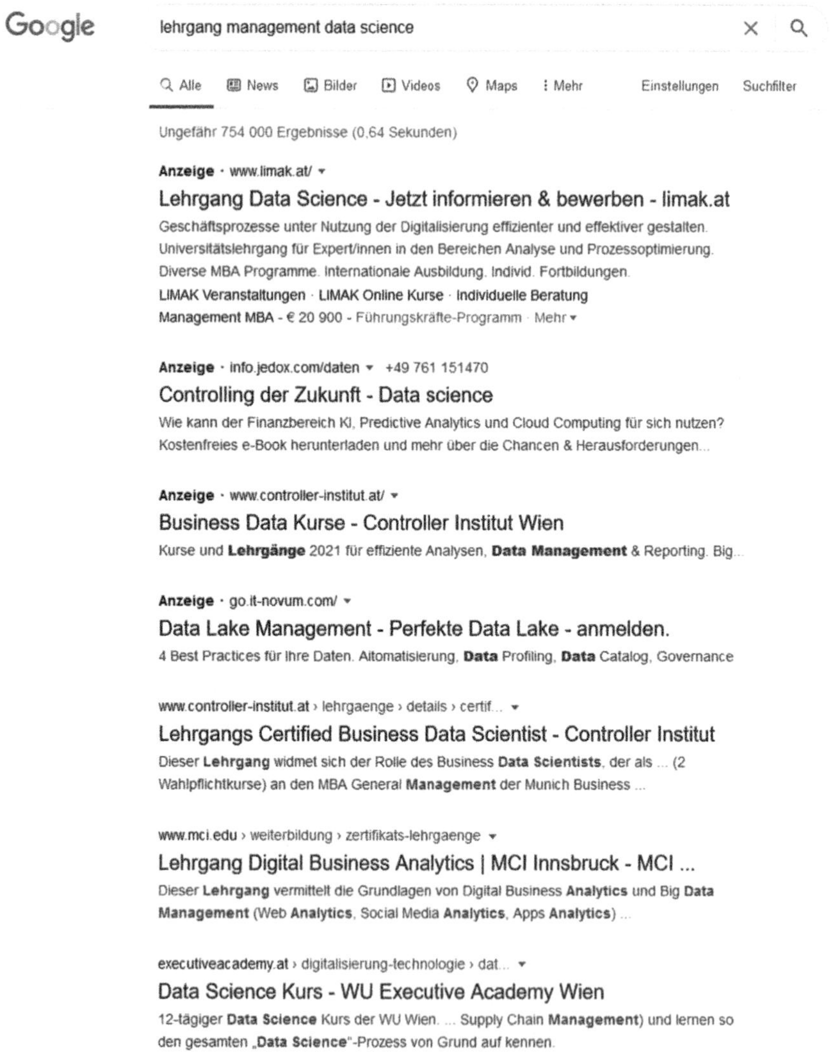

Google   lehrgang management data science   ✕   Q

Q Alle   📰 News   🖾 Bilder   ▶ Videos   ♡ Maps   ⋮ Mehr   Einstellungen   Suchfilter

Ungefähr 754 000 Ergebnisse (0,64 Sekunden)

Anzeige · www.limak.at/ ▾
Lehrgang Data Science - Jetzt informieren & bewerben - limak.at
Geschäftsprozesse unter Nutzung der Digitalisierung effizienter und effektiver gestalten.
Universitätslehrgang für Expert/innen in den Bereichen Analyse und Prozessoptimierung.
Diverse MBA Programme. Internationale Ausbildung. Individ. Fortbildungen.
LIMAK Veranstaltungen · LIMAK Online Kurse · Individuelle Beratung
Management MBA - € 20 900 - Führungskräfte-Programm · Mehr ▾

Anzeige · info.jedox.com/daten ▾ +49 761 151470
Controlling der Zukunft - Data science
Wie kann der Finanzbereich KI, Predictive Analytics und Cloud Computing für sich nutzen?
Kostenfreies e-Book herunterladen und mehr über die Chancen & Herausforderungen...

Anzeige · www.controller-institut.at/ ▾
Business Data Kurse - Controller Institut Wien
Kurse und **Lehrgänge** 2021 für effiziente Analysen, **Data Management** & Reporting. Big...

Anzeige · go.it-novum.com/ ▾
Data Lake Management - Perfekte Data Lake - anmelden.
4 Best Practices für Ihre Daten. Automatisierung, **Data** Profiling, **Data** Catalog, Governance

www.controller-institut.at › lehrgaenge › details › certif... ▾
Lehrgangs Certified Business Data Scientist - Controller Institut
Dieser **Lehrgang** widmet sich der Rolle des Business **Data Scientists**, der als ... (2
Wahlpflichtkurse) an den MBA General **Management** der Munich Business ...

www.mci.edu › weiterbildung › zertifikats-lehrgaenge ▾
Lehrgang Digital Business Analytics | MCI Innsbruck - MCI ...
Dieser **Lehrgang** vermittelt die Grundlagen von Digital Business **Analytics** und Big **Data**
Management (Web **Analytics**, Social Media **Analytics**, Apps **Analytics**) ...

executiveacademy.at › digitalisierung-technologie › dat... ▾
Data Science Kurs - WU Executive Academy Wien
12-tägiger **Data Science** Kurs der WU Wien. ... Supply Chain **Management**) und lernen so
den gesamten „**Data Science**"-Prozess von Grund auf kennen.

Fig. 8.2 Result Google query "Management Data Science" (Source: Google)

various case studies from day-to-day management practice using the various
concepts and technologies, both conceptually and operationally, in the form of
applied workshop and case study learning, as is the case at American elite
universities and in the executive sector. At this point, reference is made to the case
studies from entrepreneurial management practice in the further course of this book,
which provide a deeper insight into this topic.

8.3.4   Why the PI Team Sets the Direction

Irrespective of the current situation in the training sector, it will be up to the respective manager to make the right decisions based on the situation. That sounds simple, but it is by no means. In the form of an HR Business Partner, it also means that the important functions of an operative personnel manager are just as important as those of a specialist. Innovation through Strategic Human Resource Management SHRM (Seebacher and Güpner 2014) is only possible if brilliant employees are managed and developed according to the latest findings of HR management. Especially in such a young knowledge discipline, the rules of a supplier market apply, where job seekers can choose between several offered positions. The *war for talent* (Busol 2019) that has been proclaimed since the 1990s is nowhere else taking place with greater intensity than in new, emerging specialist and knowledge disciplines.

In order to promote and challenge young and committed employees, it is therefore necessary to talk to them about their sensitivities, activities, goals and above all their wishes and plans in half-yearly Employee Appraisal meetings. There are enough templates for such discussions either in the in-house HR department or on the Internet available, so that even as an inexperienced and experienced HR business partner, such employee discussions can be conducted professionally in the interest of all parties involved.

This information can be used to make further, upcoming decisions regarding the possible PI team expansion. Once the results of the employee interviews have been defined with regard to the future wishes of the respective PI employee(s) for more in-depth knowledge and development, and agreed with them and thus known, a competence map of the PI team can be developed.

8.4   The Predictive Intelligence Competence Model

This PI Competence Map depicts the current PI Team Competence Value for all nine Predictive Intelligence competence fields. The map is based on the *Predictive Intelligence Competence Model* (PICM), which depicts the essential areas of a Predictive Intelligence department and which can also be used on a disaggregated level as a reference framework for corresponding employees with regard to their PI suitability. The PI Competence Model (Fig. 8.3) is composed of nine areas as follows:

- Industry and Product Competence (IPC)
- Analytical Thinking (AT)
- Data Management (DM)
- Data Exploration (DE)
- Data Algorithmics (DA)
- Data Visualization (DV)
- Technology Management (TM)
- Strategic Thinking (ST)
- Leadership (LE)

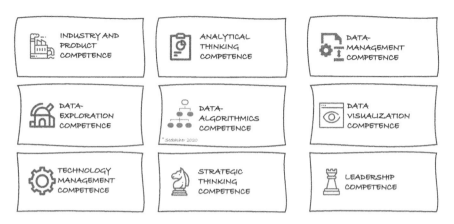

Fig. 8.3 Predictive Intelligence competence model (Source: Own presentation)

Using this PI competence model, each individual employee can now be classified. In general, there are various procedures for the classification, since such a classification must always take into account the respective age and experience background as well as the corresponding hierarchically relevant integration. Usually, common HR practice has shown that models with four to six competency levels are most practicable. This means that for each competency level, the respective behavior of the employee(s) in the respective competency field can be classified using formulated and defined *behavioral anchors*.[10] The behavioral anchors are an essential aspect of a fair and, above all, consistent evaluation that works with the same standards throughout, since they explicitly define behavior unambiguously, leaving little or no room for interpretation in terms of whether individual employees are favored or disadvantaged.

In the following section, the nine areas of the PI Competence Model are now briefly explained and discussed. To facilitate the application of the model, the relevant behavioral anchors are defined in each section on the basis of a four-level scale, which, taken together, result in a complete and finished PI competency matrices that can be used immediately in an organization. The four-level scale depicts the following levels of hierarchy or experience:

- E1: graduate, beginner, novice
- E2: advanced knowledge and sub-project management level (project management)
- E3: in-depth and proven knowledge and expertise (team leader)
- E4: expert, professional (department head, manager)

---

[10]https://en.wikipedia.org/wiki/Behaviorally_anchored_rating_scales.   Accessed: November 23 2020.

8.4.1 Industry and Product Competence (IPC)

Predictive Intelligence as part of a data-driven management requires an uncompromising connection to the business. Data as an end in itself as well as Predictive Intelligence as an end in itself does not create added value. It is therefore crucial that in the development as well as in the further analytical and creative application of predictive intelligence, the necessary knowledge about the relevant industry or industries and products is always available.

On the basis of the various projects, this IPC develops automatically or is deepened very quickly as soon as work on predictive intelligence is actively started. Another important factor is the independent, internal creation of market as well as industry updates, as the relevant employee or employees are de facto forced to continuously deal with the industry and matter. Thus, the shift of this activity from previously external suppliers to internal, in-house value creation makes sense in several respects, not only economically but also tactically and strategically.

With regard to the four competence levels, the following behavioral anchors can be derived for the area of industry and product competence:

- E1: The employee has no knowledge of relevant industries or products in the relevant area. He or she is new to the company or the business.
- E2: The employee has a rough overview of the relevant industries and knows the unit's products at a glance.
- E3: The employee is familiar with the structures in the relevant industries and also has comprehensive, structural knowledge of the products and value chains, so that he or she can not only prepare detailed analyses and studies, but also validate, discuss, and interpret them.
- E4: The employee has comprehensive operational but also structural knowledge of the industries at all levels of aggregation. He or she also knows the company's own products in relation to offers from competitors. Against this background, the employee can situate his or her entire knowledge in the overall context of strategic organizational management and thus contribute significantly to decision-making within the management opinion-forming process.

8.4.2 Analytical Thinking (AT)

The second field of competence is a very personal characteristic that can only be trained or learned to a limited extent. To a certain extent, sensitivity to analytics can be deepened, but if a person does not have a strong analytical aptitude and talent from the outset, a top PI analyst will never be able to emerge from it. Analytical thinking defines the ability to recognize and solve problems, not the expertise to solve complicated mathematical tasks.

Analytical thinking does not solve mathematical problems, but rather illuminates certain facts with the appropriate "if then" formula. Analytics recognizes dependencies or causalities, which is why recognizing connections, structuring and interpreting them and drawing the right conclusions from them are among the core characteristics. Many recruitment tests therefore work with text analysis tasks in which the candidates are asked to demonstrate their analytical thinking skills. The process of analytical thinking is divided into three steps:

- Basic problem detection
- Problem structure capturing with regard to individual parts and sub-aspects
- Problem-solving strategies development

If the ability to think analytically is mentioned in a job advertisement as a prerequisite for employment, the company needs an employee who can quickly understand and unravel complex relationships. In this context, the following four behavioral anchors can therefore be derived for the AT competence field:

- E1: The employee can recognize, understand, and interpret structures under guidance for simple and already worked out problems.
- E2: The employee is able to independently understand and capture even larger, more complex problems in the form of analyses, reports, and studies in a structured manner, identify inconsistencies, eliminate them and then work them out.
- E3: The employee is able to structure, optimize, supplement, and precisely formulate complex, not yet finally and precisely defined inquiries and problems in direct contact with internal customers. In doing so, he or she can also reference and integrate already existing data and information material and corresponding expert opinions.
- E4: The employee is able to present complex, multivariate analyses, reports, and problems in an easily understandable and clear manner at the management level in order to guide, support, and focus the data-based opinion-forming process. The employee is able to change viewing levels depending on the situation in order to actively ensure valid opinion forming at all times.

8.4.3   Data Management

Professional data management includes aspects such as methodical, conceptual, organizational, and technical measures and activities for the strategic resource data with the goal of the best possible availability, usability, validity, integrity, and security (Hildebrand et al. 2018). Professional data management must also ensure appropriate data consistency for the entire field of predictive intelligence.

In the context of the classic definition of data management in relation to business processes and operations, the focus in the area of predictive intelligence is shifting towards the operational management of data and, above all, the various internal and external sourcing systems. This requires a close coordination and cooperation with the topic of data extrapolation, which is constantly looking for new relevant data and data sources, which then have to be operatively supported by data management in the further course of the project.

In the field of data management, in particular, there is a need to sharpen the focus of training in the area of predictive intelligence, because external data and source systems are much more important in the PI environment. As discussed earlier, the current discussion and content of business analytics and data science focus almost exclusively on product and process data, which is a major difference to predictive intelligence as part of data-based corporate management.

In this context, this competence involves the ongoing monitoring of updates of the relevant databases, changes in structures in the databases that would lead to changes or errors in the internal PI system, right through to the control of units used in the various systems, such as currencies, units of measurement and the like.

Against this background, the following four behavioral anchors can be defined for the competence field of data management:

- E1: The employee can refer to experiences in dealing with spreadsheets and is able to implement defined evaluations for existing data.
- E2: The employee has an overview of the external data and database landscape and can refer to corresponding experience in the use of these sources, but also the active integration into a simple table system of such data sources. The employee is able to take over, clean up and prepare the data for a defined content field and to validate results independently with regard to validity, reliability, and objectivity.
- E3: The employee can independently cover and set up one or more industrial value chains from a data management perspective and manage and ensure ongoing operations. The employee is proactively able to discuss optimization in terms of ongoing data management with internal stakeholders and thus contribute to the continuous improvement of data management standards.
- E4: The employee has already designed and established several data management systems. He also has comprehensive conceptual-strategic knowledge about best practice in data management. In this context, the employee is able to proactively contribute on all levels to a modern PI infrastructure.

8.4.4 Data Exploration

The field of data exploration focuses on the ability to identify possible sources of data internally and, above all, externally and to evaluate them with regard to data quality and connectivity. Clearly defined processes must be created and compliance with them must be ensured. The entire field of data discovery must be covered by data exploration experts. These experts will become more and more important in the future, as there are more and more freely accessible data sources on the market that need to be found and scanned.

Data exploration is also becoming more and more of a technology issue when you consider the possibilities of marketing automation solutions or web crawlers. In this respect, data exploration managers themselves must be technology-savvy and also work closely with technology management and IT. The explorative data analysis (EDA) or explorative statistics is in itself a subarea of classical statistics and has developed from it. It examines and evaluates data of which only a limited knowledge of their interrelationships is available. EDA techniques are mainly used in data mining.

It was John W. Tukey[11] in the 1970s who also significantly shaped the modern concept of data exploration. He argued that too much emphasis in statistics is placed on the processing of *given* hypotheses. Tukey therefore advocated using data in the context of data exploration rather to obtain possible *new* hypotheses and then to test them. In the context of Predictive Intelligence, data exploration is understood and used in an essentially creative way. The explorative character is the one that, in the long run, contributes a decisive added value, especially in combination or extension with Artificial Intelligence, but also in the prediction of events and developments, since new hypotheses produced from the data can be incorporated into new algorithms and models in the form of possible, new, previously unknown contexts.

This means that there will be interesting career opportunities for data exploration experts in the context of predictive intelligence. The following four definitions show how such experts can be classified using the four levels of behavioral anchors:

- E1: The employee has basic and first experience with databases and a basic understanding of how they work.
- E2: The employee has successfully completed a corresponding basic course of study and has gained initial practical experience in this context. The employee can handle precisely defined data exploration tasks and incorporate feedback.
- E3: The employee already has in-depth experience in the identification, selection, and validation of various data sources and systems. The employee has detailed knowledge of the subject area and can already use this knowledge to set up data exploration or to analyze and optimize an existing data exploration infrastructure. The employee can introduce other colleagues to the subject area and manage them.
- E4: The employee has extensive experience in building, optimizing, and further developing data exploration infrastructures. He has already designed and implemented one or more such infrastructures himself. He is able to proactively inform the company management about possible new data sources and to evaluate and validate them in a strategic context.

8.4.5 Data Algorithmics

This area is certainly one of the most exciting, but also one of the most unoccupied in terms of training and current human potential. Data algorithms come from the field of classical mathematics and statistics, but through applied research and work in

---

[11]https://en.wikipedia.org/wiki/John_Tukey. Accessed: November 23, 2020.

connection with technologies in the field of Artificial Intelligence, their competence has developed from a techno*cratic* to a techno-*creative* one. This change goes hand in hand with that in the previously described competence field of data exploration, which is also developing away from a *reactive* approach based on existing hypotheses and thus reactive approaches to a *proactive* one in the sense of the development of new hypotheses and insights.

From the perspective of organizational etymology, it would be de facto a completely wrong step not to proactively use such degrees of freedom in relation to data, which are created by new approaches and technologies. These newly added degrees of freedom in data represent a view beyond the edge of one's own nose, which is only just beginning to open up due to ever-larger data volumes but also ever better and more powerful possibilities in the area of data management and, based on this, in data algorithms.

What was previously rather frowned upon in the field of classical mathematics and statistics has mutated into the all-important success factor in the context of data-driven management. Because modern data algorithms can recognize many previously unknown correlations and based on these, derive very important, previously impossible corporate strategy insights and immediately integrate them into new predictive models and scenarios. The predictive intelligence units of companies will soon be able to implement themselves what top strategy consultants had to laboriously work out and process manually just a few years ago, without being able to prove and validate the derived strategy theses, mostly by implication.

The task of a data algorithmists is to constantly develop new approaches in the field of secondary and tertiary methods, to test them and subsequently integrate them into the current predictive intelligence system. A data algorithmist is a designer who designs, elaborates, and creatively develops calculation paths. The data-algorithmic competence can be classified by the following four behavioral anchors:

- E1: The employee studies mathematics, statistics, operation research, or one of the new courses of study in the field of data science or business analytics. The employee has no additional practical experience but has a creative affinity to his personality structure.
- E2: The employee has a degree in mathematics or statistics or a data science program and is characterized by a solid, stringent but also creative way of working and thinking. The employee has already developed and designed the first secondary methods in projects.
- E3: The employee already has between 3 and 5 years of practical experience in the field of data algorithms. He has developed numerous secondary and tertiary methods and accompanied their implementation. The employee has profound knowledge in classical algorithms and also has extensive creative competence in algorithmic development. The employee is able to introduce younger colleagues to modern PI algorithms in an inspiring way and to support their development. The employee has first experiences in handling and using procedures of artificial intelligence.

- E4: The employee is capable of translating complex facts and questions into corresponding PI algorithms on an operational as well as strategic-conceptual level. He also has extensive experience in the functioning and application of artificial intelligence methods.

8.4.6   Data Visualization

This field of competence does not only focus on the graphic preparation and design of data and information inherent to this concept of visualization. Against the background of the ever-improving possibilities of the dashboard and online design templates, the field of competence of data visualization is also changing. More and more free and freely accessible platforms offer many different templates for various content areas. Similar to the content management platform WordPress,[12] the Colorlib[13] and CreativeTim[14] platforms offer free dashboard templates.

Data visualization in the *narrowest* sense of the word focuses on the design in terms of graphics and structure. Data visualization in the *broader sense* also considers logical-conceptual aspects in order to make the dashboards easier to use and read for the user of data analysis. The point is to immediately focus on correlations and the insights and possible conclusions that can be derived from them through smart preparation. Experienced *data visualizers* are experts in simplifying the complex.

In all PI projects, the graphic development of the elaborations has been similar. Once the initial elaborations had been completed, the skills in handling the Excel table or the PowerBI solution matured accordingly, the PI employees tried to transfer as much of the data that had been elaborated and analyzed as possible into colored dashboards and graphics. In this phase, caution must be exercised, as there is a risk that internal customers will be unnecessarily overwhelmed and fall by the wayside. This must be prevented at all costs.

At this point of the PI journey, as a manager, the aim is to bring the KISS principle back to the employees' minds:

- Keep
- It
- Small and
- Simple

Less is more. Data visualizers are also the ones that have to decide what should or must be shown and what not. Data visualizers can be compared to content managers

---

[12]https://wordpress.com/. Accessed: 15 October 2020.

[13]https://colorlib.com/wp/free-dashboard-templates/. Accessed: 15 October 2020.

[14]https://www.creative-tim.com/blog/web-design/free-dashboard-templates/.   Accessed: 15 October 2020.

in the field of marketing, because their task is to place the "story." They will have to be measured by whether the data was immediately understood by the target group in order to be able to validly discuss and debate a matter under focus and subsequently make a decision. A good visualizer is an employee with a good feeling for connections and their presentation. He must be selective in his approach to the content at hand and, in view of the big picture, translate a chain of arguments into easily understandable diagrams and dashboard designs.

On this basis, the following behavioral anchors can be derived for the four levels of competence:

- E1: The employee has experience in creating simple data graphics using common data or table applications.
- E2: The employee has already independently processed large amounts of data into different views and dashboards that build on each other and, against this background, can point to comprehensive technical skills in handling such applications.
- E3: The employee can independently outline extensive questions in the form of graphic concepts and explain possible future mapping options ex ante on the basis of storyboards. The employee has a broad ability in handling data and designs and contributes actively and significantly to the uniform, easily understandable data visualization for the organizational unit concerned.
- E4: The employee has extensive experience in the conception but also the realization of data visualization for simple to complex questions. Against the background of his expertise, he is able to identify good data visualizers on the one hand, and on the other hand, he is able to motivate and engage a team of data visualizers and to develop them further. The employee can support discussions on the management level and directly identify and derive possibilities for further optimization of existing design templates and translate them into concrete adaptation measures.

8.4.7 Technology Management

The area of technology management must take care of the PITechStack, as it was already described and discussed in detail in the previous chapter. This also involves the selection of possible new elements of the PITechStack and, within this context, the exact elaboration of template-based comparative analyses between different solutions. Especially in larger corporate structures, it is important to be able to efficiently and effectively use and benefit from in-house IT competence. Strict and comprehensively elaborated documentation is therefore of crucial importance when it comes to the decision preparation of possible new elements for the extension of the PITechStack.

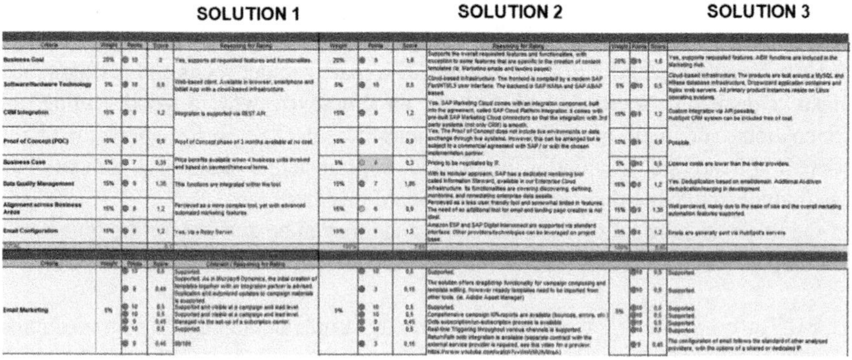

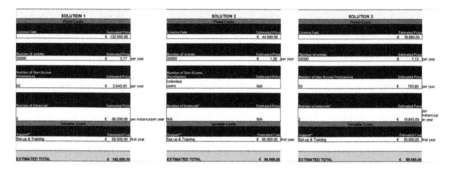

Fig. 8.4 Sample solution evaluation template (Source: Own representation)

Fig. 8.5 Sample cost model comparison template (Source: Own representation)

The PI technology manager must pay attention to the following aspects:

- Which key features are required?
- How are the potential providers positioned in the general benchmarking (e.g., in the Gartner ranking)?
- How do the solutions perform in a direct operational comparison? Here, the use of defined and coordinated Key Performance Indicators (KPIs) has proven to be a good approach, on the basis of which the solutions can be compared very accurately (Fig. 8.4).
- What do the cost models look like and where are the cost drivers (Fig. 8.5).
- What do the PI-RoI considerations look like in relation to the PITechStack solutions available? Here it is important to define relevant KPIs for the PITechStack in general but also for the specific applications in the PITechStack. In most cases, these are cost optimizations through automated and thus accelerated processing of activities or realized sales in the form of additional sales or short-term sales optimizations.

- How compatible are the various solutions in terms of integration or connection to the existing corporate IT infrastructure? Ideally, this criterion should also be taken into account when making a direct comparison.
- From the point of view of content, how does the PI team prioritize a purchase decision?

On the basis of these criteria, a possible investment decision can be validly prepared and prepared in coordination with the company's own IT.

The following four behavioral anchors can be derived for the area of technology management:

- E1: The employee has basic knowledge of the current state of development of the PITechStack landscape and can describe and recognize the different types of existing solutions against this background.
- E2: The employee has comprehensive knowledge of the current status of the PITechStack map and can validate various solutions with regard to their areas of application and orientation in the context of their use in their own organization. The employee has initial experience in preparing documents for the decision to purchase a possible solution in the relevant subject area.
- E3: The employee has a deep insight into the PITechStack map and can refer to comprehensive interface knowledge in the area of business and IT. The employee can conduct content discussions with the in-house IT department regarding IT strategic aspects and content in order to continuously evaluate and optimize the technology management for the PI area, both operationally and conceptually, in terms of user and operator friendliness.
- E4: The employee can present and represent the PITechStack strategy on a corporate strategy level. His comprehensive operational as well as conceptual knowledge enables him to recognize relevant developments in the market, to relate them to the organizational PITechStack, and to assess their relevance for the PITechStack landscape in order to ensure a sustainable *state-of-the-art* PITechStack.

8.4.8   Strategic Thinking

This area of competence is de facto not a PI-specific area of competence but is of crucial importance in the context of this topic area and the current orientation in data science and business analytics already discussed. Together with the competence area "Analytical Thinking," *Strategic Thinking* ensures that Predictive Intelligence as part of data-driven corporate management is not an end in itself. Only if the transfer or the interactive and intensive connection with the business can be established successfully, the entire potential of a modern applied Predictive Intelligence can be raised by an organization.

In this context, it is also about the necessary acceptance of the topic, which can only be realized through a common and transparent approach. The better the internal customers understand what Predictive Intelligence can do and for which diverse questions it can be used to support them, the better it will develop within an organizational environment. What has been shown again and again in the various projects is an enormous, shared creativity that arises when everyone pulls together on the PI strand on the basis of a common understanding.

Since the entire topic area of predictive intelligence as the core of data-driven management is still a young knowledge discipline, its content can only be mastered through organizational learning. Authenticity therefore plays an essential role in this context, because it is about the awareness that many things can and will only emerge in the course of time. Those managers who openly dealt with their own partial ignorance towards their colleagues and internal customers in the various projects were also those who went through the development steps more quickly and effectively together with their organizations. The reason for this was simply that by openly committing to the *Predictive Intelligence Journey* (PIJ) and thus the necessary joint learning, the sense of "we" is strengthened and all those involved are much more actively involved and help shape and master this journey.

Strategic thinking in the context of Predictive Intelligence can be classified using the following four behavioral anchors:

- E1: The employee is studying in the field of economics and social sciences or management and has gained first experience in the field of management consulting.
- E2: The employee has between 3 and 5 years of professional experience in a corporate development department or as management consultant. He has shown in various projects that he can derive a well-founded picture of a situation on the basis of data and information in order to design possible scenarios and causalities in the form of action alternatives. For this purpose, the employee can fall back on a set of common management concepts and instruments, which he intuitively selects and uses correctly.
- E3: The employee has extensive conceptual and strategic experience in the environment of modern business practice. He or she is able to document, interpret, and evaluate complex contents and contexts methodically and structurally stringent. In addition, he can present and discuss these with support also on the management level.
- E4: Due to his extensive operational experience and practice, the employee has the necessary know-how to translate all business issues into predictive intelligence structures and to accompany their elaboration with regard to stringency and congruence. Against this background, the employee can select and justify an option from a number of possibilities as a recommended course of action. Thanks to the comprehensive strategic thinking skills, complex issues can be captured, processed, and immediately adopted in new thoughts and options.

8.4.9   Leadership

The competence field "Leadership" is probably the most important one when it comes to the long-term success of a new unit Predictive Intelligence but above all also the change process towards a data-driven corporate management. Most projects have shown that the dimension of this almost paradigmatic change of perspective is often underestimated. In many organizations, the management is of the opinion that the own company or unit is already data-driven. This opinion is based on the fact that ERP and CRM systems are established in the companies and are used more or less actively and meaningfully.

On closer inspection, however, it turns out that such systems are only used to a fraction of their full potential in most cases and that the data held in the systems are completely inadequate in terms of validity and completeness. There are many reasons for this, which will not be dealt with in detail at this point, since many brilliant textbooks deal with this topic almost exhaustively anyway.

In fact, the majority of companies today are still by no means data-driven, which becomes frighteningly clear when you happen to see how essential data and information for board meetings on business and sales planning for the following period is compiled and prepared. Often such data is accessed "on the fly" via Skype-Calls and an employee from Commercial or Controlling then puts this information into a more or less stylish MS PowerPoint slight deck. Any validity check is not necessary because the employee(s) have negated requests for the provision of the data several times anyway and therefore the necessary time is ultimately lacking to perform such necessary cross-checks.

The result is sales and group planning that always has to be adjusted and corrected because the input data is based on gut feeling, the well-known "hot thumb." In the context of predictive intelligence, leadership therefore requires that a manager has the expertise and, above all, the format that allows him or her to clearly point out to the management their own organizational structural weaknesses with regard to the current situation and to data-driven corporate management, in order to then convey knowledge about the need for adaptation to a serious and value-adding predictive intelligence. This includes above all the awareness of organizational, uncompromising discipline and the appreciation of data as strategic resources and not an evil for the purpose of enabling management to create an annual plan.

How can the field of competence "Leadership" be measured or defined:

- E1: The employee has a professional appearance and a sound awareness of the value of professional handling of data and information. He or she is empathic and reflects his or her behavior, and also accepts feedback and positive criticism in order to develop further.
- E2: In initial meetings, the employee has shown that he or she is confident in the way he or she presents himself or herself to the target group and that he or she acts factually and constructively even in complex situations. He has shown that he is aware of the strategic dimension of data and thus serves as a role model for

colleagues and internal customers regarding the appreciative and valid handling of data.

- E3: The employee has already successfully implemented many different PI projects, actively acting as an ambassador of data as strategic resources. The employee is accepted throughout the organization as a PI expert and proactively involved by the organization in all aspects of data-driven corporate management. The employee has comprehensive knowledge in the area of PI but also of the company's own PI infrastructure.
- E4: The employee is involved at the top management level in all questions of corporate governance. Together with his team, he can quickly and reliably work out any business issue that arises. In addition, the employee regularly provides impulses regarding aspects of the company's development and is constantly represented and present in the management. He is involved in every decision and his word is valued and taken into account.

8.5   The Predictive Intelligence Competence Matrix

On the basis of the behavioral anchors for all nine PI competency fields, which were previously derived step by step, the PI competency matrix can then be compiled, which shows all competency fields with their four behavioral anchors at a glance (Table 8.1). This matrix is intended to serve as a frame of reference to be able to focus on and refer to the relevant aspects in the context of PI team development. On the basis of current HR practice, the fulfillment of each behavioral anchor can be measured using a five-part Likert scale, for example, from which an even more accurate picture can be derived for each of the four levels and for each potential candidate, also with regard to any development potential that may exist.

It can also be helpful to evaluate candidates and employees according to all fields of competence. Only rarely will one or more employees be available for each field of competence. In such cases, the aim is to identify which employee can best cover which areas of the PI Competence Matrix. Such an analysis can also help to provide an early assessment with regard to future decisions regarding the specialist and management careers of employees.

In this chapter, an attempt was made to describe an ideal-typical team for the field of predictive intelligence. However, one must be aware of the fact that this field is currently more than ever subject to enormous dynamics. This will also have an impact on the area of Predictive Intelligence Workforce Management. Since the entire topic of data-driven corporate management can only be successfully set up and established in the long term if the topic is authentically driven forward by the organization itself, it will also only be logical to continuously and critically address the aspects of competencies and their further development.

In this way, a PI team that perfectly complements itself and the entire organization can and will be created, which will realize sustainable added value for the company in terms of compliance with the two basic economic principles described at the beginning of this book.

Table 8.1 PI Competence Matrix

Predictive Intelligence competence tableau				
Competence areas	Behavioral anchors			
	Level 1	Level 2	Level 3	Level 4
Industry and product competence	The employee has no knowledge of relevant industries or products in the relevant area. He or she is new to the company or the business	The employee has a rough overview of the relevant industries and knows the unit's products at a glance	The employee is familiar with the structures in the relevant industries and also has comprehensive, structural knowledge of the products and value chains, so that he or she can not only prepare detailed analyses and studies, but also validate, discuss, and interpret them	The employee has comprehensive operational but also structural knowledge of the industries at all levels of aggregation. He or she also knows the company's own products in relation to offers from competitors. Against this background, the employee can situate his or her entire knowledge in the overall context of strategic organizational management and thus contribute significantly to decision-making within the management opinion-forming process
Analytical thinking	The employee can recognize, understand, and interpret structures under guidance for simple and already worked out problems	The employee is able to independently understand and capture even larger, more complex problems in the form of analyses, reports, and studies in a structured manner, identify inconsistencies,	The employee is able to structure, optimize, supplement, and precisely formulate complex, not yet finally and precisely defined inquiries and problems in direct contact with internal customers. In	The employee is able to present complex, multivariate analyses, reports, and problems in an easily understandable and clear manner at the management level in order to guide, support, and focus the

(continued)

Table 8.1 (continued)

Predictive Intelligence competence tableau

Competence areas	Behavioral anchors			
	Level 1	Level 2	Level 3	Level 4
		eliminate them and then work them out	doing so, he or she can also reference and integrate already existing data and information material and corresponding expert opinions	data-based opinion-forming process. The employee is able to change viewing levels depending on the situation in order to actively ensure valid opinion forming at all times
Data management	The employee can refer to experiences in dealing with spreadsheets and is able to implement defined evaluations for existing data	The employee has an overview of the external data and database landscape and can refer to corresponding experience in the use of these sources, but also the active integration into a simple table system of such data sources. The employee is able to take over, clean up and prepare the data for a defined content field and to validate results independently with regard to validity, reliability, and objectivity	The employee can independently cover and set up one or more industrial value chains from a data management perspective and manage and ensure ongoing operations. The employee is proactively able to discuss optimization in terms of ongoing data management with internal stakeholders and thus contribute to the continuous improvement of data management standards	The employee has already designed and established several data management systems. He also has comprehensive conceptual-strategic knowledge about best practice in data management. In this context, the employee is able to proactively contribute on all levels to a modern PI infrastructure
Data exploration	The employee has basic and first experience with databases and a basic understanding of how they work	The employee has successfully completed a corresponding basic course of study and has gained initial	The employee already has in-depth experience in the identification, selection, and validation of	The employee has extensive experience in building, optimizing, and further developing data

(continued)

Table 8.1   (continued)

Predictive Intelligence competence tableau				
Competence areas	Behavioral anchors			
	Level 1	Level 2	Level 3	Level 4
		practical experience in this context. The employee can handle precisely defined data exploration tasks and incorporate feedback	various data sources and systems. The employee has detailed knowledge of the subject area and can already use this knowledge to set up data exploration or to analyze and optimize an existing data exploration infrastructure. The employee can introduce other colleagues to the subject area and manage them	exploration infrastructures. He has already designed and implemented one or more such infrastructures himself. He is able to proactively inform the company management about possible new data sources and to evaluate and validate them in a strategic context
Data algorithmics	The employee studies mathematics, statistics, operation research or one of the new courses of study in the field of data science or business analytics. The employee has no additional practical experience but has a creative affinity to his personality structure	The employee has a degree in mathematics or statistics or a data science program and is characterized by a solid, stringent but also creative way of working and thinking. The employee has already developed and designed the first secondary methods in projects	The employee already has between 3 and 5 years of practical experience in the field of data algorithms. He has developed numerous secondary and tertiary methods and accompanied their implementation. The employee has profound knowledge in classical algorithms and also has extensive creative competence in algorithmic	The employee is capable of translating complex facts and questions into corresponding PI algorithms on an operational as well as strategic-conceptual level. He also has extensive experience in the functioning and application of artificial intelligence methods

(continued)

Table 8.1 (continued)

Predictive Intelligence competence tableau				
Competence areas	Behavioral anchors			
	Level 1	Level 2	Level 3	Level 4
			development. The employee is able to introduce younger colleagues to modern PI algorithms in an inspiring way and to support their development. The employee has first experiences in handling and using procedures of artificial intelligence	
Data visualization	The employee has experience in creating simple data graphics using common data or table applications	The employee has already independently processed large amounts of data into different views and dashboards that build on each other and, against this background, can point to comprehensive technical skills in handling such applications	The employee can independently outline extensive questions in the form of graphic concepts and explain possible future mapping options ex ante on the basis of storyboards. The employee has a broad ability in handling data and designs and contributes actively and significantly to the uniform, easily understandable data visualization for the organizational unit concerned	The employee has extensive experience in the conception but also the realization of data visualization for simple to complex questions. Against the background of his expertise, he is able to identify good data visualizers on the one hand and on the other hand he is able to motivate and engage a team of data visualizers and to develop them further. The employee can support discussions on the management

(continued)

Table 8.1 (continued)

Predictive Intelligence competence tableau			
Competence areas	Behavioral anchors		
	Level 1	Level 2	Level 3	Level 4

Competence areas	Level 1	Level 2	Level 3	Level 4
				level and directly identify and derive possibilities for further optimization of existing design templates and translate them into concrete adaptation measures
Technology management	The employee has basic knowledge of the current state of development of the PITechStack landscape and can describe and recognize the different types of existing solutions against this background	The employee has comprehensive knowledge of the current status of the PITechStack map and can validate various solutions with regard to their areas of application and orientation in the context of their use in their own organization. The employee has initial experience in preparing documents for the decision to purchase a possible solution in the relevant subject area	The employee has a deep insight into the PITechStack map and can refer to comprehensive interface knowledge in the area of business and IT. The employee can conduct content discussions with the in-house IT department regarding IT strategic aspects and content in order to continuously evaluate and optimize the technology management for the PI area, both operationally and conceptually, in terms of user and operator friendliness	The employee can present and represent the PITechStack strategy on a corporate strategy level. His comprehensive operational as well as conceptual knowledge enables him to recognize relevant developments in the market, to relate them to the organizational PITechStack, and to assess their relevance for the PITechStack landscape in order to ensure a sustainable *state-of-the-art* PITechStack
Strategic thinking	The employee is studying in the field of economics and	The employee has between 3 and 5 years of professional	The employee has extensive conceptual and strategic	Due to his extensive operational experience and

(continued)

Table 8.1 (continued)

Predictive Intelligence competence tableau

Competence areas	Behavioral anchors			
	Level 1	Level 2	Level 3	Level 4
	social sciences or management and has gained first experiences in the field of management consulting	experience in a corporate development department or as management consultant. He has shown in various projects that he can derive a well-founded picture of a situation on the basis of data and information in order to design possible scenarios and causalities in the form of action alternatives. For this purpose, the employee can fall back on a set of common management concepts and instruments, which he intuitively selects and uses correctly	experience in the environment of modern business practice. He or she is able to document, interpret, and evaluate complex contents and contexts methodically and structurally stringent. In addition, he can present and discuss these with support also on the management level	practice, the employee has the necessary know-how to translate all business issues into predictive intelligence structures and to accompany their elaboration with regard to stringency and congruence. Against this background, the employee can select and justify an option from a number of possibilities as a recommended course of action. Thanks to the comprehensive strategic thinking skills, complex issues can be captured, processed, and immediately adopted in new thoughts and options
Leadership	The employee has a professional appearance and a sound awareness of the value of professional handling of data and information. He or she is empathic and reflects his or her behavior, and	In initial meetings, the employee has shown that he or she is confident in the way he or she presents himself or herself to the target group and that he or she acts factually and constructively	The employee has already successfully implemented many different PI projects, actively acting as an ambassador of data as strategic resources. The employee is accepted throughout the	The employee is involved at the top management level in all questions of corporate governance. Together with his team, he can quickly and reliably work out any business issue that arises.

(continued)

Table 8.1 (continued)

Predictive Intelligence competence tableau				
Competence areas	Behavioral anchors			
	Level 1	Level 2	Level 3	Level 4
	also accepts feedback and positive criticism in order to develop further	even in complex situations. He has shown that he is aware of the strategic dimension of data and thus serves as a role model for colleagues and internal customers regarding the appreciative and valid handling of data	organization as a PI expert and proactively involved by the organization in all aspects of data-driven corporate management. The employee has comprehensive knowledge in the area of PI but also of the company's own PI infrastructure	In addition, the employee regularly provides impulses regarding aspects of the company's development and is constantly represented and present in the management. He is involved in every decision and his word is valued and taken into account

Source: Own presentation

Further Reading

Busol, M. (2019). *War for Talents: Erfolgsfaktoren im Kampf um die Besten*. Berlin: Springer Gabler.

Edmondson, A. C. (2018). *The fearless organization—Creating psycho-logical safety in the workplace for learning, innovation and growth*. London: Wiley.

Hildebrand, K., Gebauer, M., et al. (2018). *Daten- und Informationsqualität: Auf dem Weg zur Information Excellence*. Wiesbaden: Springer.

Rifkin, J. (2019). *Der globale Green New Deal: Warum die fossil befeuerte Zivilisation um 2028 kollabiert—und ein kühner ökonomischer Plan das Leben auf der Erde retten kann*. Frankfurt: Campus Verlag.

Seebacher, U. (2020a). *B2B marketing: A guidebook for the classroom to the boardroom*. Cham: Springer.

Seebacher, U. (2020b). *B2B marketing essential: How to turn your marketing from a cost into a sales engine* (2nd ed.). Graz: AQPS.

Seebacher, U. (2020c). *Template-based management—A guide for an efficient and impactful professional practice*. Cham: Springer.

Seebacher, U., & Güpner, A. (2014). *Innovation durch strategisches Personalmanagement: Das "Made in Germany" sichern durch Workforce und Diversity Management*. München: USP International.

Wessel, K. F. (1998). *Humanontogenetik—Neue Überlegungen zu alten Fragen*. Bielefeld: USP Publishing Kleine Verlag.

The Predictive Intelligence Case Studies

9

9.1 Why Predictive Intelligence Is Not Rocket Science

This case study is a very special case study, as it essentially consists of three small different stereotypical forms of Predictive Intelligence applications. As such, it can be seen as a blueprint for how, within an organization without specific or additional budgets and without external agency or consulting support, the hot topic of *Big Data* can be set up and sustainably developed towards predictive analytics and intelligence competence. The case study also looks at how cost-effective *quick wins* can be realized. For time and budget reasons, the entire project was set up and realized on the basis of the template-based management (TBM) approach.

9.2 Where Does the Case Study Company Come from?

The Show Case Company has its headquarters in North America. With production facilities on all continents, the company generates annual incoming orders of around $950 million. In addition, the organization has specific sales companies in certain regions such as Europe and Asia. In general, the company, BlueHill Inc., is active in four industries: environment, chemicals, mining, and process industry. The organization has 10,000 employees from more than 150 countries. The company is a typical US-based owner-managed corporation. Ray as the owner founded the company in a small barn in the 1950s and since then with ups and downs succeeded in growing his company quite successfully.

With regard to the product portfolio, it must be noted that it has not yet been finally possible to structurally cover all industry-specific value chains. Ray's vision is to develop his company from a product to a solution provider as this would help BlueHill to realize and sustainably develop competitive advantages. But this endeavor is not that easy as it takes time and money for either developing the missing products or acquiring companies with such products in their portfolio. This means that especially in the chemicals industry only very small and limited parts of the obviously very heterogeneous and complex value chains can be supplied. This in turn has a considerable impact on the aliquot market introduction costs and leads to strategic disadvantages. This situation is aggravated by the fact that competition in the chemical industry is high and few global players dominate the market. These players have many years of experience, history, and track record in the relevant applications and markets and, as a result, excellent contacts, which leads to high barriers to market entry.

The company is organized very lean and direct. Ray is overlooking all operations and tries to stay very close to the business. He is a real and authentic self-made millionaire and a sales guy through and through. Due to Ray's very active merger and acquisition activities, three production sites within the company play a significant part, one based in Austria, one based in Poland, and the last based in San Antonio, Texas. This leads to a lot of frictional losses, as top management sometimes has difficulty in stringently implementing the defined strategy due to lack of acceptance and lack of leadership strength and quality. Although Ray aims to centralize core functions, product management is decentralized and located at the various ten production sites, known as product houses. Vera is the Global Product Marketing Manager, who acts as an interface for all product managers. She coordinates, controls, and monitors all product planning and launch activities as part of the Global Marketing Team based at the BlueHill headquarter in Denver, Colorado.

The company is to a certain extent exposed to cluster risk, as almost 80% of its business is in the environment and mining industries. The chemical industry is characterized by many small projects, which means that the majority of the business generated is small but high margin. In general, the company struggles with a low EBITDA, which is in the mid-single-digit percentage range. This is due to the fact that Ray and his management team did not succeed yet to eliminate redundancies in the organization as well as existing IT. This means that all production sites do have their own independent finance and commercial department and still work on their own SME ERP systems. This means that data have to be transferred manually in order to be able to consolidate figures and do a proper order intake and cost analyses.

9.2.1 Why the Situation Became Difficult

The situation in the various industries was very different, which turned out to be an advantage for the company with regard to a certain risk balance. Especially against the background of the enormously increasing demand for lithium for battery production, mining was doing very well. The environmental industry was also about to experience a renaissance, especially when it comes to integrated water management, to increasing the efficiency of available facilities that enable virtually carbon-neutral water cycles, and to the growing world population, its growing demand for drinking and process water, which is being further intensified by global warming. These developments were also playing into the hands of BlueHill as supplier for fully digitized equipment transportation and pumping systems. The fact that more and more economies were once again recognizing pumped storage as one of the most efficient, sustainable, and environmentally friendly technologies for water and energy production was also playing into the cards for the company in terms of exploiting the potential and opportunities in this billion-dollar global market. Seawater desalination was one of the fastest growing applications in the water and wastewater management segment, and this growth would continue in the coming years and put a smile on Ray's face:

> We were fortunate to develop these four core industries, as they also represent my risk management due to their sometimes different developments. This has helped me sail through various tricky situations and a lot of headwinds since the 90s. Now I'm looking quite positively into the future with regard to the desalination industry, as we have been able to slow down some of the big players with their rigid structures and get into the big business. This allows me now to invest in the so important aspect of BlueHill's evolution into a data driven organization, as we need to know where the business is going to go and where it will come from!

The other two segments, the chemicals, and the process industries, were causing headaches for the company and its management. However, Ray was aware of the fact that a solid and strategic action plan for substantial growth in both industries would require a professional and well-planned Business Intelligence department or at least a dedicated team. Top management at the production sites did not recognize this fact and therefore all measures taken were situational and therefore not really measurable and comprehensible. Due to this the strategy and business planning was carried out as follows:

- The finance and controlling department asked the product managers and the site managers about their planning for the following years.
- The Austrian site submitted the right plans on time and with truly valid figures, while the others did not find the time to submit the requested documents even after some nice eMails from Ray.
- When appointments were made Ray and his commercial team, the other two site managers then shared their forecasts orally "on the fly."
- Ray did not like it, but the only way to proceed with the financial planning and forecasts was, to simply take the data, and have them consolidated by his commercial team.

All in all, there was no solid and truly reliable process that would have enabled the company to stringently plan and expand the business. It was not that the employees were not committed and motivated, but—as is so often the case— everything happened too late, poorly prepared and not validated, and without proper and rigorous follow-up and drawing consistent conclusions by management. Ray was sometimes too nice and some parts of the organization seemed to misuse his good-naturedness. An organization ticks like a small child, always trying to push the boundaries and test the limits. Over the years this has led to "alibi" activities and plans that have ended in endless evasions, discussions, and meetings without tangible results and without consequences.

But since the markets in which the company was active were growing steadily overall, the company was also able to grow. At first glance, therefore, the situation did not appear to be so bad, but on closer inspection, the return on investment of BlueHill was not satisfactory, as the company performed well below the market. The result was that the company as a whole had grown about 10–15% less than the relevant markets. If one considers the incoming orders of $900 million and the realized EBITDA of 5.2% in 2017, Ray ended up with ja net profit of around $46.8 million. At first glance, this figure sounds impressive, but the problem was that other comparable market players realized between 8 and 11% EBITDA and in order to be able to acquire new companies Ray would need to increase his profits in order to fill his war chest. Assuming a performance of 10% EBIDTA Ray could have almost double nis net profit up to $90 million.

9.2.2   Instead of the Watering Can Ray Needs the Spear

Ray got to know me at one of my lectures on the east coast. I reported there about our research and studies on predictive intelligence. I had been back from my lecture tour in the USA for quite some time when Ray called me and introduced himself. We immediately got into the conversation and Ray asked me for support.

He told me about his company and described his impressions to me. He invited me to come to Denver and spend a few days in his house in Aspen, knowing that I was a passionate skier. A few weeks later, it was April, I flew to him and spent unforgettable days in the Rocky Mountains. In this wonderful winter wonderland and between great runs in the world famous dry, dusty powder snow I talked to Ray about his company. I got a good picture of a true and passionate, courageous entrepreneur whose goal was to be—as he always said—a good entrepreneur who does not make profits at the expense of his employees.

Ray asked me if I thought Predictive Intelligence would help him solve his structural problems in the organization, which I immediately took off my hand and denied. But at the same time, I explained that PI could help him to assess very precisely where he could best use his hard-earned money with the greatest return in terms of business development. I explained this to him in the context of his description of how financial plans in his company are currently being drawn up more intuitively and according to the watering can principle without relying on a clean and stringent strategy.

After 1 week of skiing, we returned to Denver where I would meet the management team of Ray. I also met Gary, the designated Predictive Intelligence Project Manager. Gary was a brilliant guy and really cared about BLUEHILL. The meeting turned out to be very direct to the point. All the different *hidden agendas* and the weaknesses of the organization were discussed. I was surprised, because Gary seemed to know all this already. I had the impression that he had already made a very precise assessment of the organizational issues for himself but did not want to rush ahead. The situation seemed to be quite clear.

- Roxanna was the Commercial Manager and managed a team of four people. She was a very structured, calm, and engaging young lady.
- Pete was the Operations Manager and was responsible also for the IT of the company. He was one of Ray's longest companions and enjoyed his full confidence.
- Eden was the HR Manager, an experience one. A unique HR manager from the USA and with a background in the chemicals industry. She really had an impact on the organization and made Ray's life difficult several times. Eden was on her way to establish the HR Business Partner concept and also pushed her initiative for a dynamic, multidimensional performance and incentive management system.
- The Product Managers John, Claus, Tim, and Paul, of whom Mining Manager John was the top performer. He was a US-based, smart, and straightforward sales manager with deep roots in the mining industry. He would always overspend his budget and thereby save the others, and he had to, because Tim, who was responsible for the large environmental industry, was chaotic. Pete told me that Tim got caught in the crossfire during a management meeting because he had not delivered. But Tim managed to change the subject completely unnoticed through his gibberish and rhetoric, so that in the end he got off scot-free and the management team talked about something else trivial. John, a French Canadian, was responsible for the process industry. He was small and thin and always found ways to get himself out of trouble. Compared to Tim, John was much more subtle and elegant, but in the end, it was exactly the same trick. He always found reasons why something did not work out, and often Ray could not remember anything anyway. Last but not least there was Paul, who was responsible for chemicals. He had only recently joined BLUEHILL Inc. Paul was inconspicuous and with a background in marketing and sales and several years of experience in the industry, he was firmly established in that segment.
- The managers of the production sites also played an important role in the organizational game. One of the most colorful was Charly. He always started arguing with Ray at management meetings and never missed an opportunity to get to grips with Roxanna.

This was more or less the situation at the top management level. Everybody did what they wanted, and it did not matter if Ray wanted something or not. But Ray always seemed to succeed in bringing good ideas and clients to the table which was at the core of BLUEHILL's success. And when push came to shove, Ray could count on John and "his" mining industry, most of which was over budget anyway.

9.2.3   You Do Not Have to Be Everybody's Darling!

Then Gary stepped in and began to give an insight into his experiences with the different people in the organization. He was simply a professional and packed the whole pandemonium into magnificently formulated, precise statements without ever losing sight of the good tone. Putting it a bit more directly and less nicely, he wanted to say that, as is so often the case, the problem is right at the top.

The problem was Ray as he was not sufficiently structured and strict in its leadership and lacked a clear method to drive the company forward and let it grow. And the good thing, but even more positive was that Ray, himself, was aware of it. I admired Ray inwardly, because he was such a successful self-made man who could afford everything but still seemed so down to earth, not to take himself out of his duty and openly admit his own weaknesses. Whether it was the following year or a new market entry, nothing was discussed, analyzed, and documented professionally enough. Whoever spoke more and louder, his opinion was valid. Therefore, Gary was called in. As Vice President of Marketing and Communications, he had streamlined and upgraded the team from a chaotic B2B marketing department to an innovative department dealing with all the increasingly important topics such as lead scanning, lead generation, inbound lead management, marketing automation, customer experience and touchpoint management and many other aspects. It was Gary's team that increased the number of marketing-generated inbound leads by a triple-digit percentage, exposing that sales did not properly track these marketing-generated leads, leaving over 100 million euros in potential orders unaccounted for. Gary began to drive more and more the salesmen and the entire organization before itself. I think this was one of the reasons why Luc liked him.

To start the project, Gary and I started talking about our goal. I shared with him my thoughts and experiences from previous projects. I had to introduce him to the topic of predictive intelligence. We liked each other because we considered ourselves as "structure nerds," because we were convinced of the power and magic of structures and methods. Gary then began to draft these first working papers. I coached him on inconsistencies, and I was happy to guide him, because Gary really had a lot of knowledge, not only expertise, but also methodological knowledge. I also explained to him why the subject area was so exciting—also from a career point of view—and talked to him about the enormous potential in terms of optimizing technical sales against the background of the modest performance of product managers. I also introduced him to the Predictive Intelligence Maturity Model (PIMM). On this basis, I had Gary perform the PIMM-based PI self-assessment. Based on this assessment, we found that BLUEHILL was still at level 1 "Reactive-static Business Analysis" (Rabab) in terms of the maturity level of PI.

The result of the BLUEHILL-PI self-assessment provided us with a good basis for process abstraction and development. In a first step, Gary had to develop templates to enable BLUEHILL to define potential data sources and providers. The templates were then to be completed by the relevant people in the organization as a basis for Gary, who then had to consolidate the collected information and take the next steps in terms of discussions and negotiations with potential data suppliers and vendors.

Gary then had to design templates so that his colleagues could help him develop the underlying data model. This was an important step towards general acceptance, but also to ensure the necessary transparency about how the data is connected and processed. These templates also had to cover the various future data and research

Fig. 9.1 PI process
abstraction and development

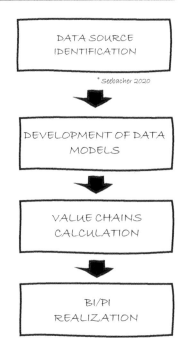

requests, so that Gary knew ex ante what and in what form would be asked and requested in the future. As part of the next step of the "Intelligence Generation" he had to provide templates to collect information on how newsletters, news updates, market studies, and reports, but also business cases, market entry studies, or strategic concepts should look like in order to meet the needs of the different stakeholders and internal customer groups in the organization.

These steps were necessary in order to take the Predictive Intelligence Maturity Model (PIMM) to the next level called "Proactive-Situational Business Analytics," i.e., no longer just to perform evaluations and research on demand, but also to keep the organization continuously proactively informed and up-to-date with relevant news and developments in the various industries. The transition from the first stage of PIMM to the next stage also meant that the need for external suppliers to provide studies and research reports was significantly reduced.

> Tip: With regard to the third step in Fig. 9.1, it is important to note that this should be done before purchasing data, because the calculation and analysis of the value chain will make clear what kind of data is required from each defined data source. It is not always necessary to purchase entire data packages or databases. Based on the elaboration and, building on that, the calculation of the value chain, you will understand which partitions or data sets your own company will need. Gary once again saved a six-figure

(continued)

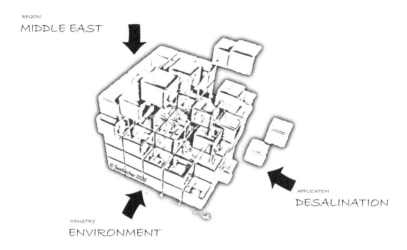

REGION
MIDDLE EAST

APPLICATION
DESALINATION

INDUSTRY
ENVIRONMENT

Fig. 9.2 Sample of multidimensional data cube structure (Source: Own representation)

> Dollar amount in narrowing down the required data sets based on the results of the value chain analysis.
>
> The goal must be to know exactly what data is needed. With this knowledge you then negotiate with the relevant data suppliers or database providers. Usually, you can get discounts of up to 50% if you sign a 2-year contract, for example. Remember: The profit lies in purchasing, also in data procurement.

Some of my clients buy expensive general news services and newsletters, which do not offer any added value when analyzed more closely. As soon as we carried out the first activities, Gary had canceled external newsletter services, saving six-figure sums in Dollar per year. Gary invested this money in the procurement of direct industry data for the multidimensional data cube, called MDC (Fig. 9.2). This data was then used for internal evaluations. The big advantage was that this data could be used again and again. This means that "doing" and not "buying" in the field of Predictive Intelligence not only pays off sustainably in the long run, but also realizes quick success and cost savings in the short run.

While Gary and I were working on the various topics of predictive analysis, he sent me his first draft templates. One of his first templates—I still remember it well—was his draft for future research requests. He felt that the sooner he knew what the organization could or might need, the better he could then prepare the draft templates for all further process steps. Although he did not initially share this research assignment template with the internal client, the template development process helped Gary deepen his understanding of the project and the expected outcome.

He then arranged coordination meetings with Ray and the product managers. Once again it was all about positioning the topic of Predictive Intelligence. Gary went through the entire process and explained what needed to be delivered by the organization.

> **Tip:** This is not about predictive intelligence per se. Do not try to explain the mechanisms and processes of PI. Focus more on the connection to the business and what needs to be done to create that connection. Create and ensure a common understanding of the outcome. Ensure absolute stringency in relation to the process you propose. Give your internal customers the opportunity to understand what you intend to do. Once you have reached this common understanding, you can start with the first PI pilots.

Gary asked specially selected colleagues to talk to him about possible PI pilot topics. He therefore arranged sessions of 30–60 min in which he briefly presented the topic and then asked colleagues to address various relevant sales topics as possible pilot projects.

9.2.4 Start Small and Show Results

Everything went pretty fast. After 4 weeks, Gary had defined relevant PI pilot topics for the first two industries in which the most important part of the business was conducted, water and mining. With this information, Gary began contacting and interviewing the identified data suppliers. In parallel, he worked on the data model. For this he used MS Excel. Dave, a business economist in his marketing team, helped him to develop this pivot tableau. Gary and Dave started to work with the first test data sets of the shortlisted providers. They inserted the data sets into the Excel spreadsheet and performed initial evaluations for specific markets.

During the meetings with the sales and product managers, Gary and Dave were able to verify the extracted data and forecasts. These meetings were a very valuable source to optimize the underlying data model right from the start. Meanwhile, Gary and Dave also pushed ahead with the value chain analysis so that he could finally select the parts and data sets from the various suppliers that he really needed. The template set for the value chain calculation was based on Excel, which enabled the various industry experts to allocate investment percentages for both purchases and services. The second version of the value chain calculation for water management was transformed into a good-looking chart, as the sales representatives also wanted to show their customers the specific products of BLUEHILL Inc. for the environmental industry.

After 3 months, Gary presented the first version of the Market Data Cube (MDC), which included market and economic data for all industries and regions. The MDC originally covered four main areas:

1. Market data

2. Social data
3. Economic data
4. Trade statistics

The MDC was initially only accessible to certain test users in order to use this important user group for ongoing tests and evaluations. Faster than expected, more and more people applied for access to the MDC. After 3 months, the mining and process industry was also integrated into the MDC and Dave continued to work on improving usability by optimizing the general user interface. This version 3 of the MDC was already using MS PowerBI and was available online 24/7 for registered users worldwide.

More and more colleagues took advantage of the benefits, and Gary and Dave had more and more time to work with data and designs, rather than spending hours and hours answering research questions. In addition, no more money was spent on hiring external suppliers and research consultancies.

Every single Dollar was invested internally and used sustainably. Dave developed a growing number of views, designs, and user group-specific dashboards. Gary continuously tracked all incoming requests, time to delivery, and direct feedback from internal customers.

After about 12 months, Gary took the opportunity to report on the project status in the management meeting, as shown in Fig. 9.3. He was able to present a truly incredible track record of the project:

Research Requests
- 85 inquiries received
- 72 applications processed
- 10 "on hold" due to unavailability of data due to budget constraints
- 3 rejected due to necessary refinement of the application
- Overall satisfaction rate (1 = bad, 10 = excellent): 9.7 (80 answers)
- Saving money with external suppliers: 175,000 (from 215,000)
- Average processing time per request: 1.9 h (project start: 12.7 days)

MDC Usage 3 Months
- 724 views
- 35 active users
- 52% increase compared to the previous time frame

As already shown, the results of the ongoing projects were impressive. With regard to the quantitative and qualitative results, three showcase examples will be described in the showcases to show what Gary has made possible with Dave, and shortly after the project start BLUEHILL Inc. opened up a completely new dimension of consistent and structured professional business planning.

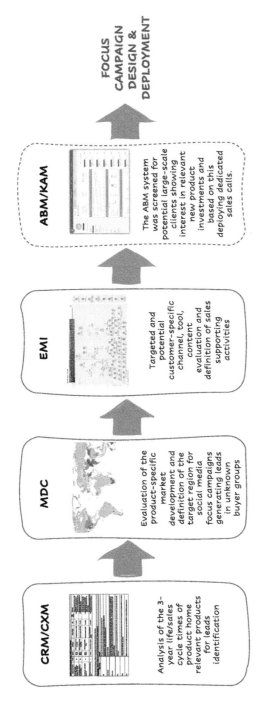

Fig. 9.3 Short-term PI for optimizing net working capital (Source: BLUEHILL Inc.)

9.3 Showcase 1: Short-Term, Operational Predictive Intelligence

The first case was not planned and just happened. Gary regularly visited all production facilities. During one of his trips, he visited the production site in Poland. The Product Home Manager gave him a tour of the plant. Gary, as he is, asked many questions, including why 30 brand new copies of the same machine were in stock. Gary actually wanted to know what specific equipment it should be. Benjamin, the local manager, told him that these machines were intended for the production of edible oil.

There would be so many in stock because essential components of the equipment would be supplied by external suppliers. However, in order for BLUEHILL Inc. to sell the finished machines at a competitive price, a larger quantity of vendor parts must always be purchased from the supplier than the customers ordered from BLUEHILL. Benjamin stated:

> As a result, many machines remain in stock for a long time until we receive a new order. This is the brutal truth, but I have no idea what to do. A major problem is, that within BLUEHILL the product homes are still not working together as one unit, This is why the other product homes are not selling our Polish products as they rather try to reach their own product-specific targets!

This, of course, has a huge negative impact on inventory turnover rates, but even more so on net working capital (NWC)[1]—at the very moment when Ray gave the order to optimize NWC. One man, one word. Gary offered to take immediate action to bring these machines to market in a timely manner (Fig. 9.3). Upon returning to the office in Denver, he searched the CRM system for customers with the same products. Based on the data from the service team, he knew that this type of machine would normally need to be replaced after 3 years. Then this customer data was compared with the MDC data in terms of market and economic data, but also project data. Based on this, MDC extracted two potential short-term sales regions, Italy and Greece. Using this information, *Event and Media Intelligence* (EMI), which was also based on MS Excel, was screened for relevant media and events in both regions. This EMI was designed on the basis of the Marketing Resource Management (MRM) approach (Seebacher and Güpner 2021), as the index-based analysis and evaluation of different marketing and communication channels in terms of performance, marketing could be used to compare their marketing return on investment (MRoI).

Carolin, campaign manager for BLUEHILL Inc. immediately initiated a focus campaign that focused on the highest scoring online and offline media channel extracted by EMI. Gary himself checked the account-based marketing (ABM)-database looking for indicators for major customers looking for similar devices, but it turned out that at that time no major customer of BLUEHILL Inc. was eligible to purchase this type of equipment.

---

[1]Net working capital (NWC).

27 machines with a price of $80,000 each were in stock. After 9 weeks, the machines were sold to a sugar factory in Mexiko, thanks to the PI-based designed and defined focus campaign conducted by Gary's PI team. The success was based on the internal ability to predict where the sale could take place. In this one case alone, the TBM-based Predictive Intelligence solution enabled a €2.2 million Dollar order intake that would not have been possible without Predictive Intelligence, and certainly not as cost-efficiently.

Without PI, BLUEHILL Inc. would either have spent too much money on advertising and trade shows or would have had to wait until another customer knew at just the right time that BLUEHILL had equipment in stock. And finally, do you think any of the external data or intelligence providers or dashboard solution vendors could have done the job?

9.4   Showcase 2: Medium-Term Operational-Strategic Predictive Intelligence

Another challenge for BLUEHILL Inc. was to stringently open up new markets. Many things at BLUEHILL Inc. happened more or less by chance. 16 months, after Gary had started the PI project, the ongoing PI activities showed and expected attractive market developments in the Central American region contrary to all external predictions and forecasts. In the management meeting, Gary presented the results and was also able to substantiate the predicted and anticipated developments. In earlier days Ray would have turned him down, but at this meeting in May 2018, Gary was asked to develop a PI-based market entry paper. Gary went through a stringent process using the PI infrastructure that had been built up in the meantime (Fig. 9.4).

It was easy for Gary because he had all the external data and the projections at hand. With the MDC he extracted the relevant forecasts for the different countries in the target region. Based on the value chain model, he was able to define exactly how high the potential sales volume would be for each application. Normally, on the second or third level of the Predictive Intelligence Maturity Model (PIMM), Gary would not have been able to dynamically calculate the worst-case, neutral, and best-case scenarios, but now, with his now three-person PI team, he could.

He entered and migrated all relevant data into the automated, TBM-based business plan template, added the data from EMI, and was able to immediately draft the forecast business plan figures for market entry.

He did this by using the margins generated for the relevant applications, which the MDC generated from the CRM system and continuously updated. The forecasts were then enriched with the data from the account-based marketing (ABM) system to gain a better understanding of possible upcoming large tenders. Based on the defined costs for personnel, office infrastructure, the formation of the required legal entity, and other administrative issues, Gary Ray was able to present a comprehensive, scenario-based market entry study within 4 weeks, including the ROI period,

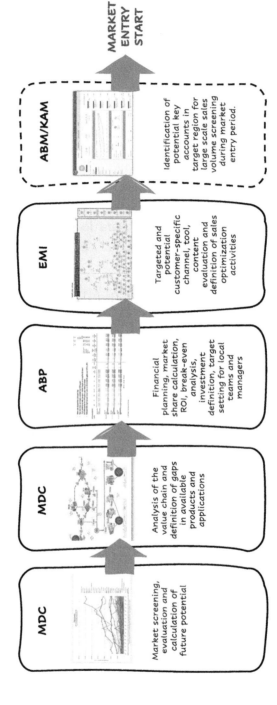

Fig. 9.4 Medium-term predictive intelligence for market entry (Source: BLUEHILL Inc.)

the required investments and also precise KPIs per time window, so that Ray would always be able to pull the ripcord if necessary.

Today, BLUEHILL Inc. is very successfully established in Central America and Gary is able to continuously monitor compliance with the business plan developed by predictive intelligence and to react immediately if necessary. He is thus one of the 10% of companies in the Americas that can already point to data-driven business management today.

9.5 Showcase 3: Long-Term Strategic-Tactical Predictive Intelligence

Finally, Gary succeeded in establishing PI as the cornerstone for all entrepreneurial measures. Gary designed an annual template-based process, on the basis of which the entire management implements the following measures:

- Definition of the strategy of BLUEHILL Inc.
- Derivation of 1-, 3-, and 5-year business figures based on value chains, applications, regions, and industries
- Reconciliation and approval of the submitted figures
- 24/7 PI-based monitoring of operational performance and deviation analysis
- Half-year report with quantified countermeasures in case of deviations from the forecast
- Review of the year and strategy adjustments

Implementing this process and ensuring that the entire organization follows this TBM procedure is a great success for Ray, Gary, and me. PI turned out to be the lever for solving Ray's structural problems in the area of corporate planning:

> Uwe helped me a lot with this focused way of getting us through his Predictive Intelligence Excellence Journey. Even though I was willing to invest, Uwe always stopped me from doing this and always was keen on first having Gary to deliver results and quick wins and only then grant him additional required resource. But Gary never approached me for additional resources or funds as he only used realized savings for getting what he needed. I am very grateful what Uwe did for BLUEHILL, especially as we could also overcome our so tiring structural and managerial issues....!

Since then, BLUEHILL Inc. has met or exceeded its targets. BLUEHILL Inc. is growing solid, steady, and healthy. Every year, the order intake grows by 10–15% and every year since then, the EBITDA has increased by 1.5–2%. Ray now looks forward to a solid and stable long-term investment and can against this background acquire one or two highly interesting companies in order to increase the product portfolio in the so important environmental industry.

9.6   Why a Glass Ball Is Not Needed

This case study showed how you can save a lot of money and how you can make a lot of money. It is as simple as it seems. But as always in life, you have to do your homework and pursue goals with method and structure—with my template-based management model. It will not help you to hire a consultant for setting up and establishing PI. It makes even less sense to continue buying studies and research externally. You can count on one hand those from which you can buy serious and valid studies.

Big Data and *Predictive Intelligence* always sound mysterious and complicated, but in the end, it is not at all, as this case study has hopefully made clear. I can only encourage you to take up the challenge, not only out of a sense of responsibility to your boss and the company, but also and above all for yourself. You grow with the task, and suddenly you are the one holding all the aces.

Further Reading

Seebacher, U., & Güpner, A. (2021). *Marketing resource management - guidebook for organizational development with many examples, explanations and instructions for action.* Graz: AQPS Inc.

Why It Remains Exciting. . .

10

It is well known that there is always a shine to new things. Indeed, it was inspiring, challenging, and exhausting to get this book off the ground. How do you describe something that you yourself intuitively and together with close, trusted, and valuable colleagues had made into a big whole from many small parts? And that, although we ourselves and all those involved were by no means aware of this in advance or could not have been aware of it at all.

The writing of this book was a concerted and structured reflection of the last 6 years in which we have been able and allowed to launch Predictive Intelligence in various companies of all sizes and industries. I would like to thank all project members, colleagues, experts, and the many executives who had placed their trust in us to address this far-reaching and important topic of Predictive Intelligence. The situation was very similar to that when I wrote the first version of my book on the topic of "Template-driven Consulting" in 2003. After 17 years, I was approached by Springer to publish a new edition of this book, because it still seems to be a much sought-after management book and an increasingly important topic.

Why do I mention this at this point? Even then, in the years before writing the book, we had unconsciously developed and used a methodology intuitively, the lasting significance of which we had only become aware of through the positive feedback of our customers. In retrospect, we then brought the Template-based Management approach (Seebacher 2020) into a concept and explored the underlying modes of operation of the approach. Many of the hypotheses could be validated and today, Template-based Management has become an integral part of business practice.

And exactly the same thing happened now in the course of the creation of this book. What we intuitively implemented out of necessity became known in the industry and led to many invitations from some of the most renowned institutions, such as the German Engineering Association (VDMA) or the German Association of Industrial Communication (BVIK), to present our work on Predictive Intelligence at symposia and conferences. It was only in this way that the renowned Springer publishing house became aware of our activities and findings and, by addressing

© The Author(s), under exclusive license to Springer Nature Switzerland AG 2021
U. Seebacher, *Predictive Intelligence for Data-Driven Managers*, Future of Business and Finance, https://doi.org/10.1007/978-3-030-69403-6_10

me personally, initiated the development of this attempt to bring the exciting and fascinating topic of predictive intelligence for achieving data-driven corporate management into book form—with the aim of making it comprehensible to non-mathematicians, non-statisticians, and non-data scientists.

It seems that what has been lived for many years in the field of education by modern universities of applied sciences has finally arrived in modern economic and social science research, namely that sustainable and groundbreaking developments in an increasingly dynamic changing economic environment must come from applied research in practice, because that is where the impulses for changing conventional approaches are set daily. Conventional mechanisms and structures are put to the test every day anew, but to see this, a corresponding systemic empathy is required, which, if one follows Jeremy Rifkin's words, many top managers and board members either seem to lack or have lost due to their too great distance from daily business practice.

In the hope that this book has made a valuable contribution to the optimization and further development of operational practice in the sense of data-driven management, I would like to thank you for the time you, the reader, have invested in reading my modest ideas and thoughts. Life is like drawing, only without an eraser. This book on Predictive Intelligence is a black-and-white sketch that can only shine in its entire colorful splendor when it is implemented operationally and filled with life and content. The color intensity and shading will develop from the acting persons and teams.

In 10 years, we will all know more about Predictive Intelligence and will look back on the beginnings. I wish you all the best for your Predictive Intelligence Journey, many interesting conversations and insights, and above all gratitude and satisfaction.

Further Reading

Seebacher, U. (2020). *Template-based management—A guide for an efficient and impactful professional practice*. Cham: Springer.

Index

A
Aberdeen Group, 11
A/B testing, 167
Account-based marketing (ABM), 86, 163, 202, 256, 257
Account intelligence, 189
Accuracy paradoxon, 96
Amazon, 28
Analysis
   primary, 167
   secondary, 167
Analytics labs, 216
Apache MapReduce, 38
Apache Yarn, 38
A-priori-principle, 25
Artificial intelligence (AI), 14, 21, 160, 168, 202, 228, 229
Artificial neural networks (ANN), 24, 40, 52, 53
As-a-service, 47, 178, 214
Authenticity, 212, 234
Auto machine learning (AutoML), 12

B
B2B marketing, 30, 175, 186
Babylonians, 1
Backpropagation, 45
Banking, 1
Bayes classifier, 52
   naive, 52
Behavioral anchors, 224
Behavioral biology, 219
Best-of-breed, 185
Big data, 24, 31, 41, 45, 91, 181
Big data architects, 211
Blanchard, K., 115
Blockchain, 155, 174

Blohm, I., 216
Blondel, V., 41
Bloomberg, 127
Bootstrap aggregating, 51
Brinker, S., 186
Brynjolfsson, E., 184
Bureau van Dijk, 126
Business analytics, 13, 193, 196, 210, 221, 227
Business partner, 210
Business-to-business (B2B), 119
Business-to-consumer (B2C), 30, 119
Buyer insights, 189
Buyer journey, 182

C
Caffe, 42
Canvasing, 217
CAPEX, 96, 153, 175
Capital ownership, 3
Carlson, S., 5
Central intelligence, 100
Centralization, 4
Chain of custody, 174
Change management, 216
Chat Bots, 22
Classification
   conceptual, 41
   deductive, 41
   qualitative, 41
Classification metrics, 25
Cleverbot, 23
Cloud computing, 174
Cloud sourcing, 65
Cloud suites, 185
Clustering models, 48
Collins, A., 184

Printed by Printforce, the Netherlands